W9-BLM-416

RELENTLESS

RELENTLESS

SEVEN MARATHONS, SEVEN CONTINENTS, SEVEN DAYS

David Gething

ROWMAN & LITTLEFIELD
Lanham • Boulder • New York • London

Published by Rowman & Littlefield
A wholly owned subsidiary of The Rowman & Littlefield Publishing Group, Inc.
4501 Forbes Boulevard, Suite 200, Lanham, Maryland 20706
www.rowman.com

Unit A, Whitacre Mews, 26-34 Stannary Street, London SE11 4AB

British Library Cataloguing in Publication Information Available

Library of Congress Cataloging-in-Publication Data

Names: Gething, David, 1975– author.
Title: Relentless : seven marathons, seven continents, seven days / David
   Gething.
Description: Lanham : ROWMAN & LITTLEFIELD, [2016] | Includes index.
Identifiers: LCCN 2016011777 (print) | LCCN 2016030549 (ebook) | ISBN
   9781442260528 (hardback : alk. paper) | ISBN 9781442260535 (electronic)
Subjects: LCSH: Gething, David, 1975– | Runners (Sports)—Biography. |
   Marathon running—History. | Extreme sports.
Classification: LCC GV1061.15.G47 A3 2016 (print) | LCC GV1061.15.G47
(ebook) | DDC 796.42092 [B]—dc23
LC record available at https://lccn.loc.gov/2016011777

∞™ The paper used in this publication meets the minimum requirements of
American National Standard for Information Sciences—Permanence of Paper
for Printed Library Materials, ANSI/NISO Z39.48-1992.

Printed in the United States of America

To my family,
Trilby, Amelia, and Madeleine.
No explanations are needed.

4. EUROPE
MADRID, SPAIN

3. NORTH AMERICA
MIAMI, USA

5. AFRICA
MARRAKECH, MOROCCO

2. SOUTH AMERICA
PUNTA ARENAS, CHILE

1. ANTARCTICA
UNION GLACIER

7 MARATH

6. ASIA
DUBAI, UAE

7. OCEANIA
SYDNEY, AUSTRALIA

ONS MAP

CONTENTS

CONTENTS

ACKNOWLEDGMENTS

I've heard people talk about a race campaign they undertook, instead of just a race they competed in. I think *race campaign* is possibly a more insightful term. Races, be they weekend sprints or intercontinental quests, are always a conglomeration of the efforts of many people. They are campaigns—the sustained efforts by many people for one ultimate goal.

These campaigns start and finish with the family who support the racer on the good days and the bad. Races, especially long-distance races, require months and ultimately years of training, preparation, planning, commitment, and, of course, financing. Family must endure this. It is a burden that often they haven't requested. Yet they do it with good grace and humility, adjusting their lives to cope with the demands of training, being supportive and positive, and occasionally injecting a dose of reality. For this I must thank Trilby White, my wife, and Amelia and Madeleine Gething, my girls. Without their love and support, and even at times their pride at having the craziest husband/dad of any of their friends, these races would be out of contention. And by the same token I must thank my parents, Lindsay and Tim Gething. I think they still have difficulty reconciling the first twenty years of my life with the diametrically opposite second twenty, but they have always been unwavering in their support.

Friends are often the people who plant that initial seed of interest, and usually they're the ones who help nurture and grow that interest from a seed into a massive tree. They provide a support that is complementary to, yet entirely different from, that provided by family. They are a source of knowledge, inspiration, motivation, and care, even if they'd often rather retain their macho facade and not admit it. There are too many who have supported me to recount, but some of those names include Richard Hall, Tim Kremer, Matt Baile, Jan Skovgaard, Mark Peters, Toby Store, Steven Purcell, Andrew Loiterton, Simon Castley, Stephen Boddington, Paolo Caputo, John Pesci, and all of the RMRH and ANTS people, especially Andy Naylor and David Howell, who both taught me some of the most important lessons in my life and are now looking down on us all from above, probably laughing at us for still being stupid enough to meet at the crack of dawn every Tuesday and Thursday to go riding together.

When I think of my coaches over the years, I'm not sure if I should list them alongside my friends, for all of the right reasons. A good coach sits in an unusual position, knowing as much as—if not more than—your family and friends about some aspects of your life. A good coach knows you sometimes better than you know yourself. A good coach is understanding, encouraging, and caring yet also subtly strict and unflinching. From your exercise data and your communications, they can decipher how your body is reacting and responding, and what you need both emotionally and physically. Good coaches are very difficult to find, but I've been fortunate to have more than one. Max Shute got me started, showed me the ropes, and built my athletic ability from nothing, with an unmatched patience and good humor. It was Nigel Gray, my current coach, who took me from that level and really helped me to excel. Through meticulous analysis, support, enthusiasm, and interest, Nigel has taken me through races that I never would have imagined I had in me: Norseman. Boston Marathon. Qualification for both 70.3 and long-course Kona Ironman World Championships. And of course the 7 Marathons 7 Continents 7 Days. For each race he has carefully formulated a unique and personal plan to allow me to achieve my best. From there he has adjusted and crafted the sessions and the weeks to maximize results. Without his intelligent and skillful assistance I doubt I would have finished, never mind won.

And, of course, this section would not be complete without thanking Kelly Falconer from Asia Literary Agency and Christen Karniski, Jessica McCleary, and Jacqline Barnes from Rowman & Littlefield. When I first sheepishly mentioned the thought of writing a book to Kelly, I thought she was going to laugh. Instead she has been a rock of support, enthusiasm, and advice, helping me to navigate a brave new world, never hesitating to give encouragement and assistance. Christen took a chance on me and gave me an opportunity despite my scant history in writing. In a truly sporting spirit, she took a punt based on a feeling, then followed up with gracious assistance and help. I am indebted to her for that.

I would like to thank the World Marathon Challenge organizers Richard Donovan and Fearghal Murphy, the photographers Dave Painter and Francisco

Mattos, and the countless others who were involved in the planning, logistics, and support of running those seven marathons on seven continents in seven days. What you all achieved was beyond amazing and an experience that I know none of us will ever forget.

And lastly I'd like to thank my fellow racers. All of you are amazing people, and each of you showed characteristics that encapsulated some of the finest elements of the human condition, from strength and bravery in adversity to humility and honor. I consider all of you true friends, and I feel we have made a bond that will live with us for the rest of our days.

My account of this race is only that: my account, my opinion, the way I saw events through my eyes. It is unavoidable that we will all have different reflections and views on the events that unfolded in that week. And on that note, there were times during the race when we were all very jet-lagged, exhausted, and mentally spent, and so if I've juggled any minor events or supporters' names, the fault is mine; please let me know and I'm happy to make any corrections in future editions. I truly hope I have done the race, and all of our collective experience, justice in the pages that follow.

In reality it's not possible to thank everybody—those people who got behind me and got behind the race, supporting with no agenda except to enjoy the moment.

For this reason, I'd say that I'm not special. But I was able to build a very special team around me. If you can do that, you are capable of anything.

INTRODUCTION

The Story of the Beginning

I never thought I'd be sitting here writing this book. Writing about the events that transpired in January 2015. Telling the story of running a race around the world, and winning, setting two world records in the process.

I never thought I'd be sitting here writing about the lead up to that race, how it all started, and how it all stood after the dust had settled. Telling the story of why my life changed, how I got to that point, and how I came back.

I never thought I'd be sitting here writing the story because I never was the sports guy. I never was the fitness fanatic. I'd never really done anything physical. Anybody who knew me back in those days wouldn't have believed it either.

I was the party guy. I secretly used to have a laugh at those health nuts behind their backs. My life was about having a good time. I worked hard. I loved going out. I ate a little too much, I drank a little too much, and I smoked too many cigarettes. Nothing terrible, nothing illegal, nothing nefarious. Just a little too much fun. There was always a good reason for a nice meal and a good bottle of wine. But as is the way with life, there came a tipping point, a time when everything came to a head. Everything suddenly became different.

This is the story of an ordinary guy who just once decided to try something extraordinary. Throw caution to the wind, see what happens. This is the story of going from being a smoker and drinker who was more than thirty-five kilograms (seventy-five pounds) overweight and for whom the idea of exercise was occasionally taking the dogs for a walk to winning one of the most difficult endurance events on the planet.

Don't worry—there's no preaching, there's no magic secret, there's no fad diet. It's simply the story of a resolve to do something, and how it all unfolded. But it is a pretty good story—at least I think it is.

—∿—

There aren't many people on this planet who can tell you the moment their life changed. For better or worse, I'm one of the people who can. My life changed on a cool November evening in 2007. I was thirty-two years old, living in a relatively rural area on the outskirts of Hong Kong called Tai Au Mun, a traditional fishing village in the New Territories that was slowly opening up to Westerners. We'd moved out there a few years after arriving in the country, seeking an after-hours sanctuary from the twenty-four-hour hustle and bustle of Hong Kong Island. *Rural* is, of course, a subjective term, and even rural Hong Kong is fairly densely populated. We were the only foreigners in the village, but the local villagers had always made us feel welcome, and in return we'd done our best to respect the local traditions. It was always a strange social dance—we spoke very little Cantonese, and they spoke very little English, but through a combination of hand gestures, smiles, and broken phrases we managed to carve out a niche for ourselves.

On that night in 2007 I was sitting outside my house with my neighbor, Ah Wai, smoking a cigarette. I don't think Ah Wai had ever been friends with a foreigner, or a *gweilo*, as he would have called me. But by the same token, I hadn't really been friends with a local villager either. We shared a passion for motorcycles, and that seemed to be enough glue to start a bond, one that strengthened as we slowly but surely destroyed my motorcycle piece by piece as we attempted to service and repair it without any instructions or experience. I enjoyed hanging out with Ah Wai. He seemed to permanently have a beer in one hand and a cigarette in the other, and it was an excuse for me to sneak in a smoke despite having told my wife I'd given up for the umpteenth time.

After a few broken fragments of conversation, we finished our cigarettes and went our separate ways. I headed back into my small house. Village houses in Hong Kong villages are all virtually identical, built to a government regulation of being three stories high and seven hundred square feet per floor. Internationally it would seem an unusual design, but in Hong Kong it was a formula that seemed to work well, like a kind of mini–high rise house. Unique, idiosyncratic Hong Kong. Our living area was on the second floor.

As I walked up the stairs on that day, I had a feeling I was in trouble. It was quiet—too quiet. My wife, Trilby, was sitting at the table in the living room.

"David, we need to talk."

It's one of the oddest phrases in the English language, at least for me. Instinctually those five words make the butterflies in my stomach start to flutter and my heart sink. My sum total of life experience has taught me that this line was never a prelude to talking about something good. I'd never been told, "David, we need to talk . . . well done on your homework." "David, we need to talk . . . I just wanted to let you know you're a great husband." "David, we need to talk . . . you really did a good job last week at work."

No, "David, we need to talk" was a universal code. Every time I'd heard those words throughout my life the real meaning was "David, you've really messed up." And generally the person saying them was in the right.

Trilby continued, "I'm pregnant with your first child. She's going to be born in three months. It's time for you to make a decision. I'll always love you however you are, but when your daughter is born, she's going to look up to you. You're going to be the center of her world. And she's going to grow up emulating you."

She paused to let it sink in.

"No matter what you tell yourself, you're not living a healthy, good life. You're overweight, you drink too much, and you smoke, even though you promised me you'd stopped. Now if that's who you're going to be, then I can't change you, but you've got to think about who you want your daughter to become."

She was right. I'd always struggled with my weight, but it had ballooned. I used to joke with my friends that I was the only husband in history who'd put on more weight than his wife during pregnancy. Hers was all baby. Mine was all beer and crisps. I'd taken to enjoying myself far too much. We only had a few months left of our lives as we knew them before the little one came along. We wanted to go out and eat at nice restaurants, have a few weekends away, and enjoy our life pre-parenthood while we could. Plus, the way I figured it, I had a nine-month free pass with my own personal designated driver—I could drink as much as I wanted and live the good life.

The only person responsible for those times was myself, but it's very easy to get caught up in the party scene in Hong Kong. Admittedly, my wife and I had both had a blast in the early years. One long succession of Friday evening drinking sessions, Saturday all-night parties, and hair-of-the-dog boozy Sunday lunches, punctuated by a hard week of work, then repeat. When she'd become pregnant, she had stopped living the wild life, but the way I saw it those pregnancy rules didn't apply to me. Until now.

It's a strange thing, but we all make excuses for ourselves. We all come to see what we do as acceptable and normal. We either turn a blind eye to our failings, gloss over them, or quite often turn them into attributes we feel we can brag about. I had seen myself as someone who worked hard and was successful but also knew how to let his hair down and party hard. I hung around with a crowd who lived life the same way. Getting home at 6 a.m. was the sign of a good night out. I was normal.

The night Trilby showed that picture of me through the lens of my baby daughter, the self-deception came crashing down.

That was the moment. I didn't say anything in reply to her statement. There wasn't really any need to. She wasn't arguing, she wasn't persuading, she wasn't really even criticizing. Trilby was just stating the facts—facts that I had to consider, information that I had to decide how to use.

Instead I just sat there at the table. And as I sat, I realized that there wasn't even a decision to make. There was no chance I'd want my daughter to grow up living an unhealthy lifestyle, overweight and grossly unfit. And at that moment I suddenly realized that was how people saw me. That charade I'd painted for myself developed a hairline crack—a crack that soon enough became a gaping fissure. The party days were over. It was time to change.

And that cigarette with Ah Wai, that was the last one I ever smoked.

However, before I go forward maybe I should go backward and let you know how everything came to such a tipping point.

—◆—

I grew up in middle-class suburban Sydney, Australia, in the seventies and eighties, the only child in a mostly happy family. I couldn't complain, although I'm sure I did on a regular basis. I had two parents who loved me, a roof over my head, food on the table, and clean clothes to wear. We were decidedly middle class, living in a middle-class house on a middle-class street of a middle-class suburb. Nothing bad. Well, except that I never really saw things in the same way as others, and I never really fit in particularly well.

My parents both worked, and worked hard. My father, Tim, put in very long hours at a large international computer company, Perkin Elmer. I didn't see him that much—he was absorbed in his work—but I do remember him taking me to his office occasionally to look at the equipment. Computers back in those days only bear a passing resemblance to what we consider normal now. I remember going into the main server room, lined with machines the size of refrigerators with large tape wheels that spun to and fro as the computer went through its calculations. I'm sure that whole room had less computing power than my smartphone does these days, but as a young boy it was certainly impressive. We were the only house I knew to have an acoustic coupler, a very primitive relative to the modem and the Internet that fit over the regular telephone and connected to the computer. The speed was so slow that you could watch the letters appear on the screen one by one, but to my friends and me it was space-age.

My mother, Lindsay, worked her way up academia to become a professor at Sydney University. She worked in the human sciences section of the campus, establishing a research unit within the nursing faculty. She worked hard to improve the lives and opportunities of others within the community, and much of her work related to integrating people with disabilities into the workforce in a meaningful and beneficial way for both sides of the equation. A published author and expert in the field, she left a legacy when she retired that continues today and has helped many.

They were not without flaws, as none of us are. My father worked far too much and had difficulty balancing his family life with his career, and my mother, well, she indulged me far too much. But in balance I was loved and cared for as much as any person could wish. I had a happy childhood, at least around the house. And one of the lessons they both instilled in me through their actions was the value of hard work.

My parents were, and still are, intellectuals. There was no real interest in or recognition of athletic pursuits in our family. The only exercise or sport I ever played during my younger years was that which was forced upon me by the school, when I couldn't think of a good enough excuse to get out of it.

This lack of athletic involvement might have been partly justifiable if I had been extremely academically talented, but unfortunately this wasn't the case either. My scholarly efforts waxed and waned, in direct relation to my interest in the subject. If I was curious about a topic, I was relentless until I'd read over every scrap of information I could find. If I wasn't interested, I couldn't fake it, and I didn't even bother trying.

My school grades were a roller coaster, swinging like a pendulum from As and high distinctions to bare pass or, in a number of cases, a fail. One year I won the academic achievement prize; the next year I came pretty close to being the bottom of the class.

At one point in my studies, I decided I wasn't really interested anymore and just stopped turning up to school. It was year ten, two years from graduation. It was an important time for studies and building foundations for the future, and I spent most of it sitting on the side of the train tracks watching the day go by. I wasn't getting into fights. I wasn't doing drugs. I just wasn't interested. And after a while the school decided they weren't interested in me either. I was asked to leave—or as the principal more diplomatically phrased it, the school could no longer meet my needs. I had to go. I was, for all intents and purposes, expelled.

There were two choices that my parents and the school could have taken. I could have been sent to a very low-pressure environment where children are allowed to make their own choices and live by the consequences, or I could go to a very strict school and have my tomfoolery forcibly ejected from my psyche. It was agreed by all that the second was the correct option. I was to go to Knox Grammar School, a private boys' school with a strong focus on military-style discipline, conformity, and rules.

That marked the start of the less happy time of my childhood. Moving to a new school was difficult, but I completely respected that everybody involved in the decision was doing it for my benefit. My old school pulled some strings to get me transferred. My parents worked hard for a living and contributed far too much of their income trying to straighten me out and do the right thing for me. Even the new school had good intentions, seeing a student they believed could be made good with their help. And maybe they were right. I guess in a strange way everything did turn out well in the end, and I wouldn't change my lot in life. But they were a few very hard years.

—⁂—

Without the social icebreaker of sport or the classroom kudos of academic ability, I struggled to make friends after arriving at Knox. That led to a fairly solitary and self-destructive existence for a while. I didn't self-harm or anything drastic, but I did overeat, underperform, and become depressed and distant. I put on a lot of weight, which as a child is even more of a stigma than as an adult. And so began a spiral of loneliness and inappropriate compensation with food or mischief. My parents did try their best to help me, my mother in particular, but I think she never could bring herself to be truly angry at the child I had become, and never really put her foot down.

Eventually the same behavior started again, but this time the school was much faster to act. When I first started not turning up to school, I was taken into the vice principal's office. He sat me down and didn't say a word. He took my file from his cabinet and slowly perused its contents. A tall but solid man, he had a thick head of white hair that seamlessly transitioned into a thick white beard, then crept up his upper lip to form a thick white mustache, and finally disappeared in a trail of white hair leading up each nostril. He breathed slowly and deeply, purposefully, and every time he drew breath, there was an intimidating hiss as the air navigated its way through his thick tangle of bristles.

"You're a bad egg. There's no place for bad eggs here. You need to see the principal," he stated flatly.

That was it. No negotiation, no reasoning, no questioning. A verdict without a trial. Well, in fairness, I decided I probably didn't have many mitigating factors anyway. I had only been caught playing hooky I figured. How bad could it be?

I realized any hope I had for mercy or understanding was gone. The school didn't get a tough reputation for no reason. The principal also wasn't one for small talk or discussion. He only muttered one sentence, and I'm sure that wasn't entirely heartfelt: "This is going to hurt me more than it hurts you."

He grabbed my hands one at a time and placed them on the oak desk, holding the sides of the thick table top. He walked to my side. A thin, long, reedy bamboo cane was brought down on me, whistling as it raced through the air toward my backside. I was astonished. I was caned a total of five times that day. I had trouble sitting for a week.

—◊◊◊—

The principal's cane had hardly been put back in its varnished black wooden box before I started getting into trouble again. I received eleven lashes of the cane while I was at that school. The straw that broke the camel's back came in the spring of 1990. My friends and I had decided to play hooky and went to hang out in the local Pizza Hut restaurant in the conservative upper-class suburb of Chatswood, not far from the school. Wearing full school uniform and with little care for our surroundings, we laughed loudly, goofed around, and smoked cigarettes. The first two would have deserved severe reprimand, but the last was unforgivable in the principal's eyes. A patron of the restaurant called the school to inform them about their wayward pupils. That evening long after school hours there was a phone call from the principal to my parents. That was a first. I knew that couldn't be good.

I was taken in for a special meeting with the principal. Knox Grammar was as stubborn as I was, and the principal would never accept being bested by a pupil. To expel me would have been to admit failure, a boy he couldn't reshape. Instead I was to learn discipline and respect through hard labor. Every Saturday I was to turn up to school. I was to be given a shovel and to dig ditches in a small scrappy yard at the back of the school grounds. After I'd finished, I was to fill them back in again. Then I was to repeat. And such were the remainder of my school days. I can't say it stopped me getting into any mischief, but I did avoid getting caught again.

They were unpleasant times, but I don't regret them. That school taught me some of the most important lessons I've ever learned—lessons that would stick with me for the rest of my life: Never let others dictate your path. Trust your own instincts. Have conviction in your beliefs. I learned mental strength and tenacity during those days, a strength that has endured for the rest of my life. I learned that when things are looking down you can push through, just keep going, put one foot in front of another and eventually you'll emerge from the other end. I learned to believe in myself, no matter what others may say.

I'm glad I took the path I did. I'm glad I didn't always turn up. I'm glad I got kicked out. I'm glad I went through the punishment at the second school. I'm glad I held together. I wouldn't have it any other way even if I could. That was a vital time. The only thing I regret is the headaches I must have given my parents.

—m—

I think it'd be fair to say I survived Knox Grammar School rather than made a turnaround. My final grades were very average, but I was just able to scrape into university, admitted to an entry-level bachelor of science program. I had always planned on being a veterinarian. Even from a very young age it was my life goal. But my later school years had certainly ensured that my marks were a very long way away from what would be needed to qualify.

University was a revelation. I knew it was different from the difficult school days I had endured. For a start, it was different because I was actually turning up. It was a good environment that stimulated and encouraged free thought rather than suppressing it. I was studying a subject that interested me—the sciences. It was only a basic science degree, a mixture of biology, chemistry, and physics. And I loved it. I soaked it up. I was fascinated.

My marks were excellent. They were good enough for the university to make a rare exception and offer me a special place. I was offered a transfer with full credit to study veterinary medicine at Murdoch University in Western Australia, considered by many to be the foremost veterinary school in the country. I didn't hesitate. It was time to leave the past behind me and truly make a new start.

If my year in basic science was interesting, my time in veterinary science was an inspiration. It was what I wanted to do, it was what I connected with, and I loved it.

The next five years of university passed quickly. The weight that I had gained during my school years fell off. I made many true friends, whom I consider close friends over twenty years later. I also met my wife, Trilby, while I was in my third year of university. She was a biotechnology student on the same campus. She was smart, attractive, and popular. What she saw in me I'll never know. But thankfully enough she still sees it to this day.

After graduation, Trilby and I went back to Sydney to start working, but after a year or two I started to itch for something more. Going back to Sydney was like opening a door into the past, a door that should have stayed firmly shut. So we decided to head to Hong Kong. It all started with a small advertisement in the back of a veterinary trade magazine. A job in the Far East. It sounded exotic. It sounded like an adventure. We were young, we had no real commitments, and life was simple. In the end there wasn't really even a decision to be made. Two months later we were boarding a plane to Hong Kong, a country we'd never even visited but where we now planned to make a life for ourselves. I'd like to think it was ambitious, but in reality it was probably rather naive.

Hong Kong is a strange place, wonderful in some respects and very dangerous in others. Living as a foreigner in Hong Kong leaves one on the periphery of any social rules or norms. Laws must be obeyed, but there is a very gray area where expatriates can essentially do what they want, as long as they aren't hurting others or grossly negligent. This was mainly a hangover from colonial days, when the foreigners tended to see themselves on a different social plateau than the local Hong Kong Chinese, and also tended to control the legal and political landscape. Officially reprimanding a foreigner for a minor infringement or silly behavior was often considered too much hassle, or may have repercussions as that foreigner was likely to know senior expatriate government or police figures. This is not to say Hong Kong is in any way lawless; it's one of the safest countries on the planet, which is possibly even more of a reason that foreigners can act out and not get themselves into trouble.

It is also a microcosm, where as a foreigner most of your friends and social circle are other foreigners, generally well educated and highly paid but also with a flair for adventure and excitement. It was a self-selecting group that had come here. And we were all in it together, bonded by our new experiences so far removed from those that we had left behind.

This reduction of societal norms and abundant supply of parties, entertainment, dining, and fun led to some very good times in Hong Kong. Trilby and I both had far too much fun. Nothing particularly nefarious, just a lot of it. Lots of eating, lots of drinking, lots of going out. We lived the high life and rubbed shoulders with people from all walks of life. It was an electrifying time. It wasn't a healthy time. An ingrained lack of any sports or exercise ethic and a taste for the finer things in life led me to put on a significant amount of weight, regularly smoke cigarettes, and drink like a fish.

And as is often the way with life, there comes a point when perspective changes. Everything is brought into focus, a mirror is placed in front of you that gives a true and unblinking reflection of the person you've become. In my case, that happened on that cool November night in 2007, after that last cigarette with Ah Wai. But, of course, you already know that part.

—⟶⟵—

When I was first becoming inspired, I read a lot of books by those who had trodden a similar path. Guys like Dean Karnazes and Rich Roll. I looked at their words and I knew that's what I wanted. And I realized that their stories had a similar theme. I read about their defining moment, their flash of self-awareness, when they realized that they were out of shape, middle aged, and heading downhill quickly. Their lives were out of balance. They were devoting too much time to work and to having a good time, at the expense of their health and their families.

I could identify. That was me.

I read about a breakthrough moment, a day when each one of them woke up and thought, "Not today. I refuse to be the person I used to be." Generally, this resulted in them putting on a pair of old running shoes and going out for a run. Wind blew through their hair, glorious oxygen filled their lungs, and they were carried away on a cloud of triumphant enthusiasm. They only realized they were still running when they were many miles away from home, or the sun was setting and they'd been out all day, or some such thing.

I could not identify. That was most certainly not me.

I'll be honest. My battle had very little to do with inspiration, and an awful lot more to do with dogged determination and perspiration. Those first few runs certainly didn't feel like I had wind beneath my wings. I felt like I was wearing concrete boots for shoes and someone had shoved a rag in my mouth to stop the air going into my lungs. But I did feel rewarded after every run, even if it was only a short run/walk combination. I set milestones for myself: First run of one kilometer. First run without stopping to walk. First run over five kilometers. First run at a certain pace. And then I'd end up trying to break my own records for time or distance. I think in part those were the two things that drove my passion in the early days of running—that good feeling after a run and the constant drive to better my own efforts and records. It wasn't a race against anybody else. It was a race against myself. At least at that stage. Sometimes I wish it could have stayed that way.

My real breakthrough came not on foot but on a bicycle. When I was first starting out, running was difficult. I was heavy, over thirty kilograms overweight, and my sum total of lifetime exercise at that point was close to zero. I had no aerobic base, no underlying fitness I could resuscitate. Running any more than a hundred meters resulted in doubling over with exhaustion. Cycling was more forgiving. I could pedal slowly on the uphills and recover on the downhills. One day, not long after my original epiphany, I was riding up one of the local hills near my house, Hiram's Highway, in Sai Kung, Hong Kong. I was wearing board shorts and a T-shirt, because, well, as a big guy, Lycra isn't very flattering. I may not have been fit but I still had my pride.

Hiram's Highway is a four-lane road with a long and fairly steep climb, and by the time I was half-way up, I was huffing and puffing and dripping sweat. They call it pedaling squares; if that bicycle crank turned any slower I would have stalled and fallen off. I was beaten. At that moment, four guys came cycling up the hill, flying past me in a line, standing up on the pedals out of the saddle and pushing away at those gears. They were lean, fit, and strong. Half of me was embarrassed at the person I was, and the other half of me was envious; each of them was the person I wanted to be. I shrugged my shoulders and resigned myself to my fate, a slow one-two, one-two, trying to winch myself up this hill one pedal stroke at a time.

Life could have ended up very differently if it weren't for one thing: when I got to the top of the hill, they were waiting for me.

"You made it," one said.

"Yeah, eventually," I replied sheepishly. I felt like I was back at school, the new pasty-faced kid surrounded by the big kids.

"I'm Matt. That's Richard, that's Tim, and that's Jan," the friendly one said. The others gave a curt nod.

"Come ride with us," he continued.

"Nah, I couldn't keep up, I'm just starting," I replied.

"Come on . . ."

He was persistent, I'll give him that.

We continued with a couple more rounds of polite requests and declines, until I finally decided why not. What's the worst that could happen?

We set off together, and less than three minutes later I was promptly dropped off the back of the pack as they sped off into the distance.

But I was stupid enough to come back. And keep coming back. I'd found something that interested me. In another big spin on that great wheel of life, I'd found a new fascination. And I was hooked. They told me they rode three times a week. Tuesday morning, Thursday morning, and a long ride on Saturday morning. *Ridiculous*, I thought. *How could anyone ever do that much exercise in a week and remain sane?* But I was going to give it a go.

Those guys, Matt Baile, Richard Hall, Tim Kremer, and Jan Skovgaard, remain close friends to this day. If I said earlier that Trilby was my source of common sense and strength, they were my source of sporting motivation and inspiration. And I still ride with them, every Tuesday, Thursday, and Saturday.

Little by little I improved. It wasn't overnight, and I wasn't naturally gifted. But with each ride I held on for a little longer before being dropped, until one day I held on for the whole ride.

This only spurred my enthusiasm. It was time to put my newfound fitness to the test. I decided a cycling race was too much, but my improvements in cycling fitness and reduction in weight had trickled down to a decent improvement in my running. I signed up for the Gatorade 8K Riverside Run. I was terrified. I somehow convinced Trilby to sign up with me. At the time I convinced her it would be a good bonding experience, but I think I probably just needed the moral support.

By the time I reached the starting line I was quivering. I looked beside me and there were a group of young men in a circular huddle, reciting the Lord's Prayer. In reflection I'm sure they were all friends from a religious group, but at the time, my first ever race experience, I had the sudden fear that they were calling on the Almighty for salvation in the desperate hour of need. My quivering descended into outright terror.

At that moment, the starting gun sounded. I started running and an hour or so later I crossed the finish line. I was jubilant. I certainly wasn't first, but I finished. And I wasn't last. That smoldering ember of athletic competition and introspection was suddenly fanned into a roaring fire. If I could do this, what else could I achieve?

The 8K run was followed by a 10K race. Next, I tried a short triathlon, known as a sprint. This led to longer Olympic-distance triathlons, then half marathons, marathons, and finally Ironman distance and beyond. My abilities also slowly improved. I went from the back of the pack to the middle and finally to the podium. I was winning local races. And soon enough I became a target. The guy to beat. Sometimes I wished I'd just kept it simple.

I was an addict looking for a fix, and as time passed the doses had to increase. The races became more and more adventurous or difficult. I ran the Boston Marathon and the Escape from Alcatraz Triathlon; I qualified for both Ironman 70.3 World Championships and Ironman Full Distance World Championships in Kona, Hawaii. I stage raced a five-day 250-kilometer ultramarathon in China and multiday bike races in Europe. To top it all, I did the Norseman Xtreme Triathlon.

Norseman was brutal, considered by many to be the hardest long-course iron distance triathlon on the planet. Held annually in Norway, it begins with a ten-foot jump off a ferry barge into a freezing fjord, immediately followed by a 4-kilometer swim in the early morning half-light, a 180-kilometer bike ride across some of the most windswept and rugged terrain on the planet, and a 42-kilometer run through remote Scandinavian countryside, culminating in a rocky climb up Mount Gaustablikk, the tallest mountain in the region. There is no official support. No winners, no losers, no prize money, no trophy. If you were one of the top guys who finished fast enough, you got to climb that mountain to claim your reward—a black T-shirt. A black T-shirt that has been only been awarded only a few hundred times in the ten-year history of the event, but a black T-shirt that in the right circles is legendary.

It wasn't long after Norseman, while wearing my black T-shirt, I started to consider what next. I felt like I'd done a lot of triathlons and quite a few running races. I'd competed around the world, and although I wouldn't claim to be world class, I could hold my head high having completed some of the most iconic athletic events on the planet. I wanted to do something different. Something that would really test my limits. A once-in-a-lifetime race, the race to end all races. I started to look at completing what runners call the Grand Slam—each of the World Marathon Majors, the most famous marathons in the world: Tokyo, London, Boston, Berlin, Chicago, and New York.

But for some reason that didn't really seem like a challenge. It was very vague and nebulous. It wouldn't be hard to go and run these races for a finish. I never had any aspirations of winning one of these professional marathons; the aim of the Grand Slam is simply to finish. To me the Grand Slam seemed like more of an exercise in luck of getting the entry, travel planning, and financing. I'm not saying it would have been easy, but it wasn't a real challenge.

It did plant a seed though. Those World Marathon Majors were held in different countries around the world. Instead of doing those races, maybe I could do one marathon on every continent. My mind raced. It was possible. But again it was vague and undefined. That could take a lifetime, it was such an uncertain achievement. And then it struck me.

I needed to run those seven marathons on those seven continents in seven days.

One of my character traits, or possibly flaws, is that I never think too much about the intricacies of a plan. It was a characteristic that had led to many achievements but had also gotten me into sticky situations on more than one occasion.

Once the concept of the seven marathons on seven continents in seven days popped into my head, the next question wasn't if—it was how. I figured for something so obscure there was only one place to turn: the Internet. That spark of interest lit a flame of curiosity, and like other previous fascinations in my life, I had to know everything there was to know. I sought exact details and definitions of continents, continental boundaries, time zones, geography, current political instabilities, climates, and seasons to help establish a preliminary list of potential countries, race sites, and suitable dates. I mapped travel routes and flight plans, trying to put that jigsaw of geographical information together, compressed into only one week, 168 hours from start to finish.

By the start of March 2014, I had maps, charts, spreadsheets, notes, and graphs. And when I'd finished and put together a potential plan, I e-mailed the only person I could find on the Internet who had ever done something similar before, Richard Donovan. I was a little bashful with initial contact. I imagined he wouldn't be too keen to help a random stranger who e-mailed him from the results of a Google search. I couldn't have been more wrong. Richard bubbled with enthusiasm at the talk of my plans.

His reply to my e-mail was deceptively simple:

> Hi David,
>   Apologies for the delay replying.
>   I'm actually organising a 7 marathons on 7 continents in 7 days trip in January 2015 . . .

Sometimes it can be difficult to interpret the tone of an e-mail, and sometimes it's very easy. From this e-mail it was clear. Richard was an enthusiast, and he wanted this as much as I did. For him this wasn't about making money as a tour operator or fame; this was the ultimate run, pure and simple. He was the person to work with.

I put my plans on hold—this sounded much more interesting. So much for all that research. However, doing it as a group, having camaraderie, support and a spot of competition—that would make it something very special.

I didn't hear back from Richard for what felt like months. And then one day in the middle of July 2014, I got another e-mail.

> Hi David,
>   I'm doing good—hope you are.
>   Yes, it's happening . . .

There were a few more lines and a couple more e-mails, but Richard was clearly a man of few words. I liked that. There was no bravado and no sales pitch. It was a simple choice of whether I wanted to run. I knew my answer. There was only one person I had to convince.

Sometimes people really surprise you in the nicest ways. Trilby has always stood by me. She's also been the filter for my endeavors, giving a quick but thoughtful mental assessment of each idea. You'd be amazed how many she rejects as either silly, impossible, or downright dangerous. I hesitantly told her the plan, not sure how she was going to take it, but not feeling entirely confident.

She looked me straight in the eye.

"Is this really important to you?" she asked. Her tone was flat but not un-emotional. She was probing, questioning, trying to determine my true feelings.

I replied that it was.

She paused for what felt like five minutes, but in reality was probably just seconds.

"Well," she continued, "it's going to be a huge commitment. It's going to be a lot of time away from your family when you're training. It's going to be a lot of time out of town and away from work when you're actually doing it. And it's going to cost a lot of money."

She paused again.

"But if it's really important to you, then I'm behind you."

I can't thank her enough for that. That was a moment of faith and a vote of confidence, an affirmation that somebody believed in me, thought I was capable of doing this, and appreciated how important it was to me. But it also took away my excuse. My get out. My reason not to go. From that moment on I knew the race was happening, and for the first time in a long time, I was scared. It felt good.

The next person I e-mailed was my coach, Nigel Gray. I've never met Nigel, at least not in person—in fact, he lives on the other side of the world—yet I consider him a good friend. Nigel got me through multiple Ironman races, transcontinental bicycles races, world championships, and ultramarathons, and I'd wager he knows me better than most. I've learned that a good coach can empathize and sympathize with their athletes, understand what motivates them, and understand how to make them respond. Through regular e-mail and careful analysis of the exercise data I upload him from my Garmin training watch, Nigel generally knows how I'm feeling physically and mentally, when to push and when to relax. Sometimes it's a little uncanny what can be deciphered from a heartbeat and a power output or run pace report. More than that, he's second only to my wife in stopping me from doing ridiculous races, or doing too many of them, and when he makes a gentle suggestion or comment I know it's time to listen.

I sent him an e-mail outlining the plan. A reply came back after a couple of hours:

> You like your crazy races don't you?
> Well I'm not going to waste time asking if you're serious. I know you are.
> I'll be honest. I don't know how to train you for this.
> Because I've never trained anyone for a race like this before.
> Because there's never been a race like this before . . .
> But I'm thinking we're going to need to do quite a lot of running.

I knew he was chuckling when he wrote it. Nigel had said more than once that if nothing else, at least I was an interesting person to coach.

From that day we started training. We had around six months in total for specific preparation, although I was already fairly fit; I'd just finished on the podium at Ironman Malaysia. We'd have a gentle start to allow time for some muscular recovery and repair, and then a constant build.

My training varied from week to week, but Nigel generally had me running four or five times a week, cycling three times a week, swimming twice a week, and doing some gym weights every couple of days. During my peak weeks, I was running around 120 kilometers a week, riding about 200 kilometers, and swimming about 8 kilometers. I'm sure a lot of professional sports people do a lot more than that, but I wasn't a professional. I was an average Joe with a wife, two daughters, two dogs, a cat, some fish, and a full-time job running a fairly large veterinary hospital with my wife. The only way to fit in the training was to get up at around four o'clock in the morning, train for two to three hours, come home, shower, play with the girls, and then be out the door to start work by eight. I'd be home again around seven in the evening and play with the girls before they went to bed. Then eat and be fast asleep by nine. I was exhausted.

Of course there's that old maxim that nutrition is the forgotten discipline of training, and I was very careful with diet. I needed to be as lean as possible going into the race. I've come to believe that if you can't see how your meal got from farm to your plate in one step, you probably shouldn't eat it. Nothing overly processed, no refined carbohydrates. I relied on a mostly plant-based diet, supplemented with a small amount of fish. Maybe it was in my imagination, but without the fish protein I just felt I didn't recover fast enough. I really cut down on alcohol to almost zero and avoided going out for dinner. It didn't take long for Trilby to wish she'd never agreed to this plan. I became a food zealot. On the inside she knew me well enough, and she knew that once I decided I was going to do something I became obsessive. It was at times a blessing and at times a curse, but I certainly was focused. I only had one target.

Six months went by very quickly, and before I knew it, that target was standing right in front of me, staring me in the face.

It was Friday the 9th of January 2015. My flight was leaving Hong Kong that evening bound for Punta Arenas, at the southernmost tip of Chile.

All of a sudden that pent-up anticipation and excitement evolved into fear and trepidation.

I couldn't escape the fact.

It was time.

THE STARTING LINE

You wouldn't be human if you weren't nervous.

—Steven Purcell, running buddy

There's something formulaic about all the races I have done, from the ten-kilometer local fun runs to the transcontinental cycling epics. A methodology, a structure, that begins with a period before the race when the competitors take measure of each other. I'm sure this happens in all competitions, from Formula One to club tennis matches, but I always find it slightly unnerving.

For us, our moment of measure came in Punta Arenas, at the tip of southern Chile, in South America, the staging point for the first leg of the race. We'd all traded a few introductory e-mails in the preceding months, but Punta Arenas was where we were all scheduled to meet for the first time face to face. The race director, Richard Donovan, had booked us all into a hotel for a couple of days to allow time for handing out race information, holding briefing meetings, preparing equipment, and making sure everyone was up to speed, and up to the task. Race details had been fairly scant up to that point.

Richard had assured us by e-mail that he had everything under control. We knew the basic plan. Seven marathons run on seven continents in seven days. The first marathon was to be held at Union Glacier on mainland Antarctica, and then we would fly back to Punta Arenas, Chile, for South America; Miami, Florida, for North America; Madrid, Spain, for Europe; Marrakech, Morocco, for Africa; Dubai, the United Arab Emirates, for Asia; and finally Sydney, Australia, where we would finish under the Harbour Bridge. And Richard had been clear: seven days meant seven calendar days, or 168 hours—no cheating with changing time zones. It meant that once the starting gun fired, we were going to have very little room for error and a very short stay on each continent. The plan was to fly in, get running as soon as we hit the ground, and then get back on the next flight without delay. After we left Antarctica, all of the flights were regular commercial airlines, so any problems or holdups might mean a missed flight and overall failure.

And as such, these few days before the race were going to be critical. We needed to all understand clearly the exact times and plans. We needed to go over the schedule in detail, and we needed to prepare.

At least that was the official reason. Unofficially, we all knew what it was, at least for us competitors. It was the crunch time, the time when we each lay our first hand of cards on the table in a week-long game of physical and mental poker. It was going to be a delicate dance of inquiry, assessment, charm, and bluff.

The flight to Punta Arenas was a long one and was strangely relaxing and therapeutic. It allowed me to start to let go of life back in civilization, to forget about some of the less pressing issues and concerns, but more than anything else to prepare myself for the coming week of racing. The physical preparation had finished more than a fortnight ago; any more now would risk overtraining and injury. It was the mental side that needed fortification. And the truth is that, mentally, I was not ready. I think to some degree I had hidden my fears away and convinced myself that it'd be all right, that it was just another race. But inside I knew this to be untrue. Stage racing is always emotionally brutal. The physical battle is draining and painful, but it's falling into the emotional abyss that will force you to quit.

I've always thought that our lives could be divided into three sections: work, family, and personal pastimes. These three compete for the only truly limited and finite resource we all have: time. Finding an ideal balance of the three is challenging, if not impossible. For the last three months my balance had shifted heavily toward work. Nothing disastrous, but the work needed to be done and it had taken its toll. I'd made sure the physical training had been done—a 4:30 a.m. daily wake-up followed by a long run, cycling, or swimming session had made sure of that. But I hadn't really even thought about preparing mentally— I'd been too busy with other things.

The flight took me from Hong Kong to Auckland, then a transfer to another flight landing in Santiago. After a brief stopover I finally touched down in Punta Arenas. It was over a day on a plane in total, which to some may sound terrible but to me was absolutely perfect. No mobile phone reception. No Internet. Nobody who knew me. Just time to think. Time to prepare and plan. And also time to get excited. I had spent such a long time focusing on the training because, to be honest, I knew that if I thought about the race too much I would be terrified. But that also meant I hadn't given myself a chance to become motivated and enthusiastic, to light that spark of desire to succeed and build it into a raging fire that would give me the fuel to get through the week.

It had been a long time since I'd been able to sit and wait and think, with no pressing task or pestering agenda. That flight wasn't that different from a good long run. Solitude, quiet, peace. An inner strength can be built in that silence. A quiet, determined resolve.

And that's what this would take: resolve. Resolve not to let minor ailments affect the outcome. Resolve not to give in to discomfort. A relentless resolve to fight on and to succeed.

—◦◦◦—

I'm not sure what I expected from Punta Arenas. To be completely honest, at that stage the only issue really important to me was my luggage showing up. Somewhere in that thirty hours and twenty-five thousand kilometers in the air I'd realized there was more than one chance for my bags to miss a connection or get lost along the way. Arriving for seven days of world travel combined with seven marathons with only what I was wearing wasn't going to be a happy experience. And of course, as luck would have it, my suitcase seemed to be pretty much the last on the carousel, probably because it had also traveled the farthest in its voyage.

It was my first time traveling to South America. Never underestimate the impact of hearing a new language spoken, something that to you is exotic and fresh but to the speaker is considered normal. To a large degree that's what makes it so exotic and inspiring: the mere fact that in these parts it's commonplace.

I've heard that economies can be compared using the price of a hamburger. But I've always thought that societies can be compared by their taxis. Perhaps it's because I don't eat many hamburgers. Taxis, more than restaurants or hotels or attractions, are a reflection of their drivers, an extension of their homes, personalized with curios and possessions. It's one of the few close interactions most travelers have with a regular townsperson.

After some negotiation and discussion at the taxi queue, I was shown to a car, an old weather-beaten sedan with a meter wedged into the dash and a crack running the length of the windscreen. And an old, weather-beaten driver. Inside, the taxi was littered with receipts, newspapers, and the remnants of a half-eaten lunch, but I was greeted by one of the friendliest smiles I'd seen so far on this trip, paired with some pleasantries in broken English. And with that we were off, and the expedition had truly begun.

Barren, austere, but with a stark rugged beauty, Punta Arenas is the capital city of Magallanes, the Patagonian region at the southern tip of Chile. Yet this capital city still had the feel of a small seaside community that refused to let modernity force its hand.

The coastline felt desolate and windswept, like something out of *The Shipping News*. Rusty skeletons of century-old ships were beached next to long-abandoned rotting wooden jetties, slowly crumbling back into the Pacific Ocean. Punta Arenas has swung from boom times to hard times and back again, with gold and wool booms, and now the oil rush creating an odd panoply of ramshackle wooden houses and elaborate Gothic manors.

It was a town of stark contrasts and opposing forces. We passed through the outlying areas, a curious mixture of farms slowly eroding back into the land and newly minted oil exploration equipment. The land seemed deserted of life apart from the occasional alpaca standing watch on a hill. We passed through the fringes of the city and its rickety houses, their red-tin roofs and walls covered in street art ranging from beautiful Spanish-style murals to hastily scrawled graffiti. We passed through the town square, bordered by a series of elaborate and at times Gaudi-esque houses reminiscent of their former glory. Finally, we arrived at the small hotel, the Rey Don Felipe, sitting on a hill behind the town and overlooking it all.

—◊◊◊—

Hotel Rey Don Felipe was the de facto staging post for the start of the race. All the other competitors were booked in there, as were most of the logistics and event staff. I was one of the last to arrive, and walking into the lobby I felt equal parts lamb to the slaughter and deer in the headlights.

There's always some pageantry at the beginning: a subtle but unmistakable evaluation of each and every one of us by our fellow competitors and by the staff. A hierarchy is formed based solely on outward appearances and rumors of previous achievements. I couldn't help but buy into it, even though I'd learned time and again that these prerace shakedowns are invariably worthless; you can never judge a book by its cover. It's usually the quiet ones you've got to watch out for. I only found out a couple of days later that most of them knew way more about me than I did about them—they had done their research, and apparently one of them was running a book taking bets on who would win.

After a few smiles and handshakes, we sat down around a crackling fireplace in the hotel lobby to try to get to know one another—after all, we were going to be spending the next couple of weeks living together. They were an enjoyable and happy bunch, and though it was early days, I had a good feeling about the race.

James Love, one of the other competitors, was the first to come up and shake my hand.

"Dave. It's been a while."

You could have struck me down with a feather. James Love. We'd run an ultramarathon together along the Silk Road in northwestern China in 2009—the brutal Gobi March, a seven-day 250-kilometer footrace through the desert, carrying all our food, clothing, and other supplies. James and I had met there and formed a bond, pulling each other through the highs and lows of the desert. It had been six years since we'd spoken. But some people you never forget.

James is the kind of guy who tells it the way he sees it but who is always fair in his appraisal. From the English Midlands near Manchester, with a viewpoint that some may describe as realistic (and others pessimistic), he never has a bad word to say about anybody, and I can attest to his strength of character from back when we were in the Gobi. He is a threat. The competitive side of me knows that James can run. That James has willpower. And that James can keep going even as others fall by the wayside. I knew then that I'd have to keep my eye on James.

It appeared that James felt the same way about me but that he was better informed. "I saw you were doing this race. You're looking fit—much less body fat than when we were in Gobi," he joked. "I looked you up, I did," he continued. "A 2:54 in Boston last year—you've come on since Gobi, and that's not the only thing you've done lately. I've seen your races on the Internet, I have."

With that, the chatter amongst the other runners became muted. I knew why. This was the sizing up. James was trying to gauge exactly how fit I was for this race and what his chances were. Everybody else figured they'd let him do the dirty work. James was completely straight down the line; he didn't mess around, he didn't mince his words, and he was an honorable, fierce competitor. He was also looking as if he'd put in a few good miles of training himself since we had last run together.

This wasn't what I had wanted. I didn't want my Boston time to come out. I didn't want anybody thinking I was anything special. It's better to be the humble one, the one that nobody watches. As soon as people think you may be competition, you become a target. It affects their race strategy, how they play their hand each day, and how they try to neutralize yours. Stage racing is always a mental game, and in a group as small as this it was always going to come down to the individual personalities and how we played off against each other.

It wasn't James that concerned me, though. It was the one in the corner. He was the quiet one who hadn't said two words to anybody since I'd been here, and he seemed to prefer his own company if given the option. He was Doug Wilson. We'd never met before, but I had seen his photo on the prerace competitor information. I hadn't bothered looking him up—or anyone else for that matter. I find that kind of research only gets me more worried, but from his photo it was clear he was an ultrarunner, and a good one. A distant stare, a mop of shaggy blond hair, a lean physique, and deep tan testified to hours out in the sun.

James caught me glancing across the room.

"He's here to win, he is," said James, gesturing at Doug.

"Thanks, James. I'm glad to see you haven't lost your sledgehammer touch when it comes to conversation."

James continued, apparently oblivious to the fact that the entire room was now listening, or perhaps reveling in the fact.

"It's between you and him, it is."

Doug stood up and walked out of the lobby, not saying a word. But he did take a good long look at the two of us first. He wasn't a talker; he was a listener, and he'd heard everything. He was evaluating and examining just as much as the rest of us. And I'll be the first to admit it—Doug was there to win.

This definitely wasn't going the way I had wanted. I'd stage raced before, and the worst way to start is by having everyone stacked against each other. We were all competitive, and we were all there to do well. That was what motivated us. That was why we had signed up for a race like this—to test our limits and come out on top. Stoking this competitive fire before the race was a very dangerous path to take. Things could end badly, with arguments and fights. At my most cynical I started to think that's what James might have wanted. His best chance was to play Doug and me against each other, have us both overcook ourselves early and burn out through a combination of overexertion and mental fatigue. James wasn't stupid. James knew how to play the game as well as anybody.

It was time to let some steam out of the pressure cooker. I laughed and told him that I wasn't here for a race; I was here for an experience. I just wanted to finish. I wanted to see seven continents in seven days. I wanted to have fun.

"Yeah, but that's what you always say, innit?" he retorted.

—⟋⟍—

The plan was to hitch a ride on a Russian-made cargo plane, an aging Ilyushin 76, to the middle of the Antarctic continent. The IL-76 was designed in the sixties as a military freighter intended to serve in the worst conditions of the

Siberian and Arctic regions of the former Soviet Union. It was built for heavy lift, short takeoff, and unmaintained runways in subzero conditions. It was perfect for what we needed. It was just a matter of waiting for the right time, for the right conditions.

Flying to Antarctica is an irregular and unpredictable experience to say the least. There is no formal tarmac runway on the Antarctic side; no control tower, no electronic beacons, no lights, nothing. Just a long strip of frozen blue ice with a few markers lining the periphery. The IL-76 weighed around 150 tons. The landing was completely visual, without any automatic instrument or autopilot function, so there could not be any cloud cover, snow, or adverse conditions. If the Antarctic weather was too warm, the ice would melt when the tires touched town and the plane would slide. Any crosswind might cause the plane to skid off the runway. Imagine driving a truck over a field of butter and not having it slip even once. Any meteorological uncertainty on the Antarctic side meant there would be no flight, and no race.

It was Tuesday, January 13, 2015, three days since I'd left behind my family and the world I knew in Hong Kong, and one day before we were going to depart South America for Antarctica, if luck was on our side. It was time for the weather briefing. The transport and logistics company had hired a meteorologist to assess the satellite images and weather reports from various government research stations dotted across Antarctica to determine a map of conditions and a probability of snowfall, cloud, wind—possible flying problems. I've always found meteorologists to be eccentric, and this one was no exception. Tall and thin, with a leathery appearance and straggly beard that suggested he'd spent more time studying the elements firsthand than reading about it in books, he seemed quiet, cautious, and concerned. This was probably the safest and best thing we should have hoped for, but it was the last thing we wanted. Our hearts were set on getting started, and right now his finger was resting on the trigger of the starting gun.

"There's a band of cloud over Union at the moment," he said, referring to the Union Glacier Ice Landing Strip we were planning to use as our access point. "There's also some low pressure readings coming from the research base sensors. This could mean snow and wind. It also might be OK. There's a westerly airflow and the clouds might pass by tomorrow morning. We'll have to wait and see."

He wouldn't be drawn on chances or percentages. He just said it was a possibility. The Antarctic logistics guys told us to go back to our rooms and pack. We needed to be ready. If we were leaving it was going to be very early in the morning, before first light. One of the logistics staff would come around to our rooms tonight to check our gear, then we'd need to be in the foyer ready to go at 4:30 a.m., everything we needed stuffed into one small carry-on bag. Oh, and we had to be dressed in our full extreme-weather gear because after those cargo bay doors closed in South America, the next time they opened it would be into the full onslaught of the Antarctic.

The room was full of nervous anticipation. None of us wanted to get our hopes up. At that moment it felt as if the decision to go rested on the opinion of the meteorologist, the final say of the pilot, and the flip of a coin. I looked around the room at the faces of my companions. Fear. Excitement. Anxiety. Regret. Jubilation. It felt like the complete range of human emotion was on display. Twelve of us in total. Twelve total strangers thrown together for what was sure to become one of the defining events of our lives. And we certainly were a mixed bag. In fact, if pressed I'd say the only common theme running through the group was a thirst for challenge and adventure.

James Love and Doug Wilson I've already mentioned. Both experienced and strong competitors, they were here looking for a win as far as I could tell. James was possibly one of the most unlikely characters. A farmer from the English Midlands, James had developed a passion for ultrarunning, he claimed, while stomping around his property chasing sheep. He was a straight shooter with a very dry sense of humor who wasn't afraid to say what he thought but generally got away with it due his boyish, likable nature. I got the feeling that although James often played the simple farmer, he was one of the canniest and most calculating racers out there on the course.

Doug, from Australia, was harder to read. He came across as introverted and brooding, somebody who often preferred his own company and had a deep interest in mysticism and spirituality. His motivations, intentions, and desires were difficult to fathom. He was definitely the enigma of the group, the quiet one.

Then there was James Danaher, or Big Jim. Big Jim was the kind of guy who bent his head slightly to pass through a doorway. He must have stood a good foot taller than me but carried himself with a gentle and peaceful demeanor. A solicitor from London, Jim was one of the only competitors who I truly believe had no aspirations apart from just wanting to enjoy the experience and say he'd run a marathon on every continent in a week.

Pierre Wolkonsky, who quickly became known as Frenchie, was the youngest in our group but often seemed to carry a wisdom greater than a twentysomething-year-old university student could have been expected to provide. He spoke little of his background, but the pieces of the puzzle suggested he came from a good family, and his father was an important industrialist. He was easily likable and more than prepared to muck in and get his hands dirty despite his rather rarefied upbringing.

From Brazil we had Marcelo Alves, an experienced long-distance athlete, author, and management guru. My impression was that Marcelo was here to test himself more than to test anyone around him. He was the kind of person who notches up personal achievements, continually trying to push his own boundaries and see what he is capable of.

Tim Durbin hailed from San Francisco in the United States. Like Marcelo, Tim was also a management consultant, and his purpose and reason for being here was again unique. Tim had a lifelong mission to run the distance around the equator, or 24,901 miles. He was currently in the middle of a running streak and had run at least a mile, often much more, every day for over the past year. He wasn't looking to end his streak any time soon, not until he'd reached his equatorial target.

Marianna Zaikova represented Finland and was the only female entrant for the full marathon distance of the World Marathon Challenge. Marianna had previously been involved in Finnish television, with roles in prime-time shows such as *Big Brother Finland*, where she developed a significant fan following. In addition to her television and media work, Marianna had a long history of experience in endurance racing, both in running and cycling events, and could certainly hold her own out on the race course.

And then there were Jon O'Shea and Ted Jackson. Jon and Ted were old friends coming into the race, and at times seemed like two peas in a pod, despite their differences. Both from England, Jon was a successful accountant and Ted was a boardinghouse master at a prestigious private school. Jon was a prolific marathoner and had run more races than he could count across more countries than he cared to remember. Jon was the true English gentleman personified, always gracious, reserved, and humble. Ted was the polar opposite. An unrepentant but good-natured rascal, Ted was the center of attention in nearly every situation I was fortunate enough to see him in. He had a way with people, a charm that saw every eye in the room focus on him, and he reveled in it. He was truly a likable rogue, one of those rare individuals whose life never has a dull moment. The two of them seemed like the most unlikely pairing, but in reality they were somehow a perfect match. I'm sure their wives both thought otherwise.

Jon and Ted had signed up for this race together and had previously done other marathons and distance races as a team. They were close, and they shared the kind of bond forged in moments of interreliance when out on the course on a very long day; however, they certainly never used this to exclude others. When

Jon or Ted were around, you were always welcome to sit and pass the time of day with them; there always seemed to be something to talk about.

Uma and Krishna Chigurupati were here for a slightly different reason and were the sole entrants in the half-marathon category. A husband and wife team from India, Uma and Krishna already held a world record for polar marathon racing. Both successful businesspeople, they had met on a previous marathon course and shared a love of adventure and travel. They were here to try to set a new record for the fastest time to run seven half marathons on seven continents in seven days.

We all had our reasons, and we all had our goals. On the face of it we were all very different people, but a group bond was already starting to form. There was a shared enthusiasm and passion, and a shared sense of nervous anticipation of what was to come. Over the week that bond would be tested more than once; we could all only hope that our combined desire to succeed was strong enough to hold us all together.

—⟋⟍—

I was one of the last to leave the briefing. I'm not sure whether I was trying to divine some extra pearl of wisdom about the weather, trying to get to know the crew and team, or just a little nervous to go back to the room, but I stayed. So did Doug, I suspect for much of the same reasons. He and I had hardly spoken since we first met.

"That meteorologist seems like a glass-half full type," I sheepishly joked, trying to diffuse some tension on both sides of the fence.

"He knows what he's talking about, that guy," Doug replied. "You should listen to him." I wasn't sure exactly what Doug was referring to, but I knew what he meant. We weren't friends, at least not at this stage, and I might as well not try to play nice and pretend we were.

That was the last Doug spoke to me for days.

By the time I had returned to my room, the sun had gone down. If I quickly packed my bags, I'd be able to wander down to the main area of Punta for a meal. I figured it would be an important one, maybe one of the last sit-down meals I would have for a while.

I laid out everything on the floor. First my race clothing: thick woolen beanie and skullcap, face mask, ski goggles, thermal base layer for both the legs and torso, running jacket, windproof thermal over-jacket and leggings, a double pair of socks, and a pair of snow-rated ultrarunning trail shoes. It looked as if I were about to accompany Shackleton on a polar expedition, but with modern gear. I'd never run on snow before. In fact, I'd never even seen snow fall. I'd lived nearly all of my adult life in Hong Kong, a country that for most of the year is humid and steamy. I attended university in Perth, Australia, a city set on a desert. My school years were in Sydney. All of these places had never seen a flake of snow in their history. It was starting to dawn on me that running a marathon in the Antarctic with no previous experience of snow may be a little ambitious, to say the least.

Next came the fuel to keep me going through the race: carbohydrate gels, protein bars, snacks, and drinks. I knew I wasn't going to eat enough when I was out there—I never seem to—but it was a matter of having it with me, just in case.

Lastly, I needed to remember this wasn't only about a marathon. We would be away for an uncertain period of time. The weather conditions affecting the flight there were equally applicable to the flight back; if the situation on the ground changed, we could be delayed. I packed a change of clothes, my tablet computer, and a ruggedized Olympus camera, specially purchased for the expedition and designed to deal with hostile environments. With a small moment of satisfaction, I left out my HTC smartphone. It had become an extension of my body for most of my working life; I was never more than a few feet away from it at any time of day or night. There was no reception in Antarctica. No mobile phones. No Internet. No e-mail. Nothing. I didn't feel entirely comfortable severing that umbilical connection with the outside world, but it was a decision outside my control, and secretly something inside me was very pleased about the fact.

I closed the latches on my small carry-on suitcase and did one more mental recheck to make sure I hadn't forgotten anything. I took a short stroll into town and down the main street to find a cozy local restaurant. A few of the other runners, Jon, Ted, and Big Jim, had kindly asked me if I wanted to join them for pizza, but I'd declined. It was a time for peace and quiet and reflection, thinking about the upcoming mission but at the same time not letting others make me nervous about it.

I ended up stumbling on La Marmita, a small family-run restaurant located a little out of the town center, apparently famous for their simple home-cooked local food. As I walked inside I knew I'd chosen well. The decoration could only be described as vibrant and would not have been out of place in a Picasso painting. Brightly colored Chilean flags, posters, and paintings were plastered on the walls; local curios and handiworks sat in every nook and cranny.

The waitress greeted me with a genuine smile and showed me to a seat. I've always felt a little uncomfortable eating alone—the lack of conversation seemed to make time drag on—but tonight it felt like the right choice, and the buzz and excitement of the restaurant helped distract my mind from worrying about the task ahead.

I threw caution to the wind and ordered an entrée of ceviche. Ceviche is a Chilean specialty, consisting of raw fish pickled in vinegar and spices. It was a risk—ceviche spoils quickly—and perhaps I should have kept it simple and safe, but I was a sucker for local delicacies and something in me felt like tempting fate. It was delicious. The main course was a heart-warming pot of soulful Chilean casserole, more than sufficient to fill my stomach and quell my rising nerves. With that it was time to meander up the quiet streets back to the hotel and try to get some much needed sleep; it was going to be a very long week.

Still, sleep never comes easy before a race. A combination of apprehension and anxiety coupled with a fear of sleeping through my alarm saw me tossing and turning though most of the night, waiting for the big unknown in the morning.

———✳———

I woke with a start. The alarm was ringing, but it was still dark outside. This was a good sign—at least I hadn't missed the flight. There was already rustling and movement in the corridor. My fellow competitors were up and about and getting ready. It was time to leave.

We sat as a group of twelve in the lobby nervously waiting for the green light. A strange parody to my arrival and our first meeting, this time we were all wearing the mandatory heavy-duty orange extreme-weather Antarctic survival suits. We must have looked like a sight to the bleary-eyed concierge at the end of his night shift.

The bus rolled up and our faces lit up. It still wasn't a complete guarantee—the final decision was down to the pilot and air crew—but the chances were looking good. We had to move. There was no exact flight schedule for Antarctic trips, just a flight window, but the window was currently open and we needed to get airborne while the weather was on our side.

We were scheduled to fly from Punta Arenas in Chile to Ushuaia in Argentina, stopping to pick up Argentinian soldiers to transport them to their Belgrano II base, located approximately eight hundred miles from the South Pole on mainland Antarctica. They were the primary reason for our trip, and I suspect they were shouldering most of the cost of the flight.

We arrived at the airport, were shuttled quickly through Chilean customs, walked across the tarmac and around the nose cone of the hulking IL-76. It looked more intimidating than I had imagined, a relic from days of the USSR long past. As we climbed the metal stairs to a small entrance door behind the cockpit, I felt we were transitioning from civilized comfort and luxury to the harsh realities of a continent where form followed function.

The interior of the plane didn't disappoint my expectations: cavernous and void of any partitioning or unnecessary amenities. Wires were hanging from the ceiling; in places paneling had been removed or fallen away, revealing pipes and tubing originally camouflaged. Russian notes and exclamations were stenciled in bright yellow Cyrillic script at various points, and I could only hope their meaning wasn't a warning important for passengers. This was not to suggest the aircraft wasn't serviceable; in fact, completely the opposite seemed to be true—it was designed not to look pretty but to work, and work it did.

The flight crew was Ukrainian, and apparently they were experts at extreme weather flying. They came aboard without any fanfare or fuss and didn't bother with any more than a passing look at their cargo of runners and support. After some preflight checks and preparations, the four massive jet engines were fired, we taxied down the runway, and with the gentlest of lifts, the massive bird raised itself aloft.

We flew for about an hour until we crossed into Argentinian airspace and landed in Ushuaia, the southernmost city in the world. We were here to pick up the soldiers, and we were to stay aboard and wait as they boarded and loaded their equipment through the massive cargo doors at the rear.

The soldiers were heading out for a yearlong posting, which included what they call wintering. The Antarctic wintering period lasts from the middle of February to the end of August, a season of permanent darkness and the fiercest weather preventing any direct contact with the outside world. No flights, no ships, nothing. If the situation goes wrong during wintering, you're on your own; there's no chance of rescue. It sounded terrifying, but to the soldiers it was a badge of honor and a highly sought-after post. I realized we had a long way to go before we could be considered the toughest and most enduring on this flight; in fact, we'd be lucky not to be the softest.

The men joked and laughed amongst themselves; they spoke little English and we spoke little Spanish. They had a camaraderie we as a group had yet to establish, but then again, they were not competing with each other. They sat huddled around their equipment toward the rear of the plane and appeared to share our feelings of nervous excitement and anticipation, albeit for different reasons.

We waited. A long time. The minutes became hours, and the jokes and humor died down into a quieter drone of conversation. I'd never sat on a plane for a prolonged period without moving. Sitting in the parked plane started to became claustrophobic and eerily silent, as if we were in the belly of a beached whale, languishing. Nobody wanted to ask why we weren't moving. We were all concerned we knew the answer—had the weather turned in Antarctica? Was the trip postponed? Or even worse, canceled?

Finally, one of us plucked up the courage to ask the flight crew what was going on. This was the first time I'd seen Ted Jackson in action, although his reputation had preceded him. The joker in the pack. The motley fool. The guy who would be the first to give you the shirt off his own back when the chips were down, and to listen to you when you had a problem, but who hid it well under a knavish charm. He was the most unlikely of all of us to be here. Stout and muscular with a big bushy beard, he certainly didn't look like a runner. He was never going to win. His goals were much nobler: to raise money for multiple sclerosis, a condition afflicting his wife. And to have as much fun as he could along the way, while enjoying as much of the limelight as he possibly could. He was the glue who would bind us together, diffuse our tensions with some comic relief. I had only just begun to realize this, and to realize we would need it.

He walked straight up the Ukrainian navigator, a disarming smile on his face, his right arm outstretched in greeting. They shook hands and after a short discussion Ted turned around. The smile broke into a grin from ear to ear, and he started singing what I think was "Ave Maria." It turned out he had been a tenor opera singer in a past life. The plane fell silent and he revealed the source of his amusement: apparently the Argentinian officials were refusing customs clearance. To their own military. It was going to take a little time and some negotiation, but it didn't seem like a major wrench in the works.

After finishing "Ave Maria," he sat back down and started a rather quieter rendition of "You'll Never Take the Falklands." The joker in the pack. We were thanking our lucky stars the Argentinians didn't hear this pro-British war ditty. Another hour passed, and the flight crew suddenly started hustling. The word had come through, approvals had been given, we could proceed. Once things happened, they happened fast, and we were in the air again after what seemed like minutes.

All aboard—next stop Antarctica.

MARATHON 1: ANTARCTICA

Union Glacier: A Trial by Fire in the Coldest Place on Earth

Why is it that you do these things? Are you trying to prove something to yourself? Or are you trying to prove something to others?

—Franziska von Kleist, my friend and neighbor

Everyone has a handful of truly unforgettable moments that get permanently etched into their memory. For me, opening the cargo plane doors and stepping out into Antarctica was one of those moments. There was an electricity in the air. Everybody felt it, everybody was part of it. There was no more magnificent place on Earth to start our epic adventure than where we were right now.

Vast whiteout, biting winds, snow flurries, and blue-tinted ice carved by the elements, over a kilometer thick down to sea level, at its depths unchanged for millions of years. In stark contrast to the massive water reserves below, the frozen air was bone dry and instantly numbed our faces and fingers; the desiccated snow crackled under our feet.

If you ever get the chance to go to Antarctica, you must take it. There's something about the place that is uniquely sublime and awe inspiring, visceral. It still feels undiscovered and untamed, bending us to its will rather than the other way around.

Roughly twice the size of Australia but nearly entirely covered in ice and snow, Antarctica is truly inhospitable and remote. It is the only continent without indigenous human inhabitants. Temperatures can drop as low as minus eighty degrees Celsius (over minus one hundred degrees Fahrenheit), although fortunately for us it was a relatively balmy minus fifteen degrees Celsius (five degrees Fahrenheit) when we arrived.

As we stepped onto the ice we were greeted by a gleaming white vista that would be bathed in sunlight for twenty-four hours a day. The clarity of the air, the intense blue of the sky—I just wasn't used to it. So crisp and cold it instantly numbed any part of my body exposed, invigorating yet energy sapping. Around us were great snow drifts, ice cliffs, and jagged, snow-covered granite mountains in the distance, but the lack of any other feature on this bleak terrain made distance and scale difficult to judge. We were drops in an ocean.

But we had no time to stop and gawk; we had to keep moving. The IL-76 had to get back off the ice before its wheels froze to the runway, and we had to get to the shelter of our base. Waiting to take us there was a massive six-wheeled heavily modified SUV. It was a ten-kilometer drive over the snow to Union Glacier Camp.

Union Glacier Camp is the only privately run base on the continent, located deep within mainland Antarctica only six hundred miles from the South Pole, situated in the Ellsworth mountain chain and near Mount Vinson, the highest peak on the continent. Union Glacier Camp is surrounded by an environment that is stunningly beautiful, but at the same time viciously unforgiving. There are no tarmac roads, no permanent houses, no trees, and no birds or animals. There are no penguins—that's only on the coast. No polar bears—that's the Arctic. Just beautiful, barren, sparkling white snow and ice.

The camp provides logistics and support to scientific expeditions, private tour groups, and some of the government research stations. At its center were three or four large tents, including a main mess hall that could accommodate around fifty people. The rest of the camp is regularly scattered with smaller one- or two-person sleeping clamshells, heated naturally by the constant glare of the midnight sun and, surprisingly, gloriously warm.

The camp is located in an area of safety, built on a solid ice foundation, but the surrounding terrain is exceedingly dangerous. The massive slab of ice that makes up Union Glacier is in a constant state of flux, slowly but inexorably pushing its way to the sea. It moves up to a meter a week, and as it travels down its path, giant cracks and clefts develop in the ice, sometimes measuring hundreds of meters in width and depth. The base staff use a special ground-penetrating radar to map the glacier and its fissures, but we were warned that nothing was guaranteed: they had lost a whole snow-tractor down a crevasse the previous season. Reassuringly, they had spent a significant amount of time mapping our course, a ten-and-a-half-kilometer rectangular loop that stretched so far that the base would be completely hidden for most of the run. We would be surrounded only by ice, snow, and distant mountains. It was beautiful.

———ɯɯ———

Antarctic mornings are an experience. As soon as you poke your head out from under the thick double-walled sleeping bag, you need to put on your sunglasses. The constant daylight is so bright it penetrates even through the fabric of the tent.

The next step is to take your clothes, which you had carefully left next to the bed the night before, and place them in your sleeping bag for five minutes to warm them up enough to put on: woolen base layer, long top and trousers, intermediate fleece layer, and outer windbreaker. The sunscreen needs to go in the sleeping bag as well, to melt it from something hard as candle wax to a pasty liquid soft enough to be applied. To venture outside without sunscreen would result in rapid snow- and sunburn.

Then it's off to the bathroom. Nothing stays on the continent, which must be kept pristine, so there are separate toilets for liquid and solid—an experience in coordination and planning if nothing else. Brushing teeth is similar to applying sunscreen. My toothpaste was as hard as a rock and needed to be chipped off and then thawed out before being useable. And then coffee. The environment was so cold it was difficult to taste anything, but the coffee was liquid and warm, and that was enough.

I woke up at 6 a.m. on my first morning in Antarctica; the rest of the camp was sleeping, apart from the skeleton night crew. Nothing else for it but to go for an early morning run. As required, I registered myself out of camp with the staff, and went off to test the roughly ten-kilometer course, marked only with small blue flags set roughly fifty meters apart. Once again they clearly stressed the need to stay on the marked course. Some new crevasses had formed near the camp recently, and these were often hidden, covered by a thin layer of snowdrift.

After running a kilometer or so it started snowing, and the camp was left in a whiteout. Running was from marker to marker, and it was otherworldly.

Another few kilometers and the snowstorm cleared, opening up a sweeping panorama of the mountains, the vast icy plains between us, and not a soul to be seen in any direction. If it was a training run it was a failure—I couldn't help myself but to stop every few minutes just to look around and soak it up. And when that wasn't enough I sat down and stared. And then I laid on my back in the snow and looked up.

But I was five kilometers from base and many thousands from civilization, and I was on a time limit. I had to get back before they grew concerned and sent out a search party. Even so, when I did finally return I had to stop myself from doing another lap. It would have to wait until the marathon proper.

After cleaning myself up and slipping back into my "casual" clothes, I headed over to the main tent. By now it was 8 a.m., and some of my fellow competitors had started stirring and getting dressed, but Jon O'Shea was the only one so far who had made it to breakfast. Jon was a true English gent, a tax accountant by day and an unstoppable athlete by night. He'd done more marathons than I'd had baked dinners, but he never made a big fuss about it. Jon was probably one of the only people there who I really believed had no ulterior motive except to enjoy himself and do what he loved. He was similar to Big Jim in that respect. Sure, Jon was looking to make the best of himself, but I really didn't get the feeling he was looking to beat anybody but himself. Every time I saw him he had a smile on his face—a trait that seemed to develop as the week went on. He was the most unlikely accountant I'd ever met.

"Good morning, David. Sleep well?" Jon asked.

"Yep, OK, I guess. I've been out for a run."

"Already? It's eight in the morning."

"Yeah, I know it's late," I joked. "I slept in today."

Breakfast hadn't been served yet, so we were able to sit and chat, get to know each other, talk about what made a person tick. There didn't ever feel a need to be on guard with Jon. More than anybody else he seemed genuinely interested in those around him, where we came from and where we were going.

The other competitors slowly shuffled in and sat down. Soon enough it was quite a tea party. Ted arrived, as did James; Pierre, the young Frenchman; Tim, my American tent-mate; and Big Jim, all of whom came to play a very important part in my experiences and adventures over the next week. Doug arrived last and sat at the end of the table but as usual didn't say much.

Jon began: "Can you believe David's already been out this morning. He's run ten Ks."

"Are you nuts?" Ted laughed. "Don't you think we'll have enough running in the next week?"

"I just wanted to get out and experience it," I replied. "I was up early. There was nothing to do, I was bored, and I didn't want to mess around in the tent and wake Tim. It just seemed like a fun thing to do. I wanted to run the course."

"Well, go on then," Big Jim said in his signature booming voice. "What was it like?"

"Spectacular. This is going to be an amazing race."

"How long did it take you?" asked Pierre.

"I dunno. I wasn't really counting. I kept stopping to enjoy the scenery. Maybe forty-eight minutes?"

I wouldn't be telling the truth if I said my reply was entirely innocent. It was a gentle statement and an implied question. Forty-eight minutes for a roughly ten-kilometer loop means that my overall marathon time could be around three to three and a half hours, especially when the ten kilometers was only a training run. Three hours isn't lightning, but it certainly isn't slow, and they all knew it. I thought it was time to throw the cat amongst the pigeons.

James didn't miss a beat. "You hear that, Doug? He's already been out and running this morning, he has. He's done a whole loop, he has. Have you been out yet?" He was pushing the needle, and nobody—including me—was stopping him.

There was a short uncomfortable silence, and then Doug stood up.

"I'm always out running. You'll never know where I'll be." And with that, he turned and walked off.

Just like our conversation in Punta Arenas, this wasn't quite the way I had planned the discussion to go, and I was quickly learning that James, for all his deceptively simple charm, was possibly the smartest of the lot of us, at least when it came to playing the stage-racing game.

———※———

The wait. The wait was difficult, more difficult than I had expected. We had to wait until the return flight was confirmed, as the Antarctic marathon had to begin as close to when the flight leaves Antarctica as possible. The moment that starting gun fires, the clocks start ticking. From then we had seven days, 168 hours, to reach the finish line under the Harbour Bridge in Sydney, Australia. No time zones, no tricks—168 hours from start to finish; 168 hours to travel between seven continents, fly over 55,000 kilometers, run seven marathons totaling over 295 kilometers, and do it all without any mistakes or errors. There was no room to maneuver.

The waiting was difficult. The uncertainty was worse. If I had known how long it would take, I could plan, adjust, count down the remaining minutes and hours. But it could be a day or, they tell me, it could be a week. It all depended on the weather being safe enough to allow that IL-76 to land again. That's a whole lot of pressure—not just atmospheric. Never mind the race. No contact with the outside world should be invigorating, but it's also very isolating. Responsibilities, family commitments, work? These aren't subject to restrictions of an Antarctic blizzard. Back in civilization, time marches on.

I tried to look at the wait as a positive. The first and probably only time I'll ever be in Antarctica. Soak it up. Surrender to it. Enjoy it. But in reality that can only last so long. It's only possible to be outside for short times before getting very cold, unless involved in vigorous activity. So most of the time is spent sitting, waiting, running over the same race scenarios with the same limited and incomplete information again and again, until you start questioning what is fact and what is hope.

Luckily the people I'd traveled with were a good bunch; conversion flowed easily. But it was good to know the gods still had a sense of humor, because as we sat bemoaning the never-ending wait, the director, Richard Donovan, knocked on my tent door. I looked at my watch. It was around nine at night, January 16, 2015, our second day on the Antarctic continent.

"Race briefing at the main tent. Right now. Be dressed and ready to run." He certainly was a man who didn't waste words.

In five minutes everything changed. It was on. Plane's on its way. The first marathon was about to begin. We'd be running through the middle of the night, but it didn't really matter—it was light twenty-four hours a day at this time of the year in Antarctica.

And I suddenly wondered if, now that I got what I wanted, I should have been more careful about what I wished for.

—◈—

It only took me a few minutes to get prepared and dressed, but by the time I'd reached the main tent most of my fellow runners were already seated, anxiously chatting, tapping fingers, or adjusting gear.

I've been to more than a few race briefings in my time, but there's only a few that I'll ever remember. This was certainly one I'll never forget.

The camp doctor, a lean and wiry little Englishman, stood up at the front of the room and cleared his throat, extinguishing the anxious chatter and noise.

"I'm only going to tell you one thing," he said sternly.

We all sat on edges of our seats to make sure not to miss any advice or information

"You sweat, you die." There was no emotion in his voice. It was just plain fact.

He explained that if we sweat, the moisture would be absorbed by the base layer shirt and fleecy top, which would almost instantaneously freeze rock hard in the Antarctic blizzard, forming a solid plate of ice that presses against the chest and saps body heat and energy.

"You will rapidly become hypothermic, and there's nothing we can do."

Great, I thought to myself. *I've spent the last seven years of my life training in the tropics, teaching my body to sweat as efficiently as possible to cool me in the warm summer climate.*

But it was the secret to this particular race: heat management at the same time as cold management. Appropriate clothing became a careful balance between wearing enough to stay warm, and not wearing enough to get hot and then subsequently freeze. I needed to dress as lightly as I possibly could, then use body heat from running to keep warm. This meant a light vest, long-sleeved T-shirt, running shorts with a windbreaker top and trousers. It wasn't much, especially in temperatures way below freezing. And here's the rub: if I stopped running and lost that source of body heat I would freeze just as quickly as if I had been sweating. I had to stay in that ideal zone somewhere in the middle . . . while running a competitive marathon.

"One more thing." It turned out the doctor wasn't finished. "Any exposed skin is a potential risk for frostbite. If it's numb, you're in trouble. If it's white, you need emergency attention. If it's black, you've lost it. Oh, I nearly forgot to mention about snow blindness . . ."

Most of us were already numb by that stage. I can only remember thinking that I had enough to worry about going into the marathon, that I didn't need any more problems, especially when I'd never even seen it snowing before, never mind run in it.

—⟋Ⱳ⟍—

The march from the main tent to the starting line was a jumpy mix of anticipation, excitement, tension, and nerves. We all lined up. We'd all trained for months. We'd prepared. We'd sacrificed time with our friends and our families. It all came down to this. It was now make or break. A multitude of thoughts went through my head in those brief moments.

Am I going to finish? All seven marathons?

Can I do it in seven days?

Will I get injured?

How will I even make it through this first stage?

And somewhere, deep inside: *Am I going to win?*

Then, the warning gun fired. And suddenly time slowed down.

I've always thought it best to be a little conservative at the start. Let things stretch out and warm up; anything else is risking an early injury. Get a feel for the terrain. Get a feel for yourself. Try to establish a reasonable pace based on the temperature, wind, and ground underfoot.

Doug clearly didn't follow the same doctrine. He went out hard. He went out very hard. In fact, he seemed to go out at what I'd consider a ten-kilometer-race pace, not a marathon pace. I knew why, though—this was throwing down a gauntlet. Establish yourself; make people think maybe you're untouchable and then you'll be left alone. It was smart. And there was only one possible response: I had to hold him.

The best strategy early in a marathon is to conserve. It's a very long way ahead. Going out hard in the first ten kilometers can make the last ten an absolute nightmare. The muscle damage and strain will haunt you, and you'll lose far more time in the second half of the race than you gained at first. Even more problematic was that this damage wouldn't go away anytime soon. It would build. This was a dangerous situation to be in for a stage race. The damage from cumulative races wasn't going to add from day to day; it was going to multiply. I knew this, and I'm sure Doug knew this, but he sure didn't act like it.

I decided to let him go a little in the first kilometer or so then slowly reel him in. My plan was to sit on his shoulder, try to gently slow him down and keep this race a little more realistic. I tried to increase the speed, but it wasn't easy. My legs were still cold, and my hands were freezing. I hadn't been running long enough to warm up. I gently leaned forward to accelerate. I'd always heard that running is a controlled fall forward, and it was time to use the physics to my advantage. Doug was a few hundred meters ahead but within reach. He must have heard my footsteps crunching the dry snow as I closed in on him. The rest of the pack were well behind but still close enough to watch this skirmish play out.

As I got closer Doug kept looking back. He wanted to keep me in sight, but his clockwork glances over his shoulder gave me the feeling he was becoming a little unsettled. Over the next couple of kilometers I slowly but surely reduced the gap, and by the third kilometer I was right behind him. I thought of staying where I was, but in running circles it's considered a little rude to sit right on somebody's feet, especially in a race. I continued past him without a word. I figured he wouldn't have much to say to me anyway. Maybe I also had a point to prove.

Our roles were now reversed, with Doug letting me go a little with the plan of reeling me back in. After two minutes at most he seemed to tire of the game and put on a surprising burst of speed, again flying past me. I couldn't keep up with that. But I could keep him in sight, and over time he slowed once more and I caught back up. We were two souls alone in a vast field of blinding whiteness, with only the occasional small blue flag to guide us. The other runners were lost to us, as was the Union Glacier Camp. It was him and me. Only him and me. And it was time to put an end to this silliness.

The game had lost its purpose. We'd both proven we could run—any more wasn't helpful. I tried to open a dialogue.

"Are we going to do this all day?" I joked. It was the first we had spoken since Punta Arenas. I didn't like the way the relationship was developing, and felt I had little control over it. We were both fierce, and we both wanted to win. We just had slightly different ways of achieving our goals.

"I'm game if you are," he replied, not even turning his head to make eye contact.

That was it. I had tried to extend an olive branch, and it had been thrown back at me. For better or worse he'd pressed a button, and I couldn't be bothered trying to be nice any more. If he wanted to try, then let him.

I wound my pace up to around 4:15 minutes/kilometer (6:50 minutes/mile). Fast. Not Boston Marathon fast, but fast. Especially on snow and ice. He fell off the back. I assume he thought I was going to slow down again after I put a gap on him, but this time I wasn't going to let up until he couldn't see me anymore. If he didn't have a target to chase, it would be very difficult for him to set his pace, and that would start weighing on him. Marathon racing depends on mental stamina perhaps more than physical. Being in the lead gives a huge boost, and not even being able to see the lead makes the whole experience much tougher.

I kept that pace up for about five kilometers, until I thought he was well back, and then I slowed it back down to around 4:30–4:45 minutes/kilometer (7:15–7:35 minutes/mile). I couldn't run at top pace forever, but opening up the throttle got my blood flowing, and it was invigorating. The next ten kilometers felt like a wonderful dream. Any runner will be able to tell you about the day when the wind was at their back, the spring in their step, when they were the gazelle. Today, I was the gazelle. I had a smile from ear to ear, I felt like nothing could stop me.

When I reached the twenty-one checkpoint, Richard, the race organizer, ran up to me.

"You're about half an hour up on second place."

"What?" I quietly mumbled, more to myself than anyone else.

—◊◊◊—

I ran out of the checkpoint with thoughts bouncing around in my head. There's often not much to think about during a marathon, and being left alone for too long is sometimes dangerous. I realized clear as a bell that I hadn't played a very clever strategy. Going out this hard was damaging. Not clever. Especially not this early. This was going to come back to haunt me, and I might end up looking very, very silly. And at that moment I imagined James smiling. He was in no way malicious, but this was the situation he had foreseen. Doug and I had gone head to head, blow for blow, punch for punch. And this was round one of a seven-round championship bout.

Being stubborn is a blessing and a curse. It sure carried me through some tough times, but it also compelled me to make some less sensible decisions in the name of pride. I didn't slow down. I didn't let him catch back up. I was in Antarctica for the first and probably last time of my life, and I was enjoying it. I was going to leave my mark.

I kept my pace steady until the thirty-two kilometer mark, and I reached the third and final checkpoint. The camp doctor from the briefing was there.

"I'll need to take your beanie," he flatly stated.

"But I'm freezing cold," I stammered, teeth chattering.

He reached and took the woolen beanie off my head and smashed it against the support table. It landed with a violent thud. It was frozen solid.

"That was on your head, cooling your brain."

At least I now had an excuse for my irrational decisions and silly race behavior.

Fortunately, I had another cap in my spares bag near the support table. It was only light but it would do. I grabbed a drink, an energy gel, and a couple of small one-time carbon heating packs. I headed out of camp for my last loop, thirty minutes ahead and holding.

The weather turned. The wind picked up, and it became cloudier. It was cold, really cold. I realized my gloves were freezing due to small amounts of sweat building up, and the scarf around my neck and face had frozen solid from the crystalized water vapor in my breath. I had no choice. I had to take the gloves off. But to expose my hands to the Antarctic weather would have been insanity. Instead I had an idea. I opened the heating packs and held one tightly in each hand, and then I retracted my hands inside the windbreaker jacket and zipped the wrist openings closed. I didn't feel any heat coming from the carbon packs, but I told myself it probably just took some time, so I ran on, after adjusting my scarf so it didn't touch my nose or face but sat on top, forming a frozen shield.

As I got to half way around the final loop, I was freezing. Everything seemed white, and I was concerned about snow blindness. It was then that I realized it was simply because everything was white. There was nothing except snow and ice, just the occasional blue flag. White valleys, white mountains, white plains. No landmarks to gain perspective or judge distance. Just freezing snow and ice. And those little heating packs didn't seem to be doing anything. There was no option. To stop would have meant much bigger problems; I had no choice to continue.

Finally, like an oasis, the mast of the communications array at the base appeared on the horizon. Then the huge blue mess tent. Then the clam shells. And finally I saw the finish line. A shot of adrenaline passed through my body. I was there, I had done it, and by the looks of it, I was going to win the stage comfortably. I increased my pace and lengthened out my stride. It hurt, but it was worth it. I ran toward the finish line and grabbed the Red Bauhinia, the flag of Hong Kong, my adopted homeland. Just like at the start, time slowed. I could see photographers clicking their cameras and then the flashes firing. The finishers ribbon wrapped my chest. I'd done it. I'd won. They told me I had finished with a lead of over thirty minutes. Apparently I'd just set a new world record for a marathon in Antarctica.

A media crew from Reuters was on hand and came over for a postrace interview. I was elated though exhausted, but more importantly my mouth and face were completely numb with cold. I tried to talk but I was completely indecipherable, even to myself. Pats on the back, photos with the organizers, and a few for the sponsors and friends back home. One down, six to go, and thirty minutes up my sleeve.

What I failed to realize, however, was that as soon as I'd stopped running I'd lost that source of body heat. I rapidly cooled, especially now that my body was low on energy. I became very cold. I started shivering, a deep, violent shiver that is reserved for those rare moments when your body really thinks it might be in serious trouble. I had to warm up and quick. There was a small hot shower in one of the tents, and I had to get there quickly. I hobbled over as fast as my post-marathon legs would carry me, uncoordinated on the slippery ice.

I struggled with my clothes as I fought to get undressed and into the shower. Taking off my shoes and socks revealed an unpleasant surprise. The ends of two of my toes were a dark purple-black. I strained to bend over and touch them and I felt nothing. I was still nearly convulsing with hypothermia, and I hoped the loss of feeling was just due to a passing swelling or irritation. It was the last centimeter of the second digit on both feet. They were my longest toes, and I realized that some sweat had built up in the end of my sealed Salomon Gore-Tex snow running shoes, which had subsequently frozen around the toe tips. My only chance was to warm them both up quickly. The camp doctor's words started playing back in my head: *If it's numb, you're in trouble. If it's white, you need emergency attention. If it's black, you've lost it.* I couldn't help but think it was frostbite.

At last I stood under a warm shower, which seemed far too short. But it was enough—I was warm enough to stop shaking and get some dry clothes on, and then wander over to the main tent to sit by the stove for a while, reheating my bones while waiting for the others to arrive.

And the best news: we all finished, and we all made it to the plane before it took off in the early hours of January 17, bound for Punta Arenas. It had been three of the most vivid days of my life. It felt as if I'd been there for a week or a month. I'd seen stark natural beauty, barren and pristine. I'd seen courage and strength from both competitors and crew. And I'd also started to see what this race was going to become. A test. A competition. A battle with our own motivations and abilities as with those around us.

MARATHON 2: SOUTH AMERICA

Punta Arenas, Chile: The Shakedown

You can only do what you can do. Run your own race. Don't worry about anyone else. If someone goes off like a hero, then let them go. Most likely you'll run straight past them later in the race as they're blown up and sitting on the side of the road with their head in their hands wondering where it all went wrong. And if not, they were better than you and there was no point hurting yourself trying to keep up anyway.

—Richard Hall, triathlon training partner and
one of the guys who got me started

I sat on the blue ice of the makeshift Antarctic runway. I was ten kilometers from our previous base camp, and thousands of kilometers from any civilization to speak of. There was a small metal hut that had been erected for passengers and staff to shelter in while waiting for the flight, but in reality it was little more than a shipping container with a few chairs to sit on and an old tin of cookies to nibble while waiting. Between the Argentinian soldiers returning from their year sojourn on the continent, Union Glacier Camp staff and my fellow competitors and crew, there wasn't much space. There definitely weren't any seats left.

I decided to spend some time outside instead. The weather was fairly mild, relatively speaking; the winds and snow that we had experienced on previous days had settled right down. After my postrace hypothermia experience, I had decided to stay positively warm, and I was wearing pretty much everything I had with me. Even sitting out in the elements, I felt relatively warm and comfortable.

It was also the last time I would see Antarctica, possibly forever. I wanted to enjoy every remaining moment and to try to commit the experience to memory, something to never forget. I believe in this I succeeded. I spent time thinking about inner Antarctica. It is one of the last places on Earth that hasn't truly been inhabited by humans, or by any other animal or plant to speak of. Such a fragile ecosystem—on one hand so hostile, but at the same time having so little tolerance for damage, pollution, or misuse. I considered my role there—I was part of the problem. After only three days on the continent I realized my view on human occupation had started to change. I'm not sure that people should travel to Antarctica without a pressing need, something that will bring benefit to more than just a few. And when I considered the base camps, I got the feeling that some of them were maintained more to stake a claim to a section of the continent, and the resources it contained, rather than for lofty scientific goals. Nobody could doubt the vital importance of the research performed and data collected in Antarctica; information gathered here has relevance on a global scale. Being there and experiencing it made me realize that all activity needs to be carefully controlled, guided, directed, and monitored.

I knew the vast majority of Antarctica was ice, but I don't think I ever fully comprehended how much ice. Around 70 percent of all fresh water on planet Earth is held there, and much of it has been frozen for the last fifty million years. If the ice were to melt, our oceans would rise so significantly that entire countries would cease to exist, the appearance of our planet would change forever, hundreds of thousands of species would be lost, and millions upon millions of people would be displaced or worse.

In a strange paradox, Antarctica is also the driest continent on Earth, as all of that water is locked in the solidly frozen ice. There is almost no rainfall in Antarctica, meaning that most of the continent is technically a desert. It was the strangest desert I'd ever seen.

I've read articles by NASA astronauts where they explain the feeling of fragility, beauty, and perfection of the planet, and how this forever changed their perspective. I believe when we see Antarctica we scratch the surface of what they have seen.

The midnight sun continued to burn over the continent, painting the surrounding mountains in a glorious half-light. I sat and I waited and I thought. And after some time, the IL-76 transport plane arrived.

—◊—

We boarded the plane at around 4 a.m. It had been three days since I last sat on that airplane, but it felt like three months. So much had changed. I read once that our brains are selective in laying down memories. The brain automatically determines the degree of novelty and originality of each experience we have, and then allocates storage and memory space proportionally. When we have new experiences, the brain allocates a much larger space, which makes the memory seem more vivid.

This memory triage is extremely important for a couple of reasons. First, it greatly helps learning. A new memory or experience is recorded in greater fidelity and detail, helping us to reassess and replay the memory to better understand. Second, it avoids the brain getting overwhelmed and cluttered with insignificant experiences.

The end result of this process is that much more of our brains are devoted to remembering periods of our lives full of new experiences. This explains why people feel like the weekend they spent sitting around the house doing the same regular routine just flew by. It unfortunately also explains why the years seem to pass quicker as we get older—the same old experiences again and again. But related to my experience in Antarctica, this memory selection process meant that my three days spent there felt more like three wonderful months. It was time to leave that alternate reality behind. It was time to get on with the week and the race.

The return journey from Antarctica took the reverse route of our inbound flight. The first leg would take us back to Ushuaia in Argentina to drop off the returning soldiers, and then it was back to Punta Arenas to start the second marathon. I put my bag in the back of the plane with the rest of the cargo, and I quickly found myself a seat. A seat was vital. There was only one task I needed to focus on right now, and that was to get some rest. We were taking some of the Union Glacier base camp staff back to civilization, and by my reckoning there were more passengers than spaces this time around. There was always somewhere to sit, but finding somewhere remotely comfortable on an old Soviet plane—that was a different matter entirely.

The primary purpose of the flight was transporting those Argentinian soldiers on their return trip. They were at the opposite end of the story to the men who had accompanied us on the flight to Antarctica. They had served their year in Antarctica; it was time to return home. I can only imagine what it must have been like, being surrounded by only a handful of other humans in a hostile and desolate environment for an entire year. They'd had minimal communication with the outside world, endured six months of permanent darkness over winter, and hadn't had a fresh piece of fruit or a vegetable for longer than I cared to think about. When they saw the female members of our running crew, the expressions on their faces were unforgettable and magical—the first women these soldiers had seen in a year.

I think I was asleep before the wheels even left the blue ice runway. That was good, very good. Recovery was going to be the deciding factor in this race. We could all run marathons—that was a given. The person who was going to survive, who was going to perform at his best, and ultimately who was going to win was the person who could recover. I knew this before going in. Coach Nigel had drilled it into me like a mantra. Every marathon was going to do damage, and the damage wasn't going to add up over the week; it was going to multiply. An ache or pain on day one could become a crippling disaster by day seven.

The equation for damage is fairly straightforward. The faster you run, the more damage you do. The longer you run, the more damage you do. The more frequently you run, the more damage you do. Now there were only two counterweights on the other side of this seesaw—good nutrition and good recovery. Whole books have been written on these subjects alone, but like most things in life there are simple rules.

I've heard it said that the most common error made by athletes is neglecting recovery. Athletes at all levels, from everyman weekend warriors to high-performance Olympic champions, make this mistake. Recovery is the body's time to heal and to rebuild. Without recovery, it is physically impossible to improve. In fact, taken to the extreme, without recovery the body can only become increasingly damaged and weak. They call it overtraining.

Everything else being equal, I've always believed that sleep was the best method of recovery. I also believe that sleep is a core component of training, just as important as exercise and nutrition. I once asked my first coach, Max, what was the number-one thing he'd tell his athletes to improve their game. His answer: "Get one more hour of sleep per night."

It is a time when the body can completely look inward, focus on repair and rebuilding, not worrying about the trials and tribulations of everyday life. The benefits of sleep are well demonstrated, both on physical and mental well-being. Human growth hormone is released during rest, with up to 70 percent of the daily production occurring in the first few hours of deep sleep. This is vital not only for repairing muscle damage but also for maintenance of bone and connective tissue.

Sleep was vital, and I was going to make sure I was getting enough. It was important for muscular and physical recovery. It was important for neurological recovery. And to be honest, the long plane flights were getting a little boring anyway; sleep had the added benefit of making the time in the air pass as quickly as possible.

Recovery is a science in itself, and sleep isn't the only trick in the book. Fluid replacement, nutrition, stretching, compression, low-resistance exercise, massage, and temperature contrast water therapy have all been touted, and I was going to use every option I had available to me to help.

I had a routine that I'd developed over the last few years of training and racing to help speed recovery. Invariably I was always exhausted when I crossed the finish line. It didn't seem to matter if it was a 5-kilometer sprint or a 226-kilometer Ironman. I put every drop of effort into the race, and if you asked me to run another ten meters beyond the finish line, I wouldn't have been able to do it.

The first five minutes after a race were pure aerobic recovery. Sit down. Get the breath back in. Let the blood course through the veins and clear some of that built-up lactic acid and metabolic waste. Next, I force myself to get up and walk, try to stimulate blood flow and movement, and not stiffen up. Walking after a race, or even a very gentle jog, is never particularly enjoyable, but it pays valuable dividends in reducing stiffness and muscle pain later.

As soon as my heart rate settles and I start to feel half human again, I know I need to eat and drink, even though I don't generally feel hungry or thirsty. Getting some proper nutrition in after a race is crucial to muscle recovery. It can be a liquid drink or something solid, but it needs to be a combination of carbohydrate and protein, in an approximately four-to-one ratio. The science shows that this recovery meal needs to be eaten within forty-five minutes of the race finishing, but the sooner the better. There are two main reasons that the meal is important: replenishment of the body's stores of glycogen and repair of damaged muscle and connective tissue. This prompt, planned meal will nearly double the rate of recovery and halve the level of fatigue for the next event, compared with not eating or just drinking water. And this was going to really add up over the week.

The next step for me after a longer race is to put on a pair of compression tights. These are leggings made of a slightly stretchy material that in theory acts to push out the toxins, prevent blood pooling, and encourage muscle repair. Since starting on this fitness journey, I've become very interested in the data and physiology of exercise and sport, and on the subject of compression the jury is still very much out. Articles in scholarly journals draw varying conclusions, contradicting each other and generally confusing the issue further. However, there are a few findings that are fairly well regarded as fact. First, the compression needs to be effective. Tights made mostly of Lycra or elastane are too stretchy and don't really compress the legs enough to be helpful. The medical-grade compression garments are the best, and if they're easy to get on then they're too loose. Second, the tights need to be put on fairly soon after exercise but should not be left on for more than three hours. Any more can start affecting circulation and hence recovery.

Last, and possibly most importantly, compression tights should never be worn outside the bedroom or hotel room, unless concealed by some baggy jeans or trousers. It's not about physiology or fashion; it's about common decency and self-pride.

———〰———

The plane briefly touched down in Ushuaia. The landing was gentle, but it stirred me from my slumber. I'd been out cold for the last five hours on the flight. I was groggy and a little dazed. It didn't really seem necessary to face the battle of the real world yet. There was one more hour flying time back to Punta Arenas, and hence one more hour to snooze away. I pulled my cap down a little to shield my eyes and drifted back into a somewhat restless sleep.

The transition back into Chile from Antarctica was uneventful. The whine of the engines on final approach and the shuddering and groaning of the airframe as the plane touched down jostled me out of my dozing once more. For better or worse, it was time to go. I shook my head to wake myself up and made myself vaguely presentable, combing my hair with my hands and rubbing my face to get the blood circulating. I had slept well on the flight, but I think I might have been the only one. Looking around the cabin there were many bleary eyes and tired faces. I'd played the recovery well, and I was feeling OK. Not great—I'd just run a marathon after all—but OK. It was ten o'clock in the morning, and it was a brisk but beautiful day. I decided not to think about the next marathon quite yet.

The plan was to go back to a small hotel near the oceanfront, have a quick shower, and get ready, and then meet in the lobby and get started. Running again as soon as possible was a good plan. I'd had enough time to rest; another few hours wouldn't have made any difference. It was better to get this over and done, and have some more time on the other side to rest, or to act as a cushion if something went wrong on the race course, and we took more time than expected.

I wheeled my suitcase up to the room, opened it, and fetched the zip-lock bag labeled *Punta*. I'd looked at the weather reports before leaving Hong Kong and had made some educated guesses about what type of clothing, socks, and shoes might be required for each marathon. Punta was windy and cool, but not cold. Marathons like this were difficult to dress for. I knew from experience that wearing too much was a big danger. I opened the window in the hotel room. It was cool to the point of being cold. If I was going to stand out in that I'd need a jacket and trousers. But if I was going to run, well, that was a different matter entirely.

I didn't have to worry about overheating quite so much as I did in Antarctica, with its distinct risk of sweat becoming ice and overheating paradoxically becoming life-threatening hypothermia, but I still had to be careful. Overheating on any race meant more sweat, more water and salt loss, more fatigue, and much more chance of cramping. Dehydration at any level affects performance. Dehydration reduces circulating blood volume, which in turn affects delivery of nutrients to the muscles and clearance of metabolites and toxins, significantly deteriorating performance. I had done the mathematics once out of curiosity. On an average marathon, the average person will lose up to a liter of water per hour in sweat and breath vapor. If not replaced, that level of dehydration can affect running pace by over 5 percent. Clothing, and hence sweating, was significant.

Punta Arenas was very windy. This was also going to affect clothing choice. I didn't want to wear baggy clothing that would flap around or act like a big parachute pulling me backward. I settled on my standard running vest, some arm warmers, and running shorts. I figured I was going to be the least dressed person on the course, but I also figured my gambit might pay off when the others realized how hot they were getting.

I got dressed, got some gels ready to have available on the course, and had a quick snack. A small meal an hour or so before the race starts is just as important as the postrace recovery food. My prerace meals are fairly similar to the postrace, a combination of protein and carbohydrate, not too heavy, not too spicy, and nothing that may upset the stomach. I settled on a protein bar and an electrolyte sports drink. Last but not least, I grabbed my sunglasses. It wasn't particularly bright outside, but it was getting windy, and some eye protection might come in handy.

My first ever coach was a guy called Max Shute. Max was a child of Mother Earth and had strong beliefs about balance and harmony. He gave me a lot of good advice and some excellent coaching, but there's one thing he told me that has still stuck with me to this day: he said that before any race, don't run if you can walk, don't walk if you can stand, don't stand if you can sit, and don't sit if you can lie down. So I laid down on the hotel bed, conserving every drop of energy to be spent later on the race course. I tried to go through the upcoming marathon in my mind. There was no point in planning—I figured those kind of prerace plans never translate to reality and can sometimes just end up bogging you down by trying to follow a naive strategy that isn't working. There was no point in mentally visualizing the course—I had no precise idea where the marathon was being held. Instead I tried to relax and think about pacing, timing my nutrition, and to some degree the competition.

It was still early days, and I wasn't sure exactly how the contest was going to develop. It was obvious that Doug was there to win, and his ego had been battered in Antarctica. He had wanted to jump off the blocks hard and make his mark. He put his plan into action and was trumped. He wasn't happy. But there was one possibility that I was considering: he might have folded his hand intentionally in Antarctica. He might have been smart enough to see that the race was going to be too hard to win outright. He might have decided that it was better to let me tire myself out and play the long game. If that was the case, he was a good runner and he was a smart runner, which was going to be a danger-ous combination.

Doug certainly wasn't the only person on my mind. There was a whole selec-tion of good runners to choose from. A really good, confident runner might have sat back a little in Antarctica to let things play out, see where everyone stood, and then come through on day two, three, or four to make his mark. These stage races are won and lost on the last day; nothing is over until it's over, and a self-assured, experienced runner would know this.

James was self-assured and experienced, and he was also very good at de-flecting attention onto others. He was the kind of guy nobody saw coming until he was right on your heels and about to steam past you.

Then there was Pierre, the young Frenchman. His manners were impec-cable, and he certainly was confident and composed, while at the same time coming across as open and approachable. He seemed reluctant to talk about his upbringing, mostly, I suspect, to avoid being typecast as a rich kid. He didn't need to worry; his actions spoke louder than any words. He was helpful and considerate to others, without a drop of arrogance. He was ten years younger than most of us, yet probably more mature. He didn't seem overly concerned about the marathons, and certainly didn't waste time squabbling or squaring up to his fellow runners.

Pierre was hard to read. Everybody came to this race with a mission, a goal, a point to prove. I reckoned I had most of them figured out. Doug, James, and I came to win. Big Jim and Jon came to finish. Marcelo, Tim, and Marianna came to prove themselves, both inwardly and to others. Ted just loved the attention. And Uma and Krishna came for the experience. But Pierre—I couldn't quite figure out why Pierre was here. I figured it was also to prove himself, to show that he didn't need his father's wealth or help to achieve greatness. I wasn't sure. He seemed too confident to need to prove himself, although we all wear masks to hide who we really are. Pierre could have been there to win. He may not have showed his true colors quite yet.

The more I thought about it, the more I realized I wasn't being constructive. It was easy to overthink it. To get caught up worrying about possibilities that weren't ever going to become realities. It was only going to lead to anxiety, and that wasn't constructive. Remember the others, but focus on your own race.

I lay for a few minutes longer, soaking up the last rest before the coming onslaught. There was no point in standing at the starting point any longer than necessary. Coach Max would have been proud.

After a short while, it was time.

—⚍—

Many of the other runners were in the lobby by the time I arrived. Most of those faces were tired. It was the second marathon we'd be running in a twenty-four-hour period, never mind all of the travel and action in between. On the other hand, it was only the second marathon of seven. I had to hope we'd all get a second wind. The only light at the end of the tunnel was that we were going to have a decent rest after this one—a night's sleep in the hotel and then an early morning flight to Santiago and onward to Miami.

Richard, the race director, was one of the last to arrive.

"Right-o, the course starts just across the road. It's going to be seven loops down the seafront and back. Let's head over."

As soon as I passed through the sliding glass doors at the hotel entrance, I wondered whether I'd made a mistake with my clothing. I was cold. I felt colder than I had on the starting line of Antarctica. I figured that had to just be in my head. But there was no turning back now.

We crossed over the road and onto a wide pedestrian walkway and cycle path that snaked along the shoreline. There was a small concrete public services building erected next to the stone and concrete beachfront path where the logistics staff had set up the flags and a banner or two. Punta Arenas architecture was divided into the elaborate fanciful and the Bauhaus purpose-built stark. This building was definitely the latter and looked something like a World War II bunker. We posed for some photographs together and then milled around placing bottles, snacks, and spare shirts on the organizer's tables. I was getting colder by the minute, and I just wanted to get started.

We lined up. Richard raised the horn. The tension built. The horn let out a surprisingly loud toot. We were off.

Ted led out with what appeared to be his signature one-hundred-meter dash for the cameras, grinning from ear to ear. Doug headed off with him. I'm not sure if he was trying to be part of the humor, or if he wanted to lead out the race. I suspected the latter, which was fine by me. It was much easier not to lead at the start of the race; easier to follow, be paced by the person in front, and not to expend any more energy or speed than needed. The big push would come later in the day, in the second half of the marathon.

The marathon course was held along a cycling and running course that followed a rocky coastline. It was barren and stark, the concrete path bordered by stubbly grass fighting against the elements for survival. A few locals walked up and down, or stopped to gaze across the ocean, but the wind was too strong and the weather too cold for anyone to be sitting and relaxing. They cast their eyes over us with a combination of confusion and amusement, wondering what kind of fool would decide to run this route for enjoyment's sake. Recreational running didn't really seem to have come to Punta Arenas.

I settled into a rhythm. I wanted to let my legs warm up for the first few kilometers, stretching and loosening the tired muscles as well as getting my body temperature up a little. It was prudent to keep Doug in sight, but there was no point in starting the back-and-forth of Antarctica quite yet.

The path followed the shoreline, but it wasn't entirely flat. Approximately half a kilometer from the start the gradient gradually started to rise as we approached a wooden footbridge that crossed a small stream outflow. It wasn't steep, but it was enough to tax the legs. Doug must have decided that this was the time, because he suddenly and substantially increased his pace. He flew up the steps and disappeared down the other side and out of sight. I was all for keeping up but he was sprinting, not running, and I didn't have that in me, not for a marathon at least.

Those words spoken by my training buddy Richard Hall came back to me: Run your own race. Don't worry about the other people out there. You can only race yourself. If someone passes you at the start, let him go. What he was saying could be boiled down into just two words: be patient. Richard was one of the people who had waited for me at the top of that hill on that fateful bike ride seven years ago. He was one of the people who fanned that spark of enthusiasm, allowing it to burst into flames. He'd done more races than I cared to think about, and it was time to listen to his advice.

Doug wasn't the only issue—Pierre and James were hot on my heels. They seemed to be playing the same game as Doug and I were to a degree, but maybe doing it with a slightly better sense of humor.

I kept to my pace and focused on running my race. I won't lie; it was definitely disconcerting to be dropped so effortlessly, but at this point there wasn't much I could do. We were on loop one of seven. There was plenty of time—plenty of time for me to catch Doug, or plenty of time for him to run away into the distance. At this stage I wasn't sure which.

It didn't take long to find out. I came up and over the wooden footbridge and a couple of hundred meters up the track I saw Doug. He seemed to have reduced his pace back to something more sensible, although he had earned himself a significant gap. And then I saw it. He glanced over his shoulder. In sports they sometimes call it a telegraph. Poker players call it a tell. It's that subconscious mannerism or gesture that gives the other players a clue about one's state of mind or intentions.

Being followed has never bothered me. I never really look backward in a race, maybe just an occasional glance on a lap turn-around to see where the opposition was. But I was starting to realize that it really bothered Doug. He kept looking over his shoulder, to the point where I was now starting to worry he might run into a lamppost. I'd noticed it a few times when we'd been racing in Antarctica, and I'd seen it again now. It was Doug's tell: when he felt under pressure he started looking over his shoulder, checking behind him for a real or imagined foe coming up on him. This told me he was feeling the exertion and it wasn't coming easily. That was enough to put a little wind back in my sails and repair some of the damage done to my confidence.

I didn't break stride. I kept my pace and continued without regard to the surroundings. The wind started to pick up, coursing straight up the coastline and blasting us head-on. This was a day for patience. It wasn't going to be fast, and it wasn't going to be easy. Steady was the key. Slowly but surely, I reeled Doug back in. I could see his shoulders sinking further with each glance backward. I couldn't understand why he kept looking backward and slowing himself down, until I realized it wasn't intentional; it was a subconscious habit.

By the time we were halfway down the southbound leg of the course, we were alongside each other neck and neck. A large graffiti mural on the other side of the road caught my eye, but I didn't slow down. I gazed out to the horizon through my dark running sunglasses. I slightly, almost imperceptibly, gave a nod, nothing else. And I ran straight past. I wasn't running quickly; I had kept the same pace right since the starting line. For what it's worth, I guess I was trying to give off that unbreakable hard-man vibe. Whether it was true or not, that was the mask that I figured was going to work with Doug. I guess he didn't want to run with me, because he let me go, deciding instead to sit a few meters behind me and try the same trick I'd used with him in Antarctica.

So there we had it. I was up front, with Doug not more than thirty seconds behind. James hot on Doug's heels, then Marcelo, Pierre, Big Jim, Jon, Tim, and Marianna, with Ted bringing up the rear, spending as much time horsing around with cameramen and innocent bystanders as running the marathon. The pecking order was starting to develop. People were settling into their places. We'd all sized each other up, we had a mental picture of where the land lay, and for the moment at least, we were comfortable to hold position. The dust was settling on round one of the skirmish. There was sure to be more, but for the moment I think everyone just found it easier to settle in and hold.

As we settled into our stride and our pace, we all had time to think. When we talked about it later, we were all thinking the same set of thoughts. For better or worse, a pack mentality was forming. Intragroup and intergroup dynamics had always fascinated me. Every social species of animal has a carefully defined set of rules and codes of conduct for their communal behavior. Every species that lives in a group has social protocols. With rules and understanding there is a balance; without them there is disharmony and fighting.

Pack dynamics follow a set of relatively simple rules. Whether the pack is a group of wild animals, a set of competitive athletes, or a bunch of office workers, the rules are pretty much the same. Even though these rules are considered fundamentally important, they are rarely discussed and are considered to be a combination of instinctual and learned social behavior. Pack dynamics tend to take a few days to develop—it takes that long for the various players to size each other up—but after a few days they are almost impossible to ignore or deny.

Fundamentally, any pack is composed of three distinct groups: the alpha, the betas, and the omegas. The alpha animal or person is the most dominant. He or she leads the pack, makes decisions for the pack, controls the pack. There is only ever one alpha in a group. The beta animals are second in charge. They will reinforce the role of the alpha, providing backup and support. Lastly, there are the omegas, the lower animals in the pack. Omegas are a vital part of the pack, traditionally playing a major role in the day-to-day operations of the group, but they follow the leader.

Within these subgroupings there is also a hierarchy. No two animals in a pack, or people in a social situation for that matter, are exactly equal. There is always a pecking order, and as long as everybody knows and understands the pecking order, there is peace, harmony, and efficient maintenance of the pack. However, the hierarchy is not set in stone. There will be long stretches of peace where everybody accepts their level, punctuated by short periods of turmoil as the order is challenged and reestablished or rearranged. The first of these periods comes fairly soon after a pack is first established. New challengers can come in the form of new entrants to the pack or young animals growing up. And if the animal or person one step up the ladder starts showing signs of weakness, the pack can quickly turn on him and demand proof of his position. If the pack is not satisfied with this validation, the senior member will quickly be demoted.

Occasionally pack dynamics can be explosive and violent, but usually it is much subtler. Most of the determination of standing in the group is conducted using innuendo and subconscious signals, whether the group is that wild pack of lions on the savannah or a bunch of office workers around the water cooler. I suspect most of us don't even realize it is happening much of the time.

This race, Punta Arenas, was our shakedown. We'd all gotten to know each other over the last few days. We'd all thrown our hats in the ring in Antarctica and laid down some foundations of who we were as runners and competitors. Now was the time to take our places on those rungs of the ladder. Positions were going to change. There would be movement at all levels as people played their hands as best as they could, but we needed to make a start. Our running order right now—that was the starting hierarchy.

—m—

I kept moving along, holding my pace. The only time I ever really worried about where the people behind me were in a race was in the last few kilometers before the finish line. That was where position became important, and people could be difficult to catch if they suddenly threw themselves at the line with a sprint finish. Right now it was better just to get the miles under the belt and not worry too much about positioning. Doug was behind me, but it didn't play on me like it played on him. Sure, I had a look at how far back he was at the turnaround at the far end of the lap. I even went so far as to count the seconds in my head from the point when I left the turnaround to when I saw him again. But this was for pacing, not for self-reassurance.

I had a habit of counting under my breath until I saw the competitor trailing me.

"One, one thousand."

"Two, one thousand."

"Three, one thousand."

The running and the adrenaline tended to throw out any regularity or reliability of my mental clock. Saying the words kept me honest. Count the seconds until you see the other guy; then double that number to allow for him running both to and from the turnaround. That's how many seconds he is behind you. For the really analytical people, it's also quite easy to calculate the distance, if you assume both people are running at a fairly similar pace. If the person is a minute behind and you're running a five-minutes-per-kilometer pace, even a fairly average math student can tell you the person is two hundred meters behind. I never felt that analytical, but I did often find amusement and distraction in the mental gymnastics. It was something to take my mind off that combination of repetition and discomfort involved in running a marathon. It was also surprisingly difficult to do simple mental mathematics when fatigued, sleep deprived, and low on energy. It must have taken me at least five minutes by the time I'd done all of my analysis. That five minutes spent was equivalent to a kilometer of running, one less kilometer until the finish line. The attraction was easy to see.

By my estimation he was around a minute back on the first turnaround. I would make sure to keep a mental note of that and take the same measurement at each turnaround point, partly to make sure I wasn't getting too excitable and running too fast or getting too lazy and slacking off, and partly just to keep my mind occupied. Besides, despite my previous assertions to the contrary, it was also good to know he wasn't catching.

I also used the counting strategy to keep an eye on James and Pierre, but it was getting hard to remember their times for the previous loop and I started doubting my own figures. If nothing else, I was trying to make sure that there were no big shifts in time and no changes in order. Good racing was largely about planning and analysis.

My other race strategy was to break the run up into segments, and target each segment rather than the whole race or even the whole loop. It would be nice to say I did this to pace myself and control my race, but the truth was that I enjoyed soaking up the scenery and trying to create a memory of each course. In previous years I'd finished races in the most stunning locations around the world, and only realized afterward that I spent most of the race staring at my feet. I could have done that on a treadmill. After one too many races like that, I made a promise to myself to live each experience. I wanted to make sure I laid down mental images and memories from each location, burning images of points of interest along the course into my brain, hopefully never to be forgotten.

This mental recording was another strategy to take my mind away and forget about the immediate discomfort, pressure, and fatigue I was feeling. I found this way I could let my mind wander, and then all of a sudden I'd feel the urge to look down at my watch and realize twenty minutes and five more kilometers of the marathon were over.

Lastly, I suspect if I spent too long thinking about the entire distance of each marathon it would seem insurmountable. It was better to focus on getting to the next memory, the next marker, the next point of interest. When I got there, well, then I'd think about the next segment. The cycle continued.

There was only one prerequisite for this strategy: I had to be able to run on remote control. It was important to be able to put one foot in front of another in an orderly and disciplined manner. I needed to be able to maintain a steady pace and, most importantly, avoid any obstacles while I drifted off in a cloud of thoughts. If I was in deep thought and ran head-on into a signpost or pole, I'm not sure which would be worse: the physical discomfort or the emotional pain of being mocked by everyone around me.

My first waypoint was the starting line—that concrete public services building, constructed in a style that was purely functional, something only a government body would build. This was a good waypoint. There was a small supportive crowd to boost the morale and an aid station with electrolyte drink and the gels I'd brought from my hotel room. Each time I hit this point I got to tick off a big psychological box—one loop done.

The wooden footbridge over the stream was next. It was a good point because there was an upward gradient leading onto the bridge and a downward gradient off it. It was one to play carefully: slow down on the uphill so as to conserve and maintain energy output, and then let the legs go on the downhill and harness gravity to recover some of the speed and time.

A couple of kilometers down the road there was a small weather-beaten children's playground next to the track, complete with monkey bars, seesaw, swings, and a slide. The elements hadn't taken too kindly to the equipment, and there were traces of rust running down most of the welds on the metal. There were a few young kids playing on the seesaw, but most of the gear was idle or blowing in the wind. Next to the kids' playground was a skateboarding area, including a small skate ramp and bowl. Some adolescent kids were hanging around, a few skating but most sitting, talking, and holding their boards.

A kilometer or so past the skate area there were a couple of roadside food trucks. They were closed when we first passed, but as the day progressed they had begun to open for business. Both were staffed by ladies of ample girth, cooking merrily while yelling friendly jibes in Spanish between the vehicles, which invariably ended with deep fits of laughing from both sides. Every time I ran past I was sorely tempted by the smell of freshly cooked churros. I'd only really discovered churros a few days earlier when walking around Punta Arenas after I first arrived from Santiago. They were the South American answer to a donut, a long sausage of deep-fried dough, sprinkled with icing sugar. The best ones had runny warm caramel inside. They must have been five hundred calories apiece, and it was lucky I had no spare change in my running shorts. I suspect I would have stopped for a snack on every loop and become the only person on the marathon to actually gain weight.

Next was the graffiti mural where I had previously passed Doug. The Chileans seemed to have a real sense of pride in good street art, and to describe this as graffiti might be underselling it. The side of a whole row of houses had been painted in vivid colors—bright yellows, oranges, and blues. Some were purely abstract, some were pictures of street scenes, and one was a clever mock-up of the interior of the house, so it looked to a casual observer like the building had no external walls. Every time I went by the mural I made it my mission to find something new in the artistry, to discover a new element or feature I hadn't previously noted.

Following the mural was the jetty out over the sea. It was constructed of wood and was in a severe state of decay, chipped away by the relentless beating of the waves and slowly crumbling back into the sea. It was a skeleton of its former self, and many seasons must have passed since it was serviceable. Its only inhabitants now were a large flock of cormorant birds, chattering among themselves.

Last was the welcome relief of the far-point turnaround: a small car park surrounded by some scrubby bushes, with a cone at one end. It wasn't much to the casual observer, but to me it was a sight for sore eyes, and the time to begin my counting of the seconds until I passed Doug coming up on the other side of the path.

—⟋⟋⟋—

I counted down the loops in my head. I really tried to avoid looking at the distance display on my watch, at least for the first half of the race. It tended to make me think about how much more there was to go, rather than how much I'd already finished.

All seemed to be going fairly well. I was still feeling great from my Antarctica experience, my morale was high, and it wasn't far enough into the race to be feeling any serious muscle fatigue or joint damage. I was happy. Yet I always feel a little concerned when all seems to be going too well, both in a race and in life in general. It's usually a signal.

I learned long ago that long-course racing was as much about dealing with unexpected issues or problems as it was about actually racing. This is probably true about life in general. In a bike race it may be a flat tire, or it may be leaky goggles in a swim event. Today, it was the sudden and urgent need to go to the bathroom. I'd been on three continents in the past week, experienced twelve-hour shifts in time zone, and eaten lots of high-energy running food. It wasn't anything medical; I just needed the bathroom.

I had to make a choice. I was on loop four of seven. Three more loops to go. I didn't think that was going to be possible. I decided there was going to be one extra waypoint on this loop. There had to be a public bathroom somewhere. I forgot the other regular scenery markers and focused on my new search. The only problem was that thinking about it made the need even more pressing. After about twenty minutes of searching, no suitable option presented itself.

I started looking at the beach next to the course. Maybe there'd be a small nook or private area. Somewhere that nobody could see. Again, nothing availed itself. There were people around. Families with children. I couldn't besmirch their local attraction. At best I'd offend, at worst I'd be arrested.

I had one hope: the public services building next to the starting line. I figured surely they must have a bathroom. As I passed over the wooden bridge on my way back I could feel my pace quicken. Things were becoming more urgent. I got to the turnaround point, grabbed the race director, and possibly sounded a little desperate when I asked him how to get into the concrete structure and where the toilets were.

"No can do I'm afraid. It's all locked up. The bathroom is back at our hotel," he replied.

Damn it. The hotel wasn't far; it was probably a five-hundred-meter round trip. But it was deeply annoying. I was starting to feel tired. I knew that at the end of a marathon I felt like I couldn't run one more step, never mind five hundred meters extra. Yet it was the only option. There was a decision to be made. Could I hold on? Could I run three more loops, probably one and a half hours, without using the bathroom? No, I decided, I could not. When it came to holding on, failure was not an option, and I wasn't willing to risk it.

OK, live with it, no point in getting upset about it, I thought. I ran straight across the road, dodged a few cars as horns honked, and ran straight through the sliding glass entrance doors and up to the concierge counter. I have no idea what must have crossed the minds of the staff. I was covered in sweat and road grime, hot, panting, and dressed in a waterlogged singlet and running shorts. I can't imagine I smelled great, and I certainly had no place being in their hotel lobby. There was no point in trying to explain myself, nor was there any time.

"I'm sorry, excuse me, could you point me to the bathroom?" I asked.

The closer I got the more urgent it became.

The poor receptionist was lost for words. She had a stunned look on her face and her chin hung down, mouth gaping. She slowly raised her left arm, pointing down the corridor. That was all I needed to know, I continued my jog with as much dignity as I could muster given the circumstances, and disappeared down the passageway and into the bathroom.

Thank goodness. Problem solved.

Now there was only the matter of the marathon, whose time clock had continued to tick for this whole extracurricular episode. I ran back out of the hotel as frantically as I had entered, sidestepped a few cars on the oceanfront road, and made it back to the pavement just in time to see Doug coming in toward the lap turnaround at the concrete building. And just in time for him to see me as well. He looked at me with a quizzical stare, and then the penny must have dropped. He didn't know the specifics, but he realized that something had happened that had taken me off the course. Given the distance from where I was standing to the turnaround and the distance he was from it, he also realized I'd just lost my lead.

There was an unwritten rule in stage racing, at least in my experience. It certainly applied to bicycle racing and I'm sure it applied to running, as well as any other sport that's competed as a multiday event: You don't attack when there's a technical issue. You don't attack when your competitor stops to tie laces, you don't attack on a bathroom break, you don't attack if someone drops a bottle and stops to pick it up. Simple as that. I'd seen it haunt even the professionals.

Two of the greats of professional cycling, Alberto Contador and Andy Schleck, turned from friendly rivals to bitter enemies in just one moment on the 2010 Tour de France. Schleck was the race leader, wearing the yellow jersey. Contador was the contender, the winner of numerous races and one of the other favorites to win. The two were neck and neck riding up Port de Balès in French Pyrénées, the final hill on that stage of the race. Schleck's chain suddenly came off his bike, stopping any further forward movement. In the heat of the moment Contador broke the unwritten rule and decided to attack, and attack hard. He gained half a minute on Schleck in that attack. Half a minute in a race that is often won by seconds.

Immediately afterward it seemed that Contador realized he'd done the wrong thing. He tried to give explanations, make excuses, and shift blame onto other team members, but as they say, it's not possible to unscramble eggs, and what was done was done. Schleck was furious and probably said more than he should have in postrace interviews. It was such a big story at the time it even got a moniker: chaingate.

Like most scandals there was fault both ways. Contador probably shouldn't have attacked, but he claimed he didn't realize and just went with the pack. Possibly there was some truth in that. However, he also had wireless radio communication with his other teammates on the race, as well as the race manager. If he didn't know what happened immediately, he did after a few seconds. He could have slowed. On the other hand, the rule is typically reserved for unavoidable technical issues that are not the rider's fault, and in this case it appeared Schleck had tried to downshift two gears at once, strongly increasing the chance of a chain slipping off. The tour is partly a test of skill, as any race is, and Schleck should have known better.

As it happened, Contador went on to win the Tour overall, but was stripped of the title two years later after being found guilty of using a performance enhancing drug. Maybe there was some kind of universal justice at play.

I wouldn't want to make a direct comparison between the 2010 Tour fracas and the experience on that marathon course in Punta Arenas, and I certainly wouldn't want to have a "toiletgate" description of the event to immortalize it, but the same forces were at play.

Doug saw me, and I saw Doug. Our eyes locked for a split second. His expression went from curious to determined. He made a decision. He was going for it. He picked up his pace from the marathon shuffle to a five-kilometer-race sprint, and he took off from the turnaround point before I had a chance to get back. He was halfway up to the wooden footbridge by the time I was back on the course.

It's hard to be annoyed about it now—I might well have done the same in his position—but I would have liked to think that I wouldn't. Maybe he didn't know the rules. Maybe he saw this as his chance to reclaim some of the glory lost in Antarctica.

I may not be annoyed now, but I was certainly angry at the time. It was my fault for going off the course, I couldn't dispute that. I was partly angry with myself, and I was definitely angry with him. I had started to develop a theory about Doug's weakness, and it was time to put that theory into practice. There was no need to increase my pace. No need to catch him. I had three more loops up my sleeve. All I had to do was sit there and let his own anxiety and apprehension build. He seemed to hate having someone following him. It affected him in a completely different way than it affected me. It made him nervous, and in turn, that slowed him down.

I passed by the kids' park. Then I passed by the skateboard park. Then I saw him. Up near the roadside churros vendors, now open and selling to a steadily building crowd. And then I saw it. He looked back over his shoulder, looking for me. My angry frown cracked into a slight smile. I was in with a chance. I could turn this around.

My pace quickened ever so slightly. I had to hold it. I didn't want to rush this and then run out of steam before the finish. I had to play my cards carefully. Slowly but surely I got closer. By the mural I was a few hundred meters behind. He looked back again, and this time he saw me. He knew I was coming.

When we got to the ruined jetty, I was only a hundred meters back, and his looking back had increased to a point where it was really affecting his running.

And as we got to the turnaround we were side by side. The course official smiled and waved as he saw us coming. I had a big smile on my face, but I'm sure Doug didn't look so happy.

It was time to extend an olive branch.

"Run together?" I asked.

"Yeah, OK" was all I got back.

I could understand he wasn't happy. He'd seen his lead erode for a second time on the course today, never mind the Antarctic marathon yesterday, and he must have been feeling like I was gnawing away at him. Sometimes you've got to put it behind you, and if we ran together I figured we could try to chat occasionally and break down a barrier. If nothing else, it might be enough of a distraction to help the time pass. Looking for new features of the mural was getting a little boring.

We ran the next lap and a half together and talked a little between our panting, but he appeared to be getting tired. Those two fast sprints, the one at the race start and the one after the bathroom break, had taken their toll on him. Running hard like that does exponentially more damage than maintaining a steady pace. Rabbit and the hare.

"I'm over," he muttered.

"C'mon," I replied. I was happy to provide limited encouragement, but I wasn't his mother, and I hadn't entirely forgotten what had happened a couple of laps ago.

"You go," he answered.

"OK, see you up the road a little; sure you'll catch back on," I said.

I picked up the pace. Prior to the challenge at the bathroom turnaround he'd been a beta in the pack hierarchy. He'd sensed weakness in the alpha. He'd attacked with all of his force. It hadn't been quite enough, or possibly it hadn't been timed and paced well enough. Either way he'd been caught, and his attack had been fended off. I wanted to show humility and respect, but at the same time I wanted to prove a point. It was time to remind him that there was a reason I was leading overall, and he needed to work with me and not against me.

I wound my run speed up by a couple of kilometers an hour. Not a sprint, but I needed to drop him off the back, and I needed to make it look easy. I strode out and didn't look back, not once. I don't know how long he held on for; I kept running until I got to the starting point turnaround next to the concrete government building. I started counting.

"One, one thousand."

"Two, one thousand."

"Three, one thousand."

I got to twenty-six, one thousand.

Multiply that by two and he was almost a minute back. He didn't look comfortable, but I think the suffering was mental more than physical. Being dropped was very difficult to stomach. I knew—it had happened to me more than once on other races. Once you're dropped, it's very hard to catch back on, and the race becomes emotional.

I kept running, crossed the bridge, and saw something that made me laugh so hard I nearly had to stop running. Ted was on the kids play equipment pretending to do push-ups and jumping jacks for a bunch of enthralled locals and an event cameraman. Race time wasn't important to him. He wasn't looking for a race time; he was looking for a good time. This was a strange way of finding it, but it seemed to work for him. He was loving every minute of it. I only found out later that he'd used the horseplay to solicit donations from the crowd, which he later spent at the churros van for a timely and delicious afternoon tea. The man was a genius. One of a kind. And completely bonkers.

I managed to pull myself together and worked my way through my tour of the waypoints and suburban monuments, had one final look at the mural, and headed for home. It was time to finish it off.

On the way back I came across the event cameraman, who had obviously drawn inspiration from Ted's antics and hired a skateboard from one of the teenagers for a fiver. He pulled alongside me as I paced toward the finish line, looking like a low-budget film crew on a special effects shoot. It was a magnificent idea and worked surprisingly well when I saw the footage some weeks later in the postevent video.

I crossed the line happy but exhausted, stopped for a couple of photos, and then collapsed onto a concrete bench attached to the side of the government building. Not particularly comfortable, but right then and there anything would do. It was at that point that I realized how windy and cold it was. When I was running, I was generating body heat and staying warm, using the same trick as I had in Antarctica, with minimal clothing but also minimal sweat. However, when I stopped and that source of body heat was removed, I was suddenly very cold. I'm sure being completely out of energy didn't help. While finishing the last lap I had committed myself to waiting for Doug at the finish line to shake his hand and say well done. I really didn't want to get into an emotional war with him. I knew how easily these things could get out of hand, and I also knew that James wouldn't have been overly upset if Doug and I started tearing strips off each other.

As I waited I got colder and colder. I wrapped myself in a poncho Big Jim had left behind at the start of the race. I felt a little bad about making it sweaty, but I promised myself I'd remember to clean it for him later. I started wondering what had happened to Doug. It felt like ages had passed.

After nearly fifteen minutes he crossed the line, shirtless and somewhat disheveled. I'm sure I looked in a similar state when I crossed. I gave him a moment or two to take some press photos and collect his thoughts, and then I went over to shake his hand and give him a celebratory man hug. It probably wasn't the right choice. He didn't seem particularly pleased or receptive. In retrospect I can understand why. My actions could have been interpreted as patronizing, although that wasn't my intention in the slightest. I think the only reason he shook my hand was for the press photographers—there was no point looking like a sore loser.

In a way I was damned if I did and damned if I didn't. If I'd have walked off after I'd finished, I may have come across as insensitive and arrogant, especially as he and I had run together for a significant part of the second half of the marathon today. I felt waiting was the right thing to do.

I'll never know whether that decision was the turning point that started the chain reaction of events between the two of us that were soon to follow.

—⟘⟒—

I hobbled back to the hotel. It was late afternoon by that stage, and there was time for a muscle soothing soak in the bathtub and a good square meal, followed by what I hoped would be a solid night's sleep in a comfy bed—I knew it was going to be one of the only chances I'd get to sleep in a proper bed on the entire trip. The flight out to Miami left in the early morning. I had some time to recover.

I'd been a little more sensible in that marathon than the first, but I'd still run hard. I'd finished in three hours and twenty-three minutes. Not a fast marathon by any stretch of the imagination—in fact the slowest I'd run for some years. It was enough though, and I'd stretched my overall lead to around forty-five minutes. It was a very good buffer. I was tired, but happy.

I walked once more through the sliding glass entranceway. I glanced at the receptionist and a look of fright came over her face. The first time she'd seen me this morning I'd just got off a fairly tough flight from Antarctica, tired and jet-lagged. The second time I was covered in sweat and manically asking for a bathroom. This time I was exhausted and walking with a limp. She must have thought me a madman.

As soon as her eye caught mine she looked away and busied herself with paperwork, hoping that she could melt into her surroundings and I'd pass her by without comment or question. I shuffled off toward the elevator, and she looked visibly relieved.

I got into my hotel room, slowly got undressed, and began my postrace ritual with a protein recovery drink. I ran a steaming hot bath and slowly slid myself in, unsure whether my weak muscles would co-operate in getting me out. I slowly drifted off into a half-sleep as I lay there in the tub, only roused as hunger pangs started to strike.

I got cleaned up and dressed, pulled on some recovery tights to help massage the leg muscles, and decided I'd treat myself to some room service and a lie-down. I order a hamburger and chips. It was a craving; not a sensible choice for recovery but it was what I desired, and I told myself I'd gone through enough today to deserve a reward.

As I waited I noticed a small green light blinking on top of my phone. I had a message or an e-mail. I was exhausted, but we never can seem to resist the siren call of the electronic harpy, be it a phone ringing, a message beeping, or a light flashing. I picked up the phone and brought it out of standby mode. There was a small icon in the upper left hand side of the screen indicating an e-mail. I clicked on it and saw it was from Coach Nigel.

Well done David,
  Amazing work.
  You must be really proud of yourself.
  You must think you're really clever.
  You've set a new world record in Antarctica.
  You've won both marathons by a huge margin.
  You've amassed a forty-five minute lead over the guy in second place.
  You must think you're really special. . . .
  But you're an idiot. You've blown it.
  If you keep going like this you can forget about even finishing this race, never mind winning it.
  The way you're running you're going to blow yourself to pieces, and you're probably going to take the guy in second place with you.
  This is a stage race, not a day race. Have a think about it. Grow up.

Nigel was kind of joking, but he also kind of wasn't. And I knew he was right. In both Antarctica and Punta Arenas, Doug and I had gone into battle. We'd both attacked and we'd both torn strips off each other. It was taking a toll on both of us. The damage was going to accumulate, the injuries were going to mount up, and at some stage if we continued acting the way we were, one or more likely both of us were going to break something that couldn't be fixed, and that would be the end of our race.

Nigel's e-mail played over again and again in my head, and my planned solid night's sleep became a restless and troubled slumber.

MARATHON 3: NORTH AMERICA

Miami, United States of America: The Forging of the Alliance

Yes, it will be very tough. But you know you can do it. Just put your head down. Avoid the temptation to go out too hard—you've still got a long way to go.

—Trilby White, my patient wife

I woke with a start and looked around the strange little room with a combination of curiosity and concern. It seemed like every morning I was waking up in a new bed in a new city, and I was having trouble keeping track. I could never sleep that well after a big race—I think it was due to a combination of sore, aching muscles and the adrenaline from the event, but not being in my own bed certainly didn't help.

My sleep had been punctuated by journeys into that twilight of the consciousness between wake and sleep, those waking dreams where half the brain is switched on and the other is still resting. My dreams felt like unstoppable rail cars rolling faster and faster, and although my conscious mind knew they were only dreams, I had no control over them. Coach Nigel's e-mail was playing on my thoughts.

I looked out of the window to the left side of my bed to try to get my bearings, and saw a patchwork assortment of brightly colored but weather-beaten little houses sitting opposite a rocky and barren coastline. Punta Arenas. We'd run a marathon down that strip of coast yesterday. The memories all came back to me as I shook off the dozy cobwebs and came to.

I looked at my watch. Five in the morning. It was still early, but I'd slept enough; it was time to get the day started. We had a long trip ahead of us: hotel to airport to Santiago to Miami. From the way the flights worked the next marathon was going to start in the early hours of tomorrow morning, so I had some time to spend on my recovery. Thank goodness. I was going to need it.

I checked my smartphone for messages and there was one from my father, Tim. I was actually a little surprised to get an e-mail from him. He'd always been a man of few words, and personal interaction and praise was rare. For some reason this marathon series had seemed to light a fire in him, and my mother later commented that he'd been up on the computer day and night checking results and reading reports.

I lay in bed and read the e-mail.

> David—I see you just won the second leg. Hopefully you will get time to read this.
> AMAZING PERFORMANCE. Well done.
> Best wishes for Miami.
> Regards, Tim

He'd cc'd my mother, Lindsay, and my wife, Trilby, on the e-mail. This seemed like a good chance to update them, and in a strange way writing an e-mail also helped me to maintain a connection with home and my family, giving me a little moral support and offsetting the homesick feeling that was slowly building.

I lay back on the bed and scribbled a reply e-mail on the phone's screen with my finger.

> Yeah, I was going to take it a bit slower but I couldn't help myself. . . I wanted to put in a bit of a time cushion so if anything goes amiss later there's some reserve.
> Not that I'm competitive, I know it's about the experience, not the win.
> The second place person put in a very spirited effort at the 25km mark but I sat on his shoulder until he melted, and when he blew up he rather fell to pieces.
> I think I've cemented myself as the one to beat, and it's always dangerous being a target, but it can also be useful for people to think you're not worth the effort to chase and to fight over second place, which is what seems to be happening now.
> But it's very early days and anything could happen . . . injury could ruin it all, so I definitely don't want to count any chickens. And it's certainly an incredible experience. I'll work out a full e-mail with a couple of photos of Punta Arenas later.
> Thanks for following, don't expect me to win every one . . .
> D.

I lay back and thought about people back home for a while. It was still early. Dawn was just starting to break through the night. I always was a morning person, but it seemed like Punta Arenas was a night owl and a late riser. I've never really been a lay-in-bed-relaxing kind of person, and I started to get fidgety after a few minutes. I thought about my options. It was far too early for breakfast; I think that opened at around 7:30 a.m. My normal choice might have been to go to the hotel gym and get some exercise, but at this point that seemed like pure folly. I settled on just going for a gentle stroll along the waterfront and watching the town slowly start to wake up.

As I swung my legs over and tried to get up out of bed, I realized there was a huge flaw in my plan. I could hardly stand, never mind go for a morning stroll. My quadriceps and my calf muscles burned with fatigue and lactic acid buildup. Suddenly I realized there was a much more pressing problem than how to fill the next two hours. I had to work out how on Earth I was going to get my legs to recover enough to run a marathon in less than twenty-four hours from now.

—⁓—

Necessity is the mother of invention, although on that day in that little hotel room in that little town, I suspect "desperation is the mother of invention" would have been more apt. My experience in stage racing had taught me that day three was generally the worst for fatigue and muscle pain. It seemed like the lactic acid, pain, and discomfort slowly built on the first day, started to beat louder and louder on day two, and then by day three it rose to a crescendo. I'd always found that by day four the pain subsided a little—not resolved, but became somewhat more manageable. It was day three by the calendar, although not day three by the racing—our third marathon was still to come. I tried to convince myself that this was to be expected. This was normal. With a little stretching and movement, the legs would loosen up. However, I couldn't rid myself of the small element of doubt, which told me that Coach Nigel's prediction had already started to come true. I'd pushed too hard.

No point in dwelling on the cause—I needed solutions, and I needed them fast. I wracked my brain. At that point, any idea was on the table, no matter how far-fetched. *First things first*, I thought. *Take an anti-inflammatory tablet.* I have always tried to avoid any kind of medication during exercise, especially anti-inflammatories. It concerned me that they might mask symptoms and hide signs that your body was trying to give you when you're pushing too hard or doing too much damage. It also worried me that medication put an additional load on the liver when it was being metabolized. Furthermore, anti-inflammatories were notorious for potential kidney side effects, especially when dehydrated either during or after a race.

Right now, however, I convinced myself it was definitely the right choice. I reasoned that an anti-inflammatory would counteract unnecessary muscle swelling and would help reduce further inflammation and tissue damage. It would also help me gather the wherewithal to walk, which seemed rather important if I was to make it down to breakfast.

I took a four-hundred-milligram ibuprofen tablet, and washed it down with copious amounts of water, trying to allay any risks of kidney damage. I figured the overhydration would probably help flush out any toxins and metabolites that had built up from my run. I'm not sure any of my logic was scientific, but it sounded rationally justifiable and that was enough for me.

The next step was to try to gently work those muscles, massaging them back to life. While I was ordering room service the night before, I'd noticed the hotel had a pool. I decided that some swimming or even aqua walking would be a low impact way to gently resuscitate the muscles. I figured I may as well pack my things first. I wasn't sure how long I was going to be out of the room, especially if I was able to combine my trip to the pool with breakfast afterward. The packing also gave some time for the anti-inflammatory tablet to start working.

After fifteen minutes or so, everything was packed and I was all ready for the hotel checkout when required later. I did that habitual sweep of the room, looked under the bed, peeled back the blankets, and checked the bins. It was probably an obsessive trait, but I had a deep-seated fear about leaving something vital in the room, especially on an expedition like this. One item lost now could result in much unhappiness later. I ran through the mental checklist of the absolute vitals—passport, wallet, Garmin sports watch, lucky running sunglasses. I was good to go. I wheeled the luggage in the small alcove next to the door, grabbed the room key, a bath towel, and a pair of running shorts that could double as swimmers, and made my way downstairs to find the pool.

I stopped by the reception desk to ask about the pool, crossing the language barrier with a combination of charades and slowly spoken English in a tone that unintentionally probably came across as patronizing or just plain silly. The bleary-eyed receptionist had just started her shift, but jumped to attention with a start when she recognized me as the crazy bathroom lunatic from the day before. She pointed me down the same hall that I'd run down previously on my mad toilet dash—apparently the pool was at the far end. I smiled and nodded thanks. Again she looked visibly relieved when I turned to leave.

The pool was decent enough, especially for a fairly small town. It was indoor, I suspect because the weather outside would have prevented swimming for much of the year. I bent down to dip a toe in. Cool, not cold. Perfect, exactly what the muscles needed. And out of the corner of my eye I spotted something else that may come in very handy: a sauna. I'd never really had much experience with saunas. The last time I'd been in one was in Norway, the morning after I'd finished the Norseman Xtreme Triathlon. All I remembered from that time was coming out feeling like I'd been steamed until medium-well doneness. I hatched a plan. I'd heard about alternating cold and hot therapy to relieve muscle pain and inflammation. I'd never tried it. I had no idea how it worked, or if it worked at all. But I was desperate.

There's an old rule: "Nothing new on race day." It means that you shouldn't try anything for the first time on the day of the race. No power meal for breakfast that you've never eaten before that might upset the stomach, no new stretches before a race that might pull a muscle, no new bike helmet or running shoes or swimming goggles that had a good chance of causing blisters or other problems. It was a simple, sensible, and time-honored tradition that any athlete worth his or her salt knew to be gospel. And part way through the biggest race of my life I was about to be foolish enough to break it.

I ducked into the changing rooms and peeled my trousers off one leg at a time, contorting my body and grimacing as I tried to undress without bending my painful legs too much. Slipping the running shorts on was no easier, nor more graceful, but finally I was done and I hobbled back to the pool victorious.

I eased myself in and unsteadily swam a few laps. The rhythmic and gentle kicking helped massage the muscles in my legs, and I started to feel like life might be able to continue. I figured that since I'd already quietly ignored the "Nothing new on race day" mantra, I may as well go the whole hog. Next I started pacing up and down the pool, doing some water walking, an exercise completely unfamiliar to me, trying to slowly build up in speed and power over each lap. My reasoning was that it would simulate walking and running, hopefully using all of the same muscles without all of the strain and impact that dry-land activity would have.

After a few more lengths of the pool and some very bemused stares from a couple of kids having an early morning pool play, I decided it was time to transition to the second half of the treatment: the sauna. I lifted myself out of the pool and walked away a little less gingerly than I had entered.

I entered the sauna. After I randomly flicked some unlabeled switches and adjusted some unlabeled dials, the pile of rocks on the top of the heater in the center of the small wooden sauna room started to warm. Ten minutes later they were positively roasting. I used a wooden ladle sitting next to the rocks to transfer some water from the bucket in the corner of the room to the rocks, to be rewarded with hissing and sizzling and a rush of steam. The needle gauge on the heat-stained thermometer nailed to the wall started to rise. I started to sweat. My logic was that the heat would dilate the blood vessels in my legs, increasing blood flow and helping the clear any built-up toxins or metabolites. I also held some degree of hope that the sauna-induced perspiration would help me sweat out those toxins, even though deep down I knew this last concept was not medically sensible or correct.

After ten minutes of ladling water onto the rocks and sweating in a room of ever increasing temperature, I decided it was time for the cold therapy again. I had convinced myself that the cool water would have a natural anti-inflammatory and soothing effect, like ice on a swollen joint. I gingerly left the sauna and climbed back into the water, starting my combination of a few laps of gentle swimming followed by a few laps of aqua-walking, under the amused gaze of the kids playing on the other side.

After my pool routine I got out and headed back to the sauna for a second heat cycle. As I was sitting there having some doubts there was a knock at the door. It was Big Jim. He was feeling about the same as I was, and had exactly the same idea. We sat and chatted for a while. It's always easier to feel rational and sensible when somebody else is there with exactly the same foolhardy idea.

I went through a couple more hot-cold cycles and started to realize I was feeling better. Quite a lot better. Whether it was a case of mind over matter or there really was a physical improvement, I came away feeling relieved. The plan seemed to work. Although I'd also have to give the anti-inflammatory ibuprofen tablet some credit, too, of course.

I shuffled back to the changing rooms and slipped back into my trousers and T-shirt, and then went on to breakfast. It was still pretty quiet when I arrived, but I did see a couple of familiar faces. I grabbed a bowl of cereal from the breakfast buffet, a couple of slices of toast, and a cup of hot coffee, and then went and sat with Jon. We said our good mornings and made some quick pleasantries, but quickly both returned to our breakfast. I started eating and realized I was ravenous. From the way Jon was wolfing down his food I think he must have felt the same. The two marathons had left us carbohydrate depleted and our bodies were trying to replenish the stores. It wasn't gourmet, it wasn't even close, but it was good.

People came and went, there were a few short conversations about how everybody was feeling, the race yesterday, the flight coming up, what Miami would be like, but I think in general most of us were feeling pretty drained, both emotionally and physically. It had been an eventful couple of days. We'd all seen things we'd never seen before and had experiences we'd never imagined. Breakfast seemed like a time for people to quietly reflect and gather their thoughts, a short period of tranquility before the upcoming storm.

—⁓—

I lingered at breakfast for a while, since there didn't seem much else to do. I'd packed most of my gear when I woke early, and although it would have been interesting I couldn't really bring myself to go for a walk. After a second plate of food and a second cup of coffee, I decided probably the best thing would be some more rest. My first coach Max's words must have been drumming through my head again: "Don't sit if you can lie down."

I wandered back to my hotel room in a considerably better state than I left it—muscles relaxed, joints comfortable, and stomach full. I had around an hour until the transit bus came to collect us for the trip to the airport. That hour passed too quickly.

We got to the airport, checked in, and after a short wait we boarded the LAN air flight to Santiago, where we were to change planes and continue onward to Miami. I must admit that after flying on the Soviet-made IL-76 cargo plane to and from Antarctica, being on a normal passenger jet just didn't seem exciting. The flights on this leg had been booked in economy class. Normally this would be completely fine, but with stiff legs, a stretch out really would have been appreciated.

The flight was fairly uneventful. I slept for most of it, doing my utmost to make the best of any potential rest time, until I was woken by excited shoulder tapping from one of the other runners, Tim. I opened bleary eyes to see most of the passengers trying to squash into the right side of the plane. In those half-dazed moments between wake and sleep my brain scrambled to try an attribute some kind of meaning to what I was seeing. People were pointing out the window. *Was the plane on fire? Had one of the engines stopped working? Were they only serving lunch on one side of the plane?* None of these seemed plausible, especially considering everybody was smiling and happy. An announcement came over the PA system: "Ladies and Gentleman, this is the captain speaking. We are passing over Tierra del Fuego National Park. If you look out the right side windows you can see Cami Lake, considered one of the great natural wonders."

My sleepy eyes widened, my focus became sharp. It was beautiful. Stunning, rugged, untouched valleys. Wild, natural, incredible Andean snow-capped mountains, with a huge lake in the center of it all, fed by tributaries draining the surrounding snow-melt. Seeing it from this bird's eye view allowed an appreciation of the magnificence of it all.

After about fifteen minutes, the air hostesses must have decided it was time to get people back into their seats, and gently used the motivation of lunch to persuade everyone to leave the view and sit down. Trolleys started to rattle up the isles, and I promptly fell back to sleep. I must have been tired.

I woke up as we landed in Santiago, drowsily stumbled off the plane and wandered to the lounge. The next leg was a connecting LAN Air flight to Miami, so there was no need to collect and recheck baggage. It was just going to be a short wait in a moderately crowded lounge.

There was a strange sense of déjà vu about being in the Santiago airport. I'd passed through on my original and protracted multistop journey from my Hong Kong home to Punta Arenas. It had been less than a week. So much had happened. When I'd passed through the first time, the hostess at the check-in counter asked to see my flight itinerary. I showed her the printout for the seven marathons flights, and she looked shocked. She proceeded to block off the seats on either side of me and told me that even though I was in economy on that original flight, she was going to make sure I got a sleep, because I was going to need it. In reflection it turned out she was right. I glanced over to the check-in counter to see if by chance she was working—I wanted to go over and thank her and let her know I was still alive and kicking—but unfortunately there were no familiar faces.

I sat in the lounge for a little while and again had that experience of being in a totally foreign part of the world. Invariably airports are melting pots—there are always faces and nationalities that are less than familiar—but the further I got from home the more that percentage of unfamiliar faces started to grow. Coming from Hong Kong, where only a few percent of the population were of Western descent, I should have been completely used to mixing with different races and types of people—and I certainly was. I realized that it wasn't the fact that I was so outnumbered by a different nationality. It was that the nationality was one I wasn't used to. And I loved it. I felt a strange child-like curiosity to study those that were fascinatingly different from my norms, even though they, of course, were the locals and I was the one who stood out. I had to be careful not to stare at intricate jewelry designs, lacework dresses, or distinctly expressive faces. An occasional glare back told me when it was time to move my eyes on.

I enjoyed sitting in this waiting lounge subtly watching and learning. The time passed quickly, and before I knew it the next flight was ready for boarding.

—⟋⟍—

I had one crystal-clear thought going into Miami: don't blow it. The last two marathon runs had been very fast, and to keep going at that pace wouldn't have been constructive—in fact it definitely would have been destructive. Coach Nigel was right. I had to control the pace. I had to be sensible. If only I had an idea of exactly how I was going to do that. It wasn't only a matter of self-control; it was a matter of slowing down the whole race before we all tore each other to shreds. As the race leader on the overall standings and generally the person in front, I had the most influence over the pack. If I ran hard, they would try to hold on and catch me. If I ran slower, they would probably slack off the pace, too. At least that was the plan.

We arrived at Miami early in the morning, around 5 a.m., and it was still dark. There is a Will Smith song titled "Welcome to Miami." I didn't really know it, but Tim, the American runner, apparently loved it with all of his heart. It seemed that, unfortunately, he only knew one line of the song, namely, "Welcome to Miami." This didn't dampen his enthusiasm, however, and he compensated for any lack of knowledge of further verses by repeating the one line over and over, with increasing enthusiasm. Every so often he threw in some hand gestures or faux breakdancing moves. It was amusing at first, but I think the rest of us were still just trying to wake up and didn't really need the motivation.

We arrived at the baggage collection carousels to hear an automated announcement on the PA system, "Welcome to Miami" in a nondescript woman's voice. This only served to spur Tim on even more, and his rendition started turning heads of other weary travelers. It wasn't possible to be irritated with him—he was having too much of a good time—and a smile broke across my face.

The luggage arrived all safe and sound, and Richard the race director gathered us over to the side of baggage carousel five.

"Alright. Everyone here? Good. Everyone got their luggage? Good," he said. It was all business.

"The vans are waiting outside. We're going straight to the marathon course. We're going to start the marathon before 8 a.m. We have a small hotel room to wash and change after.

"You're going to need to get changed into your running gear now. Be back here as soon as you can," he finished.

It was a strange combination of the power of suggestion and herd mentality. We were standing in the middle of the baggage collection area of Miami International Airport, and we as a group decided it was completely reasonable to open our suitcases then and there, rummage through our clothing, fish out some running clothes, and then head off to the nearest bathroom to get changed. In these days of TSA agents and airport security, I'm sure there were some cameras trained on us. I'm somewhat surprised we weren't questioned, but I suspect because we all seemed to act as if we were behaving completely rationally, other passengers and staff didn't overly concern themselves.

Ten minutes later I was standing back in the luggage area, now dressed in a singlet bearing the names of my sponsors and my charity, running shorts, and a pair of running shoes. I would have looked out of place had I not been standing near eleven other people dressed in a very similar fashion. Without further ado we wheeled our luggage out of the airport and toward a cavalcade of white SUVs with blacked-out windows. There was no doubt about it. We were in the United States.

Larger-than-life would be a fair description of our driver and host, Frank. He greeted us with a beaming smile and welcomed us to Miami, and to the United States. Frank was a caricature. He was as wide as he was tall, standing there in an XXL Miami Dolphins T-shirt, knee-length shorts, and loafers. I half expected him to pull out a cigar and answer a call on his pager. Sometimes it's quite amusing when the stereotypes turn out to be true.

Frank was a lovely guy, more than happy to help with luggage and organization, friendly and courteous even though it was around 6 a.m. He did a great job feigning interest in our running, although from his appearance I can't imagine he was much of a sports guy. Maybe a sports-watching guy, but not a sports-doing guy. And I fully recognized that running wasn't really a watching sport.

As soon as the luggage was packed in the trunk of the SUV and we were loaded into the passenger compartment, it was time to move. There were three SUVs in total, all white with black windows. We headed off in a convoy that must have looked like the FBI on the move. Frank certainly saw himself as a professional, and as soon as we were moving he switched from luggage and loading logistics manager to tour guide. He pointed out various significant cultural spots, including the singer Gloria Estefan's house, the local sports stadium (apparently home to his beloved Dolphins), a shipping port, and so forth. It was very interesting and it was good of him to work so hard to make our trip enjoyable, but I think most of us were just focused on the marathon that was fast approaching.

"All right, we're here," Frank declared. "South Beach."

A smile crept across my face. I realized I'd had no idea where in Miami we'd actually be running. I'd figured that it would just be a nondescript loop of road where we wouldn't cause too much disturbance to the locals. South Beach was a different matter entirely.

—◆—

South Beach has a reputation as one of the coolest places in Miami, if not the whole United States. It's an unusual mixture, half Cuban art deco and half *Baywatch*; definitely a place to be seen, full of beautiful people, beautiful houses, and beautiful cars. It was a wild contrast to the wind-swept and barren shores of Punta Arenas. The run was going be similar on paper—an approximately seven-kilometer loop up and down the seafront on a walking path that followed the beach—but that was where the similarity ended. Everything else was in complete divergence: the warm weather, the sandy beach, the wealthy tourists and locals, the manicured and landscaped gardens and parks. It was a fascinating comparison, and in truth I'm not sure which I preferred. Miami was definitely more luxe and svelte, but Punta did feel much more natural, raw, and authentic. Still, I won't deny that a little of the high life helped lift my spirits.

We got out of the SUVs and milled around the South Beach car park. Some of us chatted casually about the upcoming marathon, and we all agreed it was time to be a little more relaxed. The last couple of days had been really hard, and everybody knew it. The consensus was that a slower pace was more sensible, especially if we were all planning on finishing in one piece. I suggested around five and a half minutes per kilometer. There were some nods. We all seemed to be in agreement.

The half-light of dawn had started creeping across the horizon by the time we seeded ourselves on the starting line. We all held up the flags of our respective countries for the press photographers, and after a few quick words from the organizer and a sounding of the horn we were off. Ted took off once again, continuing on his self-styled comical mission to lead each marathon, for a short time at least. He flew off the line and must have put twenty meters on the rest of us, then sat down on a park bench and gave us all a clap and a cheer as we passed. He was certainly good value. Ted was the steam valve who released some pressure, the court jester who played a prank when things were getting a little too serious. We needed him more than we realized. He kept us sane and kept us from each other's throats.

The first loop of the race was led out by one of the organizers, Ricardo, a good-looking second-generation Cuban American whose parents had left Cuba as part of the Mariel Boatlift in 1980. Ricardo had made the clever choice of bringing a bike to ride rather than toughing out the run with us, and he cruised beside us laughing and chatting. Shaved head, black-and-white-striped Nike tracksuit, fixie bike with the beach cruiser handlebars, Ricardo was the real deal. He was great company for the run and helped take our minds off our current predicament by telling us more about the history of Miami and his place in it.

The Mariel Boatlift was apparently the largest civilian mass migration in history, according to Ricardo. It began in the latter part of 1980, after prolonged economic weakness in Cuba. The Cuban government suddenly decided that anyone who wanted to leave was free to do so, and over one hundred thousand people fled in the few months that followed, leaving the Mariel harbor in Cuba and traveling via boat to Florida. Although some have claimed that the boatlift was used by Fidel Castro to rid his country of criminals and patients from mental asylums, the vast majority of the people who left were average, honest citizens who were either seeking a better life or had ideological views that differed from the government.

The Mariel Boatlift changed Miami forever. The population dynamics, economy, culture, and even language shifted, and the effect is still obvious even today.

Jon the accountant moved up to share the lead with me as we talked to Ricardo. Jon was one of the more measured runners. He was a strong runner with untold stamina, a veteran of more marathons than most of us other runners put together, but he was generally one of the steadier back markers, and to see him up at the pointy front end of the race was somewhat of a surprise.

After a quick discussion it turned out that Jon had gotten it into his head that he wanted to lead out the first loop of the run in Miami. I'm not sure why. I asked him and he just smiled. Maybe Miami had special significance for him; maybe he'd just woken up this morning and decided that was his goal. I looked back over my shoulder to see if there were any other surprises I should know about. Doug was about twenty meters behind, James a little back from him, and then Marcelo and Pierre. We were all bunched together quite closely; maybe some of the tension and grandstanding was starting to ease.

Jon also seemed quite interested in hearing Miami-local Ricardo speak. Fortunately for us, Ricardo had quite a lot to say, as we were huffing and puffing trying to keep up with him on the bike. The loop passed quite quickly as we listened to him, punctuated by one of us interjecting an occasional question. Ricardo's views were fascinating and quite different from what I'd expected. He'd never been to Cuba, but I think somewhere deep inside he felt he had a connection to the country. His feelings for Fidel Castro, however, were very clear—in Ricardo's opinion, Castro was a dictator and had ruined the country. I'm not sure why this surprised me—after all, Ricardo's parents had fled the country, leaving family, friends, and possessions behind to escape this man. For some reason I had expected a degree of respect or even affinity for Castro, but after Ricardo had told his family's story, I could understand why affinity would be ludicrous.

As we ran down the Miami Beach boulevard, the sun slowly started to rise, bathing the foreshore in a glorious morning light. The sky was blue with only a wisp of cloud in the sky, and the palm tree fronds slowly fluttered in the early morning breeze. We were running through Lummus Park, just a stone throw from the beach, running parallel to the world-famous Ocean Drive. A policeman passed us on a Segway, patrolling the beach, but the path was otherwise fairly deserted.

We passed by the famous art deco–style buildings of Ocean Drive, a South Beach icon. We passed by the Versace mansion. We passed by the classic red-and-white lifeguard huts on the beach. And then I realized what I was doing. It was the same trick I'd used in Punta Arenas. I was subconsciously setting waypoints on the course, points that I could easily remember and could aim toward on each loop. Get to the buildings. Then get to the lifeguard huts. Then get to the next point. The marathon was too big to think about as a single goal; it was much more constructive to break it up into smaller pieces and bite them off one at a time.

As I thought about it more, I also realized I'd become quite adept at this waypoint game. I not only used it to reward myself for completing small chunks of the marathon, but I now added a new element. Each time I passed the waypoint I'd find a new feature or aspect that I hadn't seen before. The game helped keep my mind occupied. Half of the battle with any sporting event is mental. I was bemused that I'd created this accidental game in my head without even realizing it. The brain certainly works in mysterious ways.

Jon and I continued on and eventually reached the Miami Beach Boardwalk. The race director had briefly mentioned the turnaround point was on the boardwalk, so I knew we didn't have much further to go before we'd finished the first outward leg. Ricardo told us that he'd wait for us at the entrance; the boardwalk was fairly narrow and there were some steps in parts, all of which would have made riding a bicycle difficult and dangerous.

Running on the boardwalk was an immediate shock. The wooden slats had a noticeable give and springiness, and there was a mild by clearly perceivable push off with every step. It was hard to tell whether it helped or just made the legs feel more jelly-like. After around half a kilometer, Jon and I came to the turnaround point and headed back the way we came.

Turnarounds are always important in races. It was the perfect opportunity to quickly gauge where everyone else was, how they were looking, if they seemed to be strong or having any difficulty, and also their response to you. I found that last piece of information was often the most useful and the most telling. I always made it a point of giving every other runner some form of recognition, no matter how bad I was feeling. It didn't have to be much, even a nod or a smile was enough. There were two reasons for the recognition. First, and most important, it was good manners. It was respect. To not give a nod or a wave or a "Hiya" would be akin to ignoring someone. Second, the response to that little nod gave a lot of information back. A surprisingly large amount of information back. It helped tell me how the person was feeling, how tired he was, how comfortable he was, if there were any significant aches or pains, and how he felt about me. I wasn't running this race in a bubble or against myself; I was running it against eleven other people, and I needed to know how all of them were feeling and which ones I had to watch more closely.

It wasn't long until Jon and I came across Doug running the other way. It didn't take a nod or a wave to tell he didn't look happy. He had a blank forward stare, and he didn't acknowledge either of us. Jon and I exchanged a glance and shrug. To be honest, I'd given up worrying about what Doug was thinking. In fact, by that stage he'd started to get on my nerves. He'd hardly spoken two words to me for the entire race series, and I was pretty sure he saw me as his enemy. He'd come to win this competition, and I was the biggest obstacle in his way. The animosity wasn't at all difficult to see. It wasn't good to have grudges in a race environment. It was going to end up badly, and every one of us knew that. The other runners were just biding their time and waiting to see what happened, but they all knew that at some point there was going to be an explosion, and all of them wanted to be there to see it when it happened.

From the outset Doug had come across as a loner. Most of the other runners had chatted, made friends, spent time getting to know each other and talking about the race, but not Doug; he seemed to prefer his own company. Even that first time we all met in Punta before the race had started he'd spent most of the time out of the hotel wandering alone with his thoughts. His behavior in Antarctica was similar, spending most of his time at one end of the main mess tent listening to his iPod. In an event like this we all need moral support, someone to help when times get tough, and friends to help ward off homesickness. But maybe that was just his personality.

If you point a finger at someone else, then there are three fingers pointing back to you, as the saying goes, and I certainly had to share the blame for the deterioration of my relationship with Doug. If I'm honest I'd have to admit that I'd been playing him from the start. I knew he was my main opposition; I didn't need James and his book of bets from the other runners to tell me that. Without even consciously realizing I was doing it, I'd set him up more than once. It began before the starting gun was even fired in Antarctica. When I came back into that mess-hall tent at the Union Glacier base camp and gently but intentionally let everyone know I'd already done a loop of the course, I knew it would get in his head, and it certainly seemed to. I can thank James for giving the extra push when he mentioned it to Doug for a second time, but I'd started that ball rolling.

As soon as the race started in Antarctica, I knew I had to stay on his feet and wear him out; then as soon as he was tired, I had to "hit the gas" and put a big enough gap between him and me that he got demoralized and lost time.

Punta was no different. Sure, I'd felt wronged that he'd made a move on me when I had an off-the-track bathroom issue, but again I sat on him until he broke, and then increased my speed to put some time on him. I'd figured out what worked with Doug. He didn't like pressure. As soon as he felt pressure, that little tell of glancing over the shoulder began, and I knew I was getting to him. Like a dog at a bone this only made me more determined, and each time I had kept going until he couldn't take it and pulled right back to avoid further conflict and interaction.

I'm not sure whether my actions would be described as manipulative. Doug was a decent runner—as good as I was, possibly better—yet he was too easily thrown and upset. He let things get to him. I knew that and I used it against him. Everybody out on that track knew that this was a mental and a physical battle, and we were all doing our best to play both sides of the game. I'm not sure whether that makes it fair. But I do know he was completely within his rights not to like me and not to pay me any respect at that turnaround.

———✳———

Jon and I were greeted with a big smile from Ricardo as we came off the board-walk. He started pedaling just as we got close to him and continued with his tales of life in Miami. He told us that the Miami marathon was on in a few days' time, and he was an enthusiastic runner. He wanted to save his legs today, and that's why he was riding a bike instead of running with us. He continued on as my mind drifted in and out of the conversation, all the while checking off those mental waypoints on the return leg back to the starting point.

Miami was starting to wake. Lummus Park and Ocean Drive were becoming much busier, crowded with an odd assortment of joggers, cross-fit enthusiasts, yoga practitioners, dog walkers, and the occasional homeless person. It was clearly a place to be seen; girls wore tiny bikinis and guys had bulging muscles. Everybody seemed to be caught between pretending they were in their own zone and carefully scouting around to see who was looking at them, or who they could look at.

As we got closer to the starting line turnaround point, I could tell Jon was feeling the pain. He'd pushed pretty hard on this first lap, and he was starting to run low on energy. The conversation dried up and he was looking strained. But he'd set himself a goal and he was going to see it through. We ran down the final stretch of the Ocean Drive path and then turned left down South Pointe Park and to the starting line. Jon put on a final burst of speed and effort and hit that line in first place. He was elated and exhausted. Mission accomplished. And with that he settled back down to his usual jog with a contented smile on his face, pleased to finish in any position overall, as long as he finished.

Doug, however, had other ideas. As I came back from the turnaround, I saw him coming in. This time he didn't ignore me. He stared straight at me, throwing daggers. It wasn't the way I fought. I nodded cordially. To be truthful I knew it would get under his skin more if I was congenial than if I glowered back at him.

Doug must have made the decision that he was going to turn up the speed after the first loop. It made sense. Take it easy, stay in the pack, check out the course, and then make your move when you know the lay of the land. In hindsight it was obvious, a clever move on his part, but I wasn't expecting it. I had vainly thought that we were all going to run this one on autopilot, everyone just maintaining their positions and have a nice run in a beautiful place.

I think the others had the same thought as I did. James had held his position a short way back, followed by Marcelo and Pierre. It was a tight pack. Everyone was running together and seemed contented. At least that was what I had hoped, and what would have suited me best.

When I think about it, I wouldn't have been contented to be in second place either. I would have been burning to make some time back. Possibly Doug had even misinterpreted the fact that Jon, a generally slower runner, had led the first lap as meaning that everyone else was tired and weak.

As soon as he hit that turnaround, he bolted. It was typical Doug. He'd done it at the start of Antarctica; he'd done it in the middle of Punta Arena after my toilet break. He went off at a pace that wasn't fast marathon. It wasn't even half-marathon. It was a five-kilometer time trial race pace, and he stormed past Jon and me. A little experience over the last two days had taught me this game though. There was no point in trying to keep up with that. But I needed to keep him in eyesight. Doug needed to see me behind him when he started glancing.

James increased his pace slightly as well. I suspect he didn't want to let Doug get away either. James wasn't too far behind Doug in the overall time-based rankings, and second place overall was still very much a possibility. James caught up with me after a kilometer or so. I gave him a nod and a smile, and after a few words we decided to run together for a while. I liked James. He had a rather dour sense of humor, and he certainly knew how to play the game as well as anyone, but he was honest and friendly. We spoke a few sentences but mainly just enjoyed the fact that there was someone to run with and to help pace. We stayed together for the entire loop, and I watched my landmarks come and go, carefully picking out a new feature on each. The neon on the art deco building, the hedges at the front of the Versace building. The funny little lighthouse structure on the top of the lifeguard tower. The pattern of the nails and bolts holding the planks on the boardwalk down.

After the loop, Doug remained slightly in the lead, but only ten or twenty meters ahead. When we got back to the starting line turnaround, Doug decided to try the same trick again. He increased the speed dramatically, nearly sprinting off the starting line. By this time my emotions were starting to be less easy to control. It was a combination of my fatigue and raw nerves, and for some reason his sprints suddenly annoyed me. He opened up a gap of a few hundred meters. He was getting too far ahead. If I lost sight of him, it would be a big disadvantage.

"James, we've got to stick with him. You OK for that?" I groaned under my breath.

"You go, you hold 'im. I'm puffed I am," James retorted.

"All right, try to stay with me anyway, and otherwise I'll see you on the flipside," I replied.

James had sped up his pace over the last lap to hold on, and any more would be too much. It was sensible of him to pull back and conserve his strength. He was the wisest of the three of us at that point, and with a sensible strategy he might end up surprising everyone out there.

I gently increased my pace. I could feel my heart rate rising and my legs aching. I was running faster than I had intended. And at that point, Coach Nigel's words suddenly and violently came to the forefront of my thoughts, and started bouncing around my head again and again: *If you keep going like this you can forget about finishing this race, never mind winning it. This is a stage race, not a day race. Have a think about it. Grow up.*

I was torn. There was no right answer. If I stuck with him I'd be running too fast. If I let him go, I lost a mental advantage I'd spent the last few days carefully cultivating and promoting. I realized there wasn't an option. If I wanted to win, I had to maintain that mental supremacy. I had to be unassailable. I had to change the competition into being about who was going for second place, and make them forget about first place. I had to keep up.

Slowly I advanced. There was no need to rush. I figured it was better to take my time, to make him sweat. I was about two hundred meters behind him when I saw it: he turned and glanced backward. And I knew he'd seen me. Slowly as the kilometers advanced, I closed the gap, reeling him in. I could tell Doug's anxiety was building to fever pitch. The over-shoulder glancing increased to the point where he wasn't looking where he was going. It wasn't productive. He was slowing himself down, and if he wasn't careful he was going to run into something. There was no mistaking the inevitable. Tension was building. Soon enough, there was going to be an explosion.

—✺—

By its nature sport is about competition. Competition with oneself is ever present, but it's competition against others that drives sport and makes for truly compelling and memorable events. By its nature, competition forces the establishment of rivalries—two individuals or teams with similar overall abilities that square up against each other again and again until they seem to become intertwined. Rivals don't necessarily like each other. They may not even entirely respect each other. But they need each other. The classic rivalries are never forgotten and often go on to become more memorable than the event itself.

Muhammad Ali was never short of rivals, but probably his most famous feud was with Smokin' Joe Frazier. They were both considered among the greatest heavyweight boxing champions in history.

Ali was a polarizing figure; people either loved him or loathed him. Born Cassius Clay, Ali converted to Islam when he was twenty-two years old. He was a conscientious objector to the Vietnam War and was considered by many to be one of the champions of the antiwar movement. Many say that Ali was ahead of his time, both in the ring for his boxing and out of the ring for his political, religious freedom and civil rights beliefs. Ali was placed under surveillance by the National Security Agency for a period and had his own code name, "Minaret." He was arrested for draft evasion and convicted. His conviction was eventually overturned by the Supreme Court, but only after Ali had been prevented from fighting for nearly four years, potentially the best four years of his career.

Smokin' Joe Frazier was everything that Ali was not. He was the yin to Ali's yang. Whether he liked it or not, Frazier was seen by many to hold strongly conservative pro-establishment, pro-government views. Some have even suggested that Ali quietly promoted these beliefs about Frazier to help alienate him from the average man. Ali publicly suggested that Frazier was a pawn of the white establishment, and Frazier later went on to say that Ali's battle with Parkinson's was divine justice for his previous sleights. Although they had originally started their boxing careers as friends, their relationship slowly deteriorated over time to the point where they were openly hostile.

In March of 1971 at Madison Square Garden in New York City, their rivalry came to a head. They both had fair claim to the World Heavyweight Championship title. Ali had been awarded the title back in 1964, after defeating Sonny Liston, in Miami as coincidence would have it. Ali was stripped of the title when he was arrested for being a conscientious objector. In the period that followed, Frazier won the World Heavyweight Championship title by winning bouts against other boxers. But he had never faced or defeated the previous championship title holder, Ali.

The match is now known as "the Fight of the Century." There was pride and ego at stake. At a time of political turmoil and war there were fundamental beliefs and dogmas at stake. There was the World Heavyweight Championship title at stake. Neither man had ever lost a match before. They were both remarkable talents, and both had the skill and the wherewithal to win.

The fight exceeded all expectations. It was one of the few matches to go the full fifteen rounds. Both boxers had stretches where they were clearly dominant, then the tide would turn and the other man would be on top for a round. The match went back and forth, but the judges' decision was unanimous: Frazier had won. Frazier was the World Heavyweight Champion. Ali never publicly accepted defeat, saying that the outcome was "a white man's decision."

Ali went on to have two more matches against Frazier, both of which he won. But the fierce rivalry burned on, and only decades after their retirement did the two men finally decide to put the past behind them and become friends.

Ali was a technically brilliant boxer, a strategist who used an opponent's weakness to his advantage and shaped the rules of the match to play into his hands. He would mentally work away at his opponent. He knew the buttons to press, and he wasn't afraid of speaking his mind, some might say too overtly. That was his strategy—to get the opponent off balance, because an opponent off balance would lash out and miss their target.

His techniques and methods were innovative and revolutionary. There were times when he totally flipped the world of boxing on its head, and none more so than "rope-a-dope." Ali had calculated that if he acted "dopey" and leaned up against the ropes while using his arms to protect his face and torso, he could take repeated blows from the opponent, using the elasticity of the ropes to help absorb the punishment. It was a moment of genius. After a period of sustained punching and attack his opponent would tire, and Ali would bounce off the ropes and launch into a frenzied attack, catching his opponent by surprise and causing the real damage.

I am no Ali, nor am I a Frazier, but that was my plan: the rope-a-dope strategy. Sit back and let Doug tire himself out. And only when I was ready would I come out swinging.

—⁂—

Doug took off again. It was another attempt to put distance between him and me. He took off like a man possessed, and again was running a sprint pace rather than a marathon stride. I let him go; there was no point in tiring myself trying to keep up. But I did want to keep him in view.

After a kilometer or so, he started slowing down again, and I slowly started reeling him back in. The pendulum swings one way, and then the pendulum swings back. The exact same sequence of events happened again. Each time as I got slowly closer, his glancing over the shoulder became more frequent. He seemed more and more tense. And then when I started getting within fifty meters of him, he shot off up the road.

Landmarks came and went, waypoints were checked off the map, new features were found. I was running my race, and I wasn't going to change my pace or my plan for anybody. Smooth and steady was the key—Coach Nigel had been very clear about this. And in any case, Doug's sprinting and then slowing had really started to pique my curiosity; it was the oddest way I'd seen to run a marathon for a long time.

We went through one more cycle of the catch-up, sprint-off, slow-down, and reel-in. We were well past the halfway point of the marathon, but not close to the finish. He was tiring, and he yelled something and waved an arm in the air.

That's when it happened. Doug exploded. It had steadily built up a head of steam in Antarctica. It reached a boiling point during Punta Arenas. Finally, during that midmorning run down the Miami South Beach foreshore, that pressure cooker of emotion, tension, and anxiety that had slowly been increasing in temperature exploded.

"Why are you doing this?" Doug yelled at me. "Why can't you just leave me alone? It's not fair. Leave me alone."

"Dunno what you're talking about," I replied.

I tried to keep my tone as flat and emotionless as possible. There was no use in fighting back, and a small part of me knew that if I was nonchalant I would probably infuriate him even more.

"Why? I just want to win one," he continued. "Is that too much to ask? Just let me win this one."

"That's not the way it works, you know that," I stated. "It's a race. It's not you versus me; it's the first person to the finish. If I let you win, you won nothing."

"C'mon, man. Please. You've already got two. Just give me this. You can win the rest. Just give me this. Just for everyone at home."

This put me in a really difficult position. I had no idea what the right answer was. I'd never even been presented with this option before in a race. Everyone I'd ever raced had either won or fallen to the wayside trying. To let someone else win seemed very close to throwing a race or manipulating the results at the very least. It wasn't like anyone was betting on the outcome of this race, at least nobody except for James's little wager on the overall result, but it still didn't seem like the right course of action. It didn't really seem fair.

On the other hand, I knew exactly how he felt, and it wasn't a long stretch to think of myself in his shoes. We've all been there. I knew that Doug had been unwell in previous years, and thankfully he had made a full recovery, but this was his chance to prove to the world that he was back. Not only back, he was on top. In his eyes, the world was watching, and he'd made no secret of the fact he'd come there to win. His pride was on the line, and after the first two races it was hurting.

—ᵛᵛ—

An elaborate dance of personalities, desires, and agreements occurs behind the scenes in any multiday stage race. And in nearly any stage race, that elaborate dance ends up having an impact on results. Racers make agreements and deals. They work together, they work against another party, they agree to chase down leaders. They call it *gifting*. There are many reasons that races are gifted, but team tactics, public image, and future payback are the three most common themes.

Team tactics are a common reason cited for gifting. In some sports it's considered completely fair, in fact it's de rigeur. Cycling and car racing spring to mind. It's considered completely normal in these sports for teammates to work together, especially so in cycling, where different riders will have different roles and objectives within the team. Even the cycling team's manager will ride along in a car near the peloton and guide the team members, generally with the purpose of protecting the "star" rider. Other riders will ride in front of the star rider to shield him from the wind, a tactic known as drafting. They'll also chase down riders from other teams and stay close to them to keep an eye on them and gently slow them down. Finally, as the finish line approaches, the usual tactic is to have a lead-out rider, who will sprint away as fast as he can with the star rider in tow, pulling him forward ahead of the pack and protecting him from the wind and from other riders. Just before the finish line the lead-out rider will pull to the side, allowing the star rider to win.

Team tactics are controversial, and there have been initiatives to ban the use of team radios to prevent the coordination and brinkmanship, allowing the sport to go back to a more pure survival-of-the-fittest competition. However, these examples of team tactics occurred within the team, a group who are clearly and obviously working together to achieve a goal. It's a very different story when opposing teams or athletes work together surreptitiously, and that's when real ethical questions begin to be asked.

Gifting for public image and future payback occurs in nearly every stage race. An overall race leader may choose to gift a stage to another rider, especially if that rider has done much of the hard work that day, such as taking the lead, pacing the ride, or shielding the race leader from the wind. The overall race leader is really only interested in his cumulative time, the total time taken for the entire race so far, and how far he is ahead of the competition. A stage win for a junior rider would help build a career and attract sponsors, and in some cases could be a life-defining moment. A race leader who gifts a stage win in this way looks like the bigger person, gracious and willing to share the limelight with an up-and-coming star, winning public support and favor. Perhaps more importantly, the up-and-coming star now owes the race leader, and that debt will most likely be called upon at some later time when needed.

Alberto Contador, one of the recent greats of cycling, has suffered his fair share of controversy. He has attacked in races when he shouldn't have attacked, he has ridden in ways that many consider to lack sportsmanship, and by accident or design, he's generally seen as an arrogant, self-centered rider. On stage nineteen of the 2011 Giro d'Italia, one of the biggest bike races on the planet, Contador decided it was time to try to give something back. Paolo Tiralongo, a veteran professional cyclist, had never won a stage. He'd come close many times, and he'd certainly pulled his weight that day on the course. Tiralongo and Contador had once been teammates. Tiralongo had worked hard in previous seasons for Contador. But they were now rivals, with Tiralongo racing for Astana and Contador for Astana's arch-nemesis, Saxo.

Tiralongo had ridden a strong and clever race. He'd played his cards very well, and had outsmarted most of his opponents. With less than five kilometers to go, he was out in the lead—a lead he held until less than half a kilometer to the finish, when he turned and saw what should have been his worst nightmare: Contador, wearing the race leader's pink jersey.

Tiralongo's face fell. He knew what this meant. Contador was the stronger rider. Tiralongo had worked all day and was going to have his first ever stage win snatched from him in the closing meters. Contador rode past Tiralongo.

Then something happened that truly surprised everyone. Contador pulled in front of Tiralongo and shielded him from the wind. He dragged Tiralongo toward the finish line, protecting him from other riders. And just before the finish, he moved to the side and gifted Tiralongo the win. The two men embraced after the line, a thanks for a career of hard work and support, and a moment of true class that is remembered to this day. Contador won a lot of fans that day, and he reversed the tide of public opinion that was rapidly turning against him.

If only Lance Armstrong had been as gracious with ex-teammate George Hincapie when their turn to race for the line came in the 2009 Tour de France. Hincapie had the stage snatched from him in what most saw as a vicious act of betrayal from a former supposed friend, an event that had repercussions many years on and possibly played a part Armstrong's eventual downfall. But that is a different story. Sometimes, humility can lead to greater victory.

—ɷ—

The problem is that there's always a gray area in gifting, what's fair game and what's unethical. To make the issue even more complex, views on gifting vary markedly between sports. In professional cycling, gifting is considered a completely normal, tactical element of the sport, especially in stage races. In football or cricket, gifting would be considered match fixing, and would end up in fines or jail time if the participants were caught.

But in any sport there are rules, and lines that can't be crossed. What would Muhammad Ali have said if Smokin' Joe Frazier had asked him to gift that World Heavyweight Championship title in March 1971? Sure, Frazier went on to win, but to be gifted it would have changed everything. And I can't believe Ali would have agreed to a gift; it would have been unsporting if nothing else.

I thought about how I'd feel if I was in Doug's shoes. I thought about being self-centered or being a team player. I figured we weren't in a single race where one victory meant everything. This was a stage race. Sometimes it's better to lose a battle and win the war. I'll admit I also thought that a gift now would need to be repaid later, and there might come a time later when I really needed a helping hand.

It was the last thought that really played on my mind. It would be nice to say I was completely altruistic and only wanted everybody to share in victory, but even at the time I knew it was more than that. It was about the overall game. A gift wasn't a gift; it was an investment—setting the pieces in motion that could be played later as required. The only problem is that all came down to a matter of trust.

Could a deal struck now hold up under intense competition?

Would a debt be repaid when it the time came?

Or would I be throwing away a winning card in the hand now for an unproven and unreliable IOU in the future?

Since we'd met, Doug and I hadn't seen eye to eye. We were competitors, and he saw me very much as the person who was standing directly in his way. Could I really expect him to help me if I was suffering, and he was looking at a potential win? I hardly knew him, and my experiences so far hadn't been all positive. I'm sure he felt completely the same way.

On the other hand, if we worked together now we would start to build a bridge. Stage races can't be won on aggression and hostility. Good racers work together. They work with their friends. They work with people who are not their friends. By working together, everybody achieves more.

This was the thought that stuck with me, that swayed my opinion. I was sick of fighting, sick of battling every day. We needed to work together, to have a degree of camaraderie. But I needed to do it by my way. I needed to set the rules.

In theory it was a negotiation, but in reality I held all the cards, at least in his mind. I'd proven myself the stronger runner in both of the previous races, and I was ahead by a significant margin. In his mind at that stage I was unstoppable. But in my mind I knew that there was everything still to play for, and things could very easily go wrong.

I decided to start the bidding firmly.

"I can't give you time. I can't let you put time on me," I spouted, between gasps for breath.

"I just want to win one. C'mon. Just one," he replied.

I let it sit for a while and thought about his proposal while we ran together. I wasn't really in a friendly mood, but I knew the two of us had to work something out.

"We run together. We keep each other going. From now on we take turns," I stated. "I'll drop off on the last corner today. I'll let you take it. I will let you cross the line by yourself. But tomorrow in Madrid, the reverse. We run together. You let me take it.

"We hold our time positions if we work together. In Morocco and Dubai we can run together. In Sydney all is fair, no games, run however you like, best man wins."

I'd dictated a set of terms without even realizing it. But it served a multitude of purposes. First, and most important, it eliminated this constant source of stress. I knew Doug and I weren't going to be lifelong buddies. So did he. We were too different in nearly all respects. But there was no need to be at each other's throats either. If we could run together we could talk, and maybe we could put the nonsense of the last few days behind us.

I think we both realized it also served a subtler purpose. For me it served to hold him back. Even if I weakened over the next few days, he would be making an agreement not to put a lead on me. From his view, it made sure I wasn't too far ahead when we hit Sydney, and if he could recover enough and I weakened enough, he might just be in with a shot at the overall lead. Sydney was Doug's home town. All his friends would be there. A little determination mixed with some local support might well be enough to see him across the line first, and for a win overall.

Events were going to play out to the advantage of one of us, although neither of us knew who. But at that stage it was the best chance we both had, and we both knew it.

"OK," he muttered.

"Deal?" I asked.

"Deal," he replied.

I extended my hand to him midstride. We shook on it. I just hoped he understood what that handshake meant.

—✺—

I'll be honest. It was like a heavy cloud of tension had lifted. We both felt it. For the first time in quite a while we both were smiling at the same time. We started to talk a little as we ran, tried to find some common ground that we could build on.

We passed the art deco buildings. We passed the lifeguard huts. I didn't look for new features. I didn't even notice the Versace place. I'd been too busy talking. I came to realize that this unlikely alliance was going to serve another goal: the company would keep me occupied. It would keep me entertained. It would keep my mind off this race for long enough to allow me to retain my sanity.

We ran around the last loop, headed up the boardwalk at the far end and came back around. We passed James coming the other way. He had a surprised almost shocked look on his face when he saw us. Doug and I both smiled, and James gave me a high five as he passed. It was a moment that will stick with me. We'd overcome a major obstacle, and maybe we'd both become better people for it.

We made a couple of quick drink stops on that last leg back to the finish line, and as we turned the last corner we stuck to the plan. A deal was a deal. It was time to extend the hand of good faith. I gave Doug a nod and slowed. He strode off, and crossed the line with both hands in the air, looking as proud as punch.

I came in a handful of seconds later to a much more lukewarm reception. It was Doug's moment and he was reveling in it.

The cameraman gave me a wink and quietly wandered over.

"That was a really good thing you did today," he whispered.

And suddenly I wasn't so sure. A wave of self-doubt washed over me. Doug was in the limelight lapping up a victory. The green streak of envy inside me told me that victory should have been mine. The red streak of anger inside me suddenly was furious that he didn't even acknowledge me at the finish line. At least he could have given me a nod and a wave and made some passing remark about working together. I realized I must have been tired. Tired and emotional. It was time to leave before I said something I shouldn't and made a complete fool of myself. The sore loser. Better to smile and be gracious in defeat. It was, after all, our deal. But that wave of self-doubt started whispering in my ear:

You've let him win. You've given him confidence. He thought you were unbeatable. Now he knows he can win. And everyone back home thinks he's won. His friends will all be telling him he's got this. You've just blown your biggest advantage. You've thrown away your mental game. And for what? For an alliance he'll never stick to? You're a fool.

I knew I wasn't rational. I needed to get out, to get some space. To get away from all of them.

I hobbled over to South Beach and went for a swim. The water was cold. I hoped it would refresh my legs, and maybe clear my head. I realized why Doug found it so difficult coming second.

—⁂—

I realized in retrospect that this was one of my most emotional races, not only over this race series but over my whole racing career. Everything changed, and it changed quickly. The race suddenly became so much more complicated. There were multiple balls to juggle, egos to manage, and deals to honor. I wasn't sure if I'd just made the biggest mistake of the event, or if I'd behaved with dignity and class. I needed to talk to someone, and I didn't know anyone here well enough to completely confide in them and trust their opinion to be in line with my beliefs. There were only two people I could think of. I e-mailed my wife and my coach. Here is the e-mail I sent my wife the next morning, verbatim:

Hi honey, how are you going?

I'm feeling a bit down I must admit. I think it's always after a few days, when exhaustion starts kicking in and I begin to question what I'm doing. Had a bit of a strange experience today and I don't know if I've played it like a gentleman or made a huge mistake. I just have memories of being too competitive when we did Raid Pyrenees and it tainting the experience. But I hope I haven't been silly. I could have easily taken it today and I didn't. I'm not normally sympathetic like that.

I kept most of the details out of official posts because it's a bit more private, but I wanted to email you the report I sent to Nigel . . .

Hi Nigel,

I excluded some details from the general post-race email I sent out to my friends because I thought some things are better left unsaid, but for your interest . . . I agreed with your assessment about going too hard, and I actually had a chat to the #2 guy before the race.

It was a bit weird really. We agreed to run at a steady pace (5:30 mins/k's). He ran behind me for about 10km. I was just running gently chatting to another guy. #2 then got really pissed and started yelling stuff. I thought he was in trouble so I asked if all was ok, he didn't say anything. He took off like a rocket at what must have been 4min/km pace. I told the guy I was with I was going to keep the #2 rocket in sight, again #2 blew up not much further down the road. Then he had what I can only describe as a breakdown where he was going on about how unfair it all was and how I needed to let him win one for everybody back home . . .

I could see his point, I know he came to win and I'd feel the same way, but it's not really a victory is it. Anyway after about 15 mins I said ok. I agreed that I didn't want to have any time put into me, but I'd let him take line honours. I sat with him at a slow pace until the last corner then I let him go and he finished 20 secs up (I didn't want to get in the camera shots etc).

I hope I haven't made a terrible mistake . . . I've got a small worry this might come back to bite me. The camera guy who was with us the whole way came up after privately and said thanks for showing some humility.

It was a really weird experience . . . I guess stage races do this to people.

This stays between us, I don't want to look like I'm making excuses for second place or anything . . . and I wanted to get a straight victory every day but to be honest I had some sympathy for him..

D

Antarctica: Landing the IL-76 on the blue ice runway.

Antarctica: The sleeping tents of Union Glacier Camp.

Antarctica: Warm-up run before the race.

Antarctica: A training run with too many stops to gaze at the landscape.

Punta Arenas: One of the many delicious churros food stalls around the marathon course.

Punta Arenas: Gothic manors next to weather-beaten houses.

Punta Arenas: Street murals along the marathon course.

Punta Arenas: Crumbling jetties, a memory of times long past.

Miami: Palm trees and Jacuzzis behind the marathon path in South Beach.

Miami: Lifeguard huts on the beach side of the marathon course in South Beach. *Thinkstock Images.*

Miami: South Beach. *Thinkstock Images.*

Madrid: The painful test, where everything was up for grabs. *Thinkstock Images.*

Madrid: The Urogallo restaurant, a welcome sight at the end of the marathon.

Marrakech: Sometimes it's about finding how bad things can get, how low you can go . . . and still dig your way back out. *Thinkstock Images.*

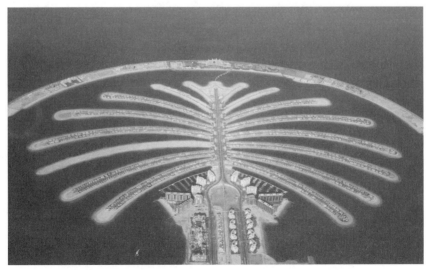

Dubai: A true embodiment of "build it and they will come." *Thinkstock Images.*

Dubai: A warm welcome from Haile Gebrselassie.

Sydney: The winding path around the Iron Cove foreshore.

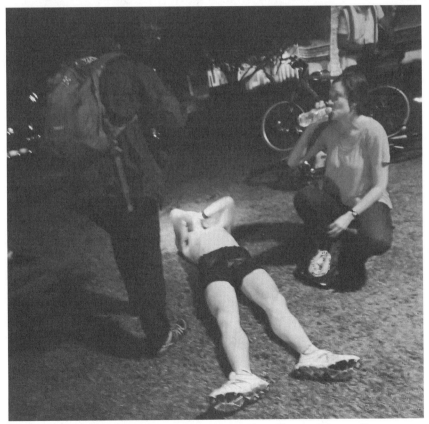

Sydney: Dazed and confused, watched by my wife, Trilby, and the media.

Sydney: Presented with the winner's trophy.

Sydney: A moment to remember.

MARATHON 4: EUROPE

Madrid, Spain: The Painful Test

Onwards and upwards, my friend, onwards and upwards.

—Matt Baile, friend and cyclist

The ocean swim at South Beach helped clear out the cobwebs. The water was cool, chilly even, not what I was expecting from Miami. In fairness it was winter in the United States in January. One of the oddities of flying around the world in a week is we'd traveled through enough latitudes and longitudes to see every season at least once. It was becoming difficult to keep track of what was normal and what to expect.

After ten minutes paddling and stretching the arms in the Atlantic Ocean it was time to get out, get cleaned up, get some food in, and get packing. The next continent was waiting, and there was limited time until our flight departed.

The race logistics staff had booked a room at the Marriott Stanton South Beach Hotel for us to share, essentially a communal shower and changing room, and for the lucky early finishers like myself, a place to put up the feet and have a little rest before we continued on our journey.

I shuffled up from the beach in my running kit, now saturated with seawater. To the uninformed observer I must have looked like the most sweaty person on the planet. Despite my best efforts, I left a trail of water behind me as I sauntered into the lobby. The concierge bore a passing resemblance to George Michael from Wham! dressed in black shoes, black trousers, and a black collared shirt. His three-day facial growth was carefully manicured into a precisely defined stubble, forming a seamless connection with his hair, all trimmed neatly to the same length. He had a single diamond ear stud in his left ear. We were definitely still in Miami.

He looked up from the laptop nestled behind the counter and his practiced greeter smile cracked into an accidental look of disdain. The thought crossed my mind that this was the second time I'd had this exact experience with a hotel concierge in the past two days. When it happens once it could be an accident. When it happens twice it's probably your fault. I decided I'd maybe start taking care of my postrace appearance a little more, at least when I entered a hotel lobby.

"I'm one of the running group," I explained. "I believe there's a room that's been reserved for us?"

A look of relief seemed to come over his face, followed by a genuine smile. If I had to guess I'd say he was just happy I wasn't a madman, and maybe he even had a little sympathy for someone who had just run a marathon.

"Yes sir, the room's all cleaned and ready for you. First guest," he replied.

I figured Doug was still at the finish line lapping it up. A small wave of annoyance passed over me again. I knew that wasn't fair to him, but I couldn't help it.

The concierge thrust two identical room keycards at me. It must have been habit; I could only really use one, but he insisted. I smiled and nodded and slowly hobbled over to the waiting elevator, water trail left behind as evidence of my path. The doors opened to reveal two women, one middle aged and one senior, presumably a mother and adult daughter on holiday together. They parted to make space as I entered the elevator. I gave them a nod and a gentle smile. There was no point in explaining my bedraggled state; it was better to pretend everything was completely normal. They seemed to have the same opinion, as they nodded courteously back and then looked at a small spot on the wall in front of them as the elevator car slowly and painfully ascended the seven floors to my level. There was an electronic bell chime, the doors opened, I stepped out, the doors closed, and for the first time since the race I cracked a smile, wondering what they must be saying now I'd left.

I moved down the hallway, following room numbers until I came to 715. There was a reassuring click as I put the keycard in the slot, and I stumbled inside. Frank the driver and his buddies had been kind enough to bring our bags up, and there was a huge stack of towels on the bed. They'd prepared, and I was eternally grateful. I gingerly peeled myself out of my seawater-soaked race clothes, winched myself into the shower, got cleaned up, put on my recovery tights and clothes, and lay down on the bed.

The next thing I knew there was fumbling and rustling at the door. I must have drifted off. I got up and opened the door. It was James. He'd come in third, only a few minutes behind Doug and me apparently. He'd done very well, especially given that he'd pretty much done it on his own without any help or pacing. I'd had Jon running with me and Ricardo on the bike for the first half, and then Doug on the second half to help me along. James was in a jovial mood, and we had a couple of laughs while I lay down and he got his things ready. He disappeared off into the bathroom to emerge ten minutes later showered and clean. We agreed it was time for a late lunch.

There was only one rule for lunch: something very close. Neither of us had the energy to go exploring. There was a beach bar downstairs, incorporated into the front of the hotel. Hamburgers and chips, but at fancy hotel prices. We were resigned to our fate. All we really wanted was food; cost was a secondary concern. We ordered. We waited. We watched some muscular guys and scantily clad girls come and go. We waited some more. Part of me thought it must have been a case of that old adage about watching a kettle boil taking forever, but when I checked my watch I realized it really had been over half an hour since we'd ordered. Marcelo stumbled down the hallway, saw us and wandered over. He smiled and sat, also fresh from a shower and hankering for some food. We tried to warn him against ordering, but either he didn't hear or really didn't care. We talked some more and waited some more, and after another twenty minutes we finally decided enough was enough and it was time to leave. At which point the food promptly arrived, accompanied by a sizable bill, which included a 20 percent tip. Only in America. We were all tired, and coupled with the thought of having to go elsewhere, we decided to make do and wolfed down our burgers. We all wished we'd ordered more, but none of us were going to wait a second time.

After lunch and a little more people watching by the pool deck, we slowly headed off to collect our bags then proceed onward to the airport. Frank was parked in his SUV out front, engine burbling away while the air conditioners hummed inside. It may have been winter, but it was still warm. As soon as he saw us he jumped out, big smile on his face.

"Good to see you boys. How ya been? How was the run?" Frank asked.

"Good, great. Tiring," James replied.

I nodded and smiled, then jumped in the back of the vehicle. Time for some rest.

We motored down the highway, Frank just as enthusiastic to point out new and exciting points of interest, but finding the crowd much more fatigued and less receptive than they were earlier in the day. Undeterred, Frank pressed on, trying harder and harder to find landmarks and sights that may leave us with positive memories of Miami. I had to hand it to him. A lesser host may have given up and turned on the radio, but not Frank. Finally, he started to run out of options. He saw a big shopping mall out of the right side passenger window.

"And that," Frank pointed at the top of the mall, "that's a roof."

To this day I'm not sure if he was testing us, he was having us on, or he was just desperate to inform. I suspect it was one of the first two. But it was enough to break through the wall of exhaustion. We all erupted in peals of laughter, and Frank cracked a broad smile, content in the knowledge of a job well done.

We left Frank at the airport, all secretly wishing he was going to continue on with us. He was one of a kind, an unexpected gem that you randomly discover on a journey such as this.

—⁂—

As soon as I sat on that plane I was hit with a wall of tiredness and fatigue. The postrace adrenaline had worn off, and I felt exhausted. I was asleep before the wheels left the ground, vaguely stirred a couple of times as we moved through bumpy air, but didn't properly wake until we'd touched down in Madrid, roughly eight hours later.

With a yawn and a stretch, I groggily disembarked into the byzantine structure that is Madrid Airport. The airport was massive and sprawling, a maze of tortuous shiny glass and steel corridors, elevators, staircases, and ramps. Navigating the airside passageways, collecting our luggage, passing through customs, and getting to the arrivals hall seemed like a marathon in itself.

Finally, we emerged from the belly of the airport and were immediately struck with how cold it was outside. I'd been expecting cool weather, but a cold snap had hit and we were all positively freezing. The wet, still air felt far more bone-chilling than the crisp, dry freeze of Antarctica, even though Antarctica had been more than twenty degrees colder. Maybe it was partly because we were prepared for it in Antarctica. Looking around it seemed that my companions felt the same way, all huddled together and waiting for a sign that we could proceed.

We were greeted by Juan and Miguel, the local fixers and organizers. It was nine o'clock in the morning, but the city seemed to be still half asleep. I figured the Spanish, like the residents of Punta Arenas, were night owls, not early risers. After a few handshakes and smiles we loaded the bags and then loaded ourselves into the awaiting coach bus, then rolled out of the terminal for a journey through the city to Casa de Campo park. Casa de Campo was once a hunting reserve, but in modern times had been transformed into the largest recreational nature park in Madrid. Among other things it houses the Madrid Zoo and an amusement park, but it also has a reputation for crime, especially prostitution, in certain areas. It certainly sounded like an interesting venue for a run.

I gazed absentmindedly out the window as the bus passed through early-morning Madrid, watching people start their day against a backdrop of gray and imposing buildings. I'd been to Barcelona a couple of times before, and its vibrant colorful street life and atmosphere seemed in stark contrast to my current surroundings in the more somber, authoritative capital. Possibly that was partly a reflection of the time of day and my own weary emotional state, but I suspect it was also just Madrid.

We passed the spectacular Royal Palace of Madrid and the adjacent Cathedral de la Almudena, and I knew we must be close. I'd seen some course recce photos and the palace had often featured in the background. With one more left turn we were there. The coach pulled up next to the lake in the eastern corner of the park, and we slowly sauntered out. I think we'd all hoped the ride was going to be a little longer, but there was no point in delaying the inevitable.

The run was fairly straightforward. A couple of the roads in the park had been closed to motor traffic, and the course followed an east to west path out and back, climbing a long gradual hill on the way out, which then became a slow descent in the reverse direction on the way back to the turnaround. It was going to be four loops up and back, and I had a strong feeling that hill was going to become mentally steeper with every pass.

It was cold, really cold, and I decided I'd underdressed. I dashed back on the bus to swap my running cap for the woolen beanie I'd used in Antarctica, and put a long sleeved windbreaker over my thermal running top.

We all meandered over to the starting line near a restaurant on the lake, El Urogallo. Apparently *urogallo* was Spanish for "wood grouse," one of the birds that the park was famous for, once hunted and now only shot with the birdwatcher's lens.

I avoided the journalist from the local newspaper. It was nothing personal, I just didn't want to jinx myself by estimating my race results—even if there was a strong chance that I was going to win, assuming my accord with Doug held up. I was hoping the run today would be a friendly one; we could jog it out and try to continue to build on the foundation of respect and trust we'd started constructing the day before.

We lined up on the starting line. Richard the organizer raised his arm in the air. The starting gun went off. I had a mental image of a startled wood grouse suddenly thinking he was back in the bad old days.

And with that gunshot started a very unexpected and disconcerting course of events.

When considering friendships and rivalries, one episode in cycling history stands above all others: the 1986 Tour de France battle of Bernard Hinault and Greg LeMond.

Cycling has often been referred to as an individual sport practiced by teams, and nowhere is this more true than in the Tour de France. The Tour generally runs for twenty-one days, covering over 3,500 kilometers. All riders belong to teams, and teams generally consist of an assortment of skills and specialties—but there is only one rider on each team who is a potential Tour winner. All of the other members of the team will cooperate to protect and assist their potential winner, giving him the best possible chance of getting over the finishing line first. Without this protection and assistance, the potential winner has very little chance of beating the other teams.

Greg LeMond and Bernard Hinault both rode for the same team, La Vie Claire. They were both stars—LeMond was the young up-and-coming American talent and Hinault a seasoned professional, the all-conquering French legend.

Greg LeMond was a phenomenon, one of the few riders who could blend overall strength, sprinting, time trial racing, and climbing. And as an American, he was a complete shock to the European-dominated racing scene. LeMond never seemed to feel entirely comfortable in the limelight, and in some cases he seemed to shun it completely. He was respected as a humble and quiet achiever, a person who believed in honor and believed in his team, as well as in himself.

Bernard Hinault was possibly the polar opposite of Greg LeMond, with the exception of their shared desire to win. They called Hinault "the Badger." He was an aggressive rider, always on the attack. He could channel strength and determination unheard of for most riders. He never gave up. And he was most fierce when he was under pressure. Hinault commanded the other riders, both on his team and off. He was uncompromising and unflinching, and was feared as much as he was respected. When the 1984 Paris-Nice race was interrupted by striking local shipyard workers blocking the road, Hinault rode directly into the protest, dismounted his bike and started punching the strikers. He was unpredictable, and he would not be stopped.

Hinault was already a cycling icon by the time he teamed up with young-gun LeMond. He'd been cycling professionally for over ten years and had notched up an impressive palmares of wins and achievements, including five Tour de France victories. He'd won the 1985 Tour, with LeMond supporting him and some would say pulling him to victory after a big crash. That 1985 win was Hinault's fifth victory, equaling the record for the most ever Tour wins. The desire to win one more and be the sole record holder must have been excruciating. However, he had given his word in 1985 that in return for LeMond's support and assistance for the win, Hinault would swap roles the next year and help LeMond to his first-ever victory in 1986.

Before the 1986 Tour de France, Hinault and LeMond appeared to have formed a close bond. After agreement had been reached in 1985, Hinault made a number of public and private statements that both he and the entire La Vie Claire team were there to get a win for LeMond. It will never be known whether his intentions were always otherwise or whether the lure of a sixth and record-breaking victory was just too much to resist, but even from the start of the race, Hinault didn't seem to be playing by the team rulebook.

The race began with an individual time trial, a stage where each rider competes independently against the clock. Hinault set a ferocious pace, throwing down an unexpected gauntlet and giving all the signals of a rider intent on winning the Tour for himself.

In addition to this opening stage shock, LeMond felt like the team owner and the team manager were not completely behind him as their overall champion, and over the next few days he started to question their race tactics and plans.

It was during stage twelve, the first of the stages through the mountainous Pyrenees region, that Hinault made his intentions very clear. Instead of protecting and helping his teammate LeMond, Hinault went on the attack. Astonishingly, he worked with Pedro Delgado, a rider from an opposing team, and streaked away up the mountains. Bewildered and unsure what to do next, LeMond suddenly realized that Hinault had opened up a five-minute lead. In a race where places are decided by seconds, a five-minute lead could be race defining.

LeMond tried to regain lost ground, but it was all but impossible. Hinault and the rival team's Pedro Delgado reached the final stages of the race together, far in front of the rest of the peloton. Hinault pulled to one side and let Delgado win the stage, a move seen by LeMond as a reward or gift for Delgado's help and testimony to an arranged betrayal. Delgado won the stage, but with the huge amount of time gained on LeMond, Hinault took the overall lead and the yellow jersey.

Hinault was later asked by a reporter why he attacked his own teammate, to which he answered, "Because I felt like it."

Over the next four days the same pattern was repeated. LeMond, now aware of the betrayal, used every inch of his skill to claw back the time that Hinault had taken, with LeMond eventually regaining first place and an overall lead of two minutes, forty-five seconds. The tables were turned once more during stage eighteen: Alpe d'Huez, the penultimate climb, probably the most famous stretch of road in cycling history. Hinault attacked with everything he had.

He couldn't help himself. It was his last chance. He knew he needed to break LeMond. This time, LeMond wasn't falling for it. He rode as hard as he could, sprinting out of the saddle, and caught Hinault. LeMond didn't miss a beat, and rode past Hinault. With his back against a wall and quickly running out of options, Hinault then made one final plea deal with LeMond to team up, ride together to defend against the other riders. They rode together on that legendary climb of Alpe d'Huez.

Hinault claimed that he wanted to shield LeMond, to protect him from fans. The team owner told LeMond that Hinault must be allowed to win the stage for publicity reasons. They rode the last kilometer side by side and raised their hands together in celebration. LeMond slowed down a little to allow Hinault to take the stage.

It seemed like the deal had been re-formed; there was a truce, and old friends turned bitter rivals had become old friends again. Hinault had taken one of the greatest and most famous stages of the race, but LeMond hadn't lost any time overall. They crossed the line with huge smiles and hugged each other.

And then, almost like a slow-motion train wreck, Hinault's pathological trait reared its ugly head. It only took one hour. In a postrace televised live interview with both Hinault and LeMond, the reporter asked Hinault who was going to take the overall victory.

"I only hope the strongest man wins the tour," Hinault replied.

LeMond was stunned. Furious. Hurt. He couldn't understand how Hinault could turn around once again and stab him in the back, especially after he'd just let Hinault win the stage.

Even the reporter looked surprised. It was an answer nobody had expected. Everyone had watched the finish less than an hour ago and had all understood the strong message that had been sent. It seemed a clear truce.

"You are going to fight one another?" the reporter asked incredulously.

Hinault replied, "The tour is not finished. There could be a crash, many things can still happen. But if we have a war, it'll be a fair war and the stronger one will win."

LeMond couldn't even bring himself to make eye contact for the rest of the interview. He could only have been thinking of the 1985 Tour, where he protected Hinault after he was injured in a major crash, and ensured Hinault the victory. He could only have been thinking of the deal that had been made, a deal that appeared to be evaporating in front of his eyes.

Hinault finished with "Why don't we let the final time trial decide."

Hinault was known as a very strong time trialist, one of the best.

To make things worse for LeMond, there was a rumor going around the riders that one of Hinault's old teammates or friends, or even a member of the public, was going to sabotage LeMond, to crash him, give him tainted food or water, vandalize his mechanicals. LeMond was paranoid, possibly rightly so.

Stage twenty was the final individual time trial, a race where each rider battles the clock. LeMond had a lead of two minutes and forty-five seconds. Hinault rode hard and set a blisteringly fast time. LeMond was the final rider of the day, a position reserved for the yellow jersey holder. He came into a corner fast, possibly too fast. LeMond claimed there was oil on the road, deliberately put there. He crashed spectacularly, but wouldn't be stopped.

LeMond picked up his bike and dusted himself off. He started riding again, only to find his wheel was rubbing, and had to stop and switch to a replacement bike. His lead was being chipped away. LeMond rode like there was no tomorrow—and crossed the line only twenty-five seconds behind Hinault, retaining the overall lead and the yellow jersey.

LeMond had won. Hinault knew it was over. He looked crestfallen. Hinault claims he let LeMond win, but history seems to remember Hinault's motivation and the course of events very differently. LeMond was the first American to ever win the Tour, and went on to be one of the greatest cycling champions of all time. Hinault, a national cycling hero and legend, will always be tainted by those days of the 1986 Tour.

—⚶—

With the shot of the gun on that starting line in Madrid began one of the most difficult runs of the entire race. It was the fourth marathon. The middle of the race. Fatigue and apathy was starting to set in, but the end of the final marathon was still far too distant to consider. More difficult than anything else, however, was that I hadn't expected Madrid to be tough; I wasn't prepared. I had imagined a jog through a beautiful, warm, sunny Spanish park. What I received was a tough, hilly run on a cold and bleak winter's day, a run that was a mental battle as much as a physical one.

Doug sprinted off the starting line. *Strange*, I thought. *This isn't what I expected. Maybe he's just stretching out and opening up a little. No need to be concerned,* I told myself. *Just stick to the plan, keep a pace I can maintain, and see what happens.* I was sure things would settle down in time.

The run started off with a gentle uphill climb, a gradient of a few percent at most. It didn't seem too bad at the time, but even on the first loop I knew that climb was going to hurt more with each passing. I kept Doug in sight, but I didn't work particularly hard to catch up with him. Better to keep contained, pace myself.

I settled on running with James. Company always makes the race pass by quicker. We shared a few words between gasps, but for the most part we focused on the run. Doug had set off with quite a blistering pace, especially given that this was the fourth marathon we'd run over just a handful of days. There was no point in trying to keep on his heels quite yet. We passed through a quiet, beautiful promenade, lined with evenly spaced poplar trees.

When we reached the top of the hill we came upon a large intersection. The road spidered out in five different directions. James and I took a few confused glances before we spotted a race volunteer on the far side of the intersection waving and directing us down a wider road on the left. I could see Doug again, not too far, probably a few hundred meters up the road.

We were running fast. Too fast. Faster than we had run any of the previous marathons up to this point. I struggled to understand the plan. Running this hard was going to come back to haunt all of us, if not later today on this marathon then definitely later in the week. It didn't seem sensible, and as my feet hit the ground the thought started drumming into my head: Something was going on here. This wasn't right. This wasn't the plan. I hadn't quite figured out what Doug's new plan was, but I could guess.

I figured there was no point in getting overly concerned. The situation would play out. Motivations would become clear. We came to another intersection. There were bollards up on the side street, presumably placed by the organizers to keep the road free from any early morning traffic, and I assumed also to keep us runners on the correct path. I noticed a small puddle on the side of the road near one of the bollards, and I thought I'd make a splash to help break the monotony of a run. It's a silly habit, but as long as a puddle wasn't too deep I'd learned a way to land my shoe at an angle so the water would splash outward, keeping my shoe dry. It had to be done quickly and correctly, otherwise the shoe would get wet. It's odd the little tricks and games we all subconsciously develop to keep our minds occupied or distract us when we're out on a long run.

I lined up the puddle as I approached, making sure that I'd time it correctly so my foot would land in the center without breaking stride. I took one more step and slightly curved my foot to land in the water with the inner edge of my right foot first, causing the splash to wash out away from me. I landed it perfectly, but instead of being rewarded with a splash, I hit solid ground and my foot slid out to the side. It took me a minute to figure out had had just happened. And then it struck me. It wasn't water. It was ice. The puddle had frozen solid. At the point I realized Spain really was much colder than I'd expected. I also realized that was enough of the silly games; I was lucky not to trip and injure myself.

"Ice," I pointed out to James. I thought I should make sure he didn't make the same mistake.

"Yup, of course," he replied.

The only outcome of my silly game was to make me look silly.

As we carried on the road seemed to narrow a little. The neat rows of poplar trees had been replaced by scrubby bush and grass banks, and the road gently curved and sloped downwards. I realized that the length of the run course was actually over a long slowly rising and declining hill. Four loops for the marathon, meaning eight hill climbs and hill descents in total, counting the outward and return journeys. That really wasn't going to be fun, especially not at this pace.

Finally, as the edges of the road started to become crumbled and mud encroached on tarmac, I saw a large red and white cone in the center of the road. There was a man standing next to the cone, stopwatch hanging from his neck. That cone had to be the turnaround marker, and the man must have been a race official. Seeing the turnaround marker was a relief on any race. It defined the end of the course. It meant I'd seen the entire course, there were no surprises, I knew what was coming up on the next round, and I could plan. It also allowed me to set my waypoints, my little visual cues and goals that kept me motivated and interested and helped to break up the run.

At the moment, though, I had a more pressing problem. I could see Doug at the turnaround. He was about 250 meters ahead, and his lead seemed to be increasing. It was very odd, especially considering our conversation yesterday. But it didn't take a rocket scientist to figure out what was going on. Running angry is never a good strategy, especially in a race. Invariably you run too hard and fast when angry. You don't pay attention to your body's warnings or signals. There's a strong tendency to light a fire inside, fan the flames until it's an inferno, and then unceremoniously explode. I had to stay cool. I had to slowly reel him back in, take my time making back up the lost ground, and not overcook myself in the process.

He came back from the turnaround, heading toward James and me. I tried to make eye contact with no avail. He looked straight ahead. I gave him a nod. No acknowledgment, at least no acknowledgment directly. Instead, he broke into a sprint. It didn't seem like a sensible course of action so early in the marathon, but at least it answered my internal dialogue. He was going for it. He was going to try to win this race. And he was going to try to do it by a significant margin. I'd been played.

—ɯ—

I'd been stupid. I should have known better. Maybe it was divine retribution for entering into an agreement with another runner. I had justified it to myself before by telling myself that these types of alliances happen in every sport, especially so in stage racing. Now I was questioning that. I questioned my motivations. I knew in my heart I hadn't let him win one in Miami for his pride with his friends back home. I'd done it to take him out of the game. I'd agreed to let him win Miami as long as our race times were similar, and then I win Madrid, he takes Morocco, and then we finish even in Dubai. With that agreement I'd been trying to make sure that my forty-five-minute lead would hold until Sydney. It meant that if I was having a tough day on any of the marathons, he would keep me going. On the flipside, if he was having a rough time, I'd help him too, keeping him in the game; not a problem for me as long as I kept those forty-five minutes. Furthermore, if we worked together we also helped protect each other from James eating into our lead. We'd be able to keep each other going and give support, a luxury James didn't have. It was a mental game of cat and mouse, and I was now realizing that a mousetrap I hadn't even seen coming had just sprung, catching me square across the neck.

Racing is a mental game—even short races, but definitely in long races. Long races were won by the person with the best game plan, and the ability to execute that. I'd taken many victories against stronger opponents through the virtue of the mental game. An hour ago I was feeling rather cocky in the knowledge that I had sewn this race up, or so I believed. Now I had that sinking feeling of realizing that my imagined checkmate chess move had instead left my king exposed, and my opposition was quickly moving to exploit my foolishness.

My head was a mixture of emotions and feelings. Part of me felt angry. I was angry that a deal was being broken in front of my eyes. I'd always thought a person's character is evidenced by their ability to stick to their agreements. There's that old phrase that an honorable person's word is his bond. If you make a deal, you stick to it, even if the conditions don't entirely suit you. Especially when the conditions don't entirely suit you. That's when your word means something. I felt angry.

Part of me felt hurt. I felt like I'd offered an olive branch, and it had been accepted. I'd given a victory to someone who needed it, someone who at that moment was feeling the strain and was starting to break. The thoughts went through my head: we weren't friends, I owed him nothing, and yet I gave him a victory and let him bask in a glory that rightfully should have been mine. But I'd kept it secret and let him have his day, and this was how he'd repaid me?

And a large part of me felt really stupid. I'd tried to make an alliance. If I looked deep in my heart, I'd done it nearly entirely for my own benefit. I didn't want him to win. I wanted to contain him, to prevent him being a threat—in a sense even to hold him back. It was a race tactic, but now I was starting to think maybe I wasn't playing fair. There was no doubt we were all subtly playing each other off. James wasn't even that subtle about setting Doug and I up head to head. I thought I was the one who had been cunning and clever, orchestrating them all with one fell swoop like some athletic Machiavelli, but I realized that in fact I was the one who'd been having my strings pulled like a puppet.

I wasn't that stupid, though. I realized then and there that this was shaping up to be the turning point of the entire race series. Unless I could put a lid back on this little Pandora's Box, I was going to be in trouble. If Doug could beat me when I was trying my hardest, it would completely shift the dynamic—a change in the pack leader and in the mental attitude both for myself and for him.

I circled past the turnaround, uttering a quick "Thanks for the help" to the race official on the way through. Never hurts to be courteous, even when under pressure. As soon as I turned I could feel the gradient change to a gradual uphill slope. We were climbing back up that hill. Doug's sprint seemed even more adventurous now that I realized he'd been doing it against the slope. I figured that was a mistake. Cooler heads will prevail.

As I kept Doug in sight I noticed something. He wasn't turning to look behind him. He'd lost his tell. He wasn't under stress. He was confident after yesterday's win. Which meant he was going to be more difficult to overpower. And I'll be honest that a part of me knew that if I was to overpower him today and overpower him for the rest of the race, I had to clobber him. I had to shatter that confidence and put him straight back into line as being the number two guy who follows orders, not gives them. It wasn't a nice thought, but it was the truth. We all knew the mental game was going to win this race.

I tried to settle my emotions and formulate a plan. There was no point running him down over a few kilometers; it was better to sit behind, slowly advancing. Maybe he wasn't looking behind him, but he'd catch a glimpse of me when the road changed direction at the top of the hill, and again when we got back to the starting point turnaround. I needed to let him know I was still there and not slowing down any, let that play on his mind a little and give me some time to think and work out what my next step was.

I ran up the slope past the shrubby bushes. I noticed they looked like ash trees, a close relative of olive bushes, and made a mental note; the first waypoint. I ran past the bollards and the slippery ice. I noticed the ice had a small cobweb of cracks around its periphery; the second waypoint. I reached the five-fingered intersection at the top of the hill; third waypoint. I noticed there was a radio antenna not too far from where the road split in all the different directions. I ran down the hill on the other side, keeping Doug in my sight, slowly closing the gap. I could see him just up ahead of me, passing down the poplar-lined promenade. I noted that the poplars were quite mature, the trunks thick and sturdy. And finally we came back to the turnaround at the race start. Doug reached the turnaround not long before I did and didn't stop for a drink or snack. He was certainly putting in the effort. But again he was making sacrifices that I figured might come back to haunt him. This was the only point to get more water or to take on some nutrition, and it was important to stay strong and hydrated, especially when we were only a quarter of the way through the race.

He sprinted off the line again, partly for the cameras and partly for my benefit, to send a message that he was feeling strong. I figured it was time to keep my head. I grabbed a lemon Gatorade and a small Spanish cupcake from the table set up by the organizers, jogging off with both hands full. I quickly crammed the cake in my mouth between breaths and washed it down with a few swigs of the drink. I've never been an expert at eating or drinking while actually running, but today I didn't have the luxury of time. I was mostly successful, and what didn't go down my throat spilled down my front.

Doug was passing up the promenade again, but he hadn't really made much ground. His sprint must have been fairly short-lived. By the time we approached the top of the hill I was sitting comfortably on his heels, clawing my way back to just a meter or so behind him. I knew the next few kilometers were going to be crucial. We were both playing our best cards in this poker game, and it was about time to finally call the hand.

As I reeled him in my emotions started strengthening again, mixing around in the pit of my stomach and slowly increasing in temperature until they would boil. A head of steam was building up that would be impossible to contain. I knew I needed to be careful. There was no point in being furious or emotional. In fact, I decided that was the exact opposite of what I was going to do. I needed to clear my mind.

I pulled up next to him as we approached the icy puddle and bollards. No time to look for a difference and check off the waypoint this time.

"Thought we had an agreement," I said flatly. I kept my voice as level and calm as possible, while at the same time trying to get enough air through my lungs to continue running at this pace.

"Yeah, sure," Doug replied in a noncommittal tone.

"Doesn't seem like it," I continued. "You've been running hard, too hard. I thought we agreed to run together."

"Hey, I'm just running, man," Doug replied. "It doesn't mean anything. I'm just running." He laughed a little. I figured that was a nervous laugh. I was basically calling him out, questioning his word.

"No, Doug, you're not. You're running very fast," I continued flatly. I was determined not to appear emotional. I needed to look like I was in control. It was like a game of chicken. One of us was going to blink. I was certain it wasn't going to be me.

"I'm fine. I feel great. I can run like this all day," he continued. An equal mix of a boast and a challenge.

"No Doug, you can't," I said softly.

I let it hang for a while. I wanted him to think about it. To make a choice. I really didn't know which way it was going to go. I figured there were two ways this could now proceed. If he capitulated, he knew the race was over. He would have thrown down the gauntlet, but the gamble hadn't paid off. I pretty much knew he wouldn't try again if he yielded today, and so did he. And our previous agreement would stand.

Or, he could fight. He could tell me then and there to go to hell. He would run as hard as he could and see where we both stood when the dust settled.

I'll admit I was angry or at least annoyed, and at that moment I didn't really care which choice he made. I was determined to win either way. But at the same time I didn't want to fight. For all of the talk about games and plans and strategies, I was tired. If we battled it out, we'd fight both emotionally and physically until one of us couldn't go on. I'd much rather we just put our differences aside and run together. If it was my choice, I'd choose to team up again. But it wasn't my choice.

It was his choice, and only his choice.

We ran side by side for a kilometer or two. Neither of us said a word. The air was so thick with tension you could have cut it with a knife. It was that game of chicken. The first one to speak was the first one to blink. We ran past James, who was heading back in the opposite direction back to the starting turnaround. He gave a small knowing smile when he saw us. He knew we were fighting. After the race he told me he looked at our expressions as we passed. We both had a stony face and a thousand-yard stare. He said he put even odds on one of us throwing a punch we both looked so angry. I started to wonder if we were two grown men acting like little children. Two playground bullies lining up to try to see who was the top dog.

Doug blinked.

"I wasn't trying anything," he mumbled sheepishly. "Today's yours."

He was climbing down from his position. The decision had been made. I felt an internal sigh of relief.

"No worries," I replied.

Those few short and simple words spoke volumes. The direction of the race just took a monumental shift. A shift for the better. Partly, selfishly, because I'd stacked the deck in my favor again. He'd made an agreement. Then he'd become overconfident. He'd thrown down a challenge. He'd overplayed his hand, and I had called him on it. In those few short and simple words, he'd admitted as much and admitted that he'd follow, not lead.

But more than that, it was a shift for the better because it was a relief. Finally, we'd squared up properly against each other. We'd both run as hard as we could and laid our cards flat on the table, and we'd sorted out that all-important hierarchy. When there is order, there is peace, and I think both of us now felt more at peace. We could run together, try to build a bridge, and work on being friends. We could enjoy the coming marathons, or at least survive them, and we knew that we had each other's backs if times got tough.

I trusted him from that point on. I don't know why, but I knew inside he'd be good to his word. They say leopards can't change their spots. But when I thought about it, I realized that I didn't see Doug as a liar or a cheat. He had to make sure he'd made a fair deal, a deal that served his interests as much as mine. He had to test to make sure he couldn't win by himself. He had to figure out that we were better as a team than as enemies. I might well have done the same in his shoes, although I'd like to think I would have tried the challenge before I'd entered into the agreement.

It certainly wasn't an end to our battle, but it was a truce for as long as the agreement held. Two more races: Morocco and Dubai. Then it was Sydney, and all bets were off.

—⚊⚊—

We didn't talk much for rest of the loop. Both of us were thinking through what had happened and what it meant. And both of us needed a break, emotionally and physically. It had been a tough marathon so far, and we were only half way through. Hopefully the next twenty kilometers would be easier.

I broke the silence as we approached the starting line turnaround.

"We should stop, get a drink and food."

Doug looked visibly relieved; he'd run straight through the aid station the last time as we'd both raced past the starting line turnaround. He must have been feeling thirsty and running out of energy. We both took a quick pit stop, threw some food and sports drink down our throats, and then I tapped him on the shoulder, and he replied with a nod. Finally, we seemed to be working together.

We passed James coming down the promenade as we were passing back up. He gave us another knowing smile and a nod. I guess he'd been watching the soap opera play out with some amusement and was hopefully glad that previous differences had been settled for the time being. In some regards it served James's interests to have us fighting, but at the same time having open hostility in a stage race makes the atmosphere unpleasant and difficult for everyone. We were all here to enjoy our experience, even if our definition of enjoyment was a little more strenuous than the average person's. I think James knew, as did Doug and I, that it was better for everybody now.

The last two laps passed fairly quickly. Doug and I stayed together. We didn't talk much, just an occasional thought or comment followed by a grunt of acknowledgment. We were both feeling our way, trying to figure out this cooperation was going to play out. But we were at peace.

On the last loop I threw caution to the wind. I really needed to use the bathroom. I mentioned it to Doug.

"Be quick; I'll jog slowly. I won't take off," he suggested.

I figured I may as well take him up on his offer. I didn't think I could wait until after the race finished. A toilet miscalculation would have been a major embarrassment for me, and a source of constant amusement and jokes between the others for the rest of the trip. I wouldn't want to take Ted's place as the joker of the pack. Anyway, I figured it'd be a good test that our agreement was solid, a proof.

I dashed off the run course and used the facilities as fast as my body would allow me, and then rushed back out. Doug was only a hundred meters or so up the road, just slowly trotting, true to his word. I caught up in no time and said a quick thanks for waiting. "Yep, no worries," he replied.

It was about the last we spoke on that lap, but we ran together amicably, both tired and just looking for the finish line. We reached the junction at the top of the hill and I noticed the radio antenna. The thought suddenly crossed my mind. I hadn't checked off a waypoint or found a new feature on one of the landmarks for the past twenty kilometers. My mind had been elsewhere, taken up with my own thoughts and mental wanderings. I figured that had to be a good sign. Maybe things were starting to look up.

As we came down the mall for the last time, Doug said one word: "Go." He slowed back down to a trot, and let me take the lead a little before the last turn into the finishing straight. It was the same as I'd done for him yesterday. He'd allowed me to take the glory and the cameras, and had avoided the limelight and the attention himself. It was payback for the last race. It was a kind gesture, and I got the feeling that we were going to be just fine, at least for a while.

I crossed the finish line smiling but exhausted. It had been a long day. A combination of the fast run over the first half of the marathon, the cold temperatures and the intense emotional experience left me feeling drained on all fronts. I crossed the line and nearly crumpled. I summoned enough strength to thank the local organizers for the beautiful course, and then jokingly berated them for also finding so many hills to throw in. The reporter wandered over and asked for a quick interview on camera. I warned him I wasn't probably at my best, but at the same time I was probably at my most candid. He laughed and commented that the aftermath of the race makes far better viewing than all of the happy smiling fresh faces before the event anyway. I can't remember the exact interview, but I do remember that I appeared exhausted.

Doug came across the line as I was doing the interview. He waited for me to finish then came over and shook my hand.

"Well done. Tough today," he commented.

I gave a wan smile in return. "You too. I'm exhausted."

Richard the race organizer walked over to us.

"Well done guys. Good run. There's a shower in the back of the restaurant over there," he pointed in the direction of the Urogallo.

"Go over and get cleaned up, then order something from the menu. I'll take care of the bill after everyone has eaten."

—m—

We grabbed a change of clothes from the bus and both hobbled over to the Urogallo restaurant. I felt like I couldn't walk another step. I had no idea how I was going to run a marathon again soon. Still, that was a problem that was going to have to wait. For now I needed to stick with the plan. Get cleaned up; get some food in, especially some protein; get some compression tights on to help my legs recover; get some rest.

Doug told me to have the first shower. I don't think it was a winner's privilege; I think he was just being a gentleman. The shower was in the back of a tiny storage area at the rear of the restaurant, only accessible via a small gate on the far corner of the building. In reality it was probably only an extra fifty-meter walk, but if felt like I was pushing through waist-deep molasses. My leg muscles were cooked.

I entered the small covered storage area and locked the gate behind me. The next step was to negotiate my way around stacks of old cookware, a rusty disused oven and a stack of old magazines whose edges had started to crinkle and rot from repeated accidental dousings of shower water. Pictures of half-naked pinup girls had been stuck to the walls. I cracked a smile—the stereotypes of the Spanish men being Don Juans with the ladies might have had some truth.

With a series of uncomfortable groans, I managed to slowly pull off my cold-weather long running tights and long-sleeved shirt. Next was my thermal undershirt. Every contortion seemed to trigger another muscle twitch or spasm. Finally, I stood there, naked, in front of a mirror next to the shower. I glanced at the person reflected; he looked like a shell of the person he was a week ago. Muscles hung limply from bones. Skin appeared baggier and thinner, but at the same time was pinched into every crevice and across every swelling. It was half due to dehydration, and half from losing my reserves of body fat. I'd tried to be as lean as possible coming into the event. Body weight is everything in running, and I was the thinnest I'd been in the last twenty years. But when I saw myself in the mirror, haggard and drawn, I wondered whether I should have started the marathons with a little more reserve.

The shower was rejuvenating. I was still exhausted, but I felt clean. I felt like this chapter of the race had come to an end. I could put it behind me and move on. A lot had been achieved. A huge amount. I'd won the day, but that was a minor victory compared to the successful reformation of the truce between the two of us. For more than one reason, that truce could possibly win me the whole event.

I didn't waste time in the shower. I knew Doug was waiting, and I guessed that James and Pierre probably weren't far behind him. I dried myself up, got dressed, chuckled like a schoolboy as I passed the pinup girls again, and passed through the gate and around the corner, into the restaurant.

"All yours." I motioned to Doug, who was sitting waiting with a blank, tired stare on his face. He nodded, got up, and wandered off.

The main area of the Urogallo was humming. The lunchtime crowd had arrived, and there were people sitting at the bar, people sitting at tables, and people standing with drinks in hand. From the light red color of liquid in their glasses I guessed it was sangria. Waiters buzzed around, collecting plates and taking orders. A barman mixed drinks while a sous-chef went to work on a large leg of ibérico ham mounted on a wooden block mounted near the register. It was certainly popular, and any other time I would have loved to sit and soak up the atmosphere, but right now I needed to rest and recover.

I noticed there was a gazebo area on the other side of the main dining area that appeared quieter. There were still guests, but it seemed to be reserved for business lunch meetings and discussions as opposed to the hijinks and high-spirited atmosphere of the central section. A waiter approached and greeted me with a big smile and a machine-gun fire of Spanish. I must have looked a little startled. He looked confused and took a deep breath, ready to try his greeting a second time. I caught him as he opened his mouth.

"Sorry, I don't speak any Spanish. Is English OK?" I asked.

"Of course, Señor. Are you here for lunch?" he replied.

"Yes, I'm with the runners. They said I could eat here and it had been arranged already."

"Of course, of course, welcome. Would you like a seat?"

He waved his outstretched arm from left to right as he swept across from the bar to the tables.

"Could I sit over there, in the quiet area?" I asked. I was as friendly as possible, but I'm sure I looked like a wreck.

"Of course, Señor. Come with me."

He led me to a small table for two on the side of the gazebo opposite the lake, and handed me a menu. It was in Spanish, but I could hazard a guess and a rough translation of the dishes.

The waiter briskly marched back the way he came and returned with a bowl of bread and a jug of water. I figured I needed food quickly to try to replenish what I'd lost. I'd heard once that you should eat some protein as soon as possible after a marathon, and the faster you get food in the better the recovery. I ordered a tortilla Española (Spanish omelet with potato and ham) and bacalao (salted cod), as well as a green salad. I figured my eyes must have been bigger than my mouth, but I was starving and the portions were probably tapas sized.

I gnawed on the bread as I waited, greedily breaking apart the crusty roll and dipping it into a small saucer of olive oil and balsamic vinegar. And then that wave hit me. I was suddenly exhausted. Absolutely exhausted. I don't know whether the adrenaline of the race had worn off or whether the food hitting my stomach triggered my sleepy gene, but I could hardly keep my eyes open. I propped my head up with my hands, elbows resting on the table. I closed my eyes for just a second.

And was awoken what must have been ten minutes later when the waiter plonked a huge fluffy omelet cut into inch sized squares and a cod big enough to feed a family in front of me, followed by a bowl of salad. To say I'd over-ordered was putting it mildly. Doug walked in, showered and changed. I gave him a smile.

"Join me. I've ordered way too much. Happy to share," I offered.

"Thanks, no, vegan," he replied.

I think in reality that was probably an excuse. We were both dog tired, and neither of us was up for small talk and niceties. Although we had an agreement, we weren't best buddies, and we had seen the more ruthless sides of each other out on that racetrack today. I'm sure he was also feeling what I'd felt the day before. Even if it was an agreement and a plan, nobody liked to lose. Nobody liked to give it away. I knew exactly where he was coming from. It added an additional drain on to the already overwhelming day.

"No worries. Understand," I responded.

I ate a few squares of omelet and about half of one side of the fish, washed down with some water. Sangria might have been a better anesthetic for the legs, but even in my dilapidated state I knew that wasn't a good idea.

I figured it was time for some proper rest. I asked the waiter if he could pack the rest up. There was no point in wasting it, and the race organizers and supporters were going to be out on the course for some time to come. The waiter collected up all of the plates and scurried back out to the kitchen, returning a minute later with two packages wrapped in foil and a bill for me to sign.

I wandered back across to the starting line and handed the omelet and fish to the organizers. The surprised smiles on their faces was worth any hassle. They'd been standing there all morning in the chilly winter air, doing all they could to help keep the runners on course and motivated. They needed a little thanks and pick-me-up, too.

I slowly limped back over to the tour bus, hauled myself up the entry stairs using the handrails, and collapsed into my seat. Five minutes later I was deep asleep. I stirred a couple of times when other runners got off and on the bus, but all in all I was out cold for over two hours as the back-marker runners came across the line. Finally, with a full stomach and a clear head, I felt contented. My body let go and allowed me to properly rest.

—ɯ—

As an epilogue to the story of Madrid, the newspaper reporter sent me a photo he took of us all lined up on the starting line before the marathon. I showed the picture to a friend as I told her the story of that day. The first thing she noticed was that Doug and I were standing on opposite sides of that line.

"I thought you guys were friends or something. Doesn't look like it," she commented.

She was right. We could not have stood further away from each other if we tried. The other runners were all smiling and waving for the cameras. Not us. We both had our game faces on, a look of stubborn determination. Subconsciously I think neither of us believed that the agreement we'd made in Miami was yet valid. Both of us set out to prove ourselves and test the resolve of the other to their limits. We had both decided it was to be a day of reckoning before the starting gun had even fired.

We just didn't know it at that stage.

6

MARATHON 5: AFRICA

Marrakech, Morocco: The Unraveling

I don't think this is possible. I mean I don't think you're going to be able to do it. It's not possible to run that many marathons back to back. And even if you can, something's going to give . . . the flights, the timing, the logistics. I just don't think it's going to work. . . . But if you do make it, could you wear some of our sunglasses as you cross the line?

—Tim H., potential sponsor

There's really no way to tell it except for the way it was. If Antarctica was my highest moment, Morocco was most certainly my lowest. We landed in Marrakech at midnight. It was a chilly eight degrees Celsius. It was raining. It was dark. It was miserable. It was the third continent that we had visited in the last twenty-four-hour period, due to the way the flights had worked out. The course was a dimly lit three-and-a-bit-kilometer loop on the outskirts of the city around an abandoned industrial estate, which we were to circumnavigate eleven times in the wee hours of the morning.

Compared to my expectations, the flight over had been surprisingly acceptable. Ryanair from Madrid. It was only a few hours in the air, but as opposed to the relative luxury we'd experienced in business class so far, we had expected the worst. I will be honest, I found the Soviet-built IL-76 cargo plane more comfortable than the Ryanair flight, but after the Madrid and Miami marathons I think I probably could have rested on a bed of nails and I'd still have slept.

Big Jim had let it slip on the starting line in Madrid that it was his fortieth birthday. What a way to celebrate. We'd all wished him our best, but at the time all of our minds were solely focused on the Madrid marathon that was about to begin. We were all too tired after the run, and the Ryanair flight to Morocco was the first time we'd all been together again, had a chance to eat something, had a little rest, and regained our enthusiasm. It was time for a formal celebration.

There's always a spark that lights the fire, and in our group that spark always seemed to be Ted Jackson. The logistics people had organized all of our seats at the front of the plane, so we were first on and first off, minimizing any delays to starting the next marathon. But it also meant that Ted was near the cabin attendant and the cabin PA system. At least he had the good graces to wait until we were airborne and at cruising altitude before he started his mischief.

A likable rogue, I think that's the way most would describe Ted, with an unlikely combination of charisma and bravado that allowed him to get away with harebrained schemes and pranks that most of us wouldn't have dreamed of. As soon as the fasten seat belt cabin lights went off, he was unbuckled and out of his seat, grin on his face and glint in his eye. He merrily strode over to the cabin attendant and whispered something in her ear. She looked a little unsure, so his smile widened and he tried again. In return he received a slight nod and a tacit approval.

At the top of his lungs, the would-be tenor opera singer started bleating his best rendition of "Happy Birthday Big Jim," with a note loud enough to carry through half the plane, despite the whine of the jet engines not thirty meters away. It was a testament to his thoracic capacity and diaphragmatic strength if nothing else, and probably went some way to explaining how he managed to suck enough air in on each marathon to power his rather solid frame around the course.

Passengers looked up with a surprised and shocked look on their faces, but this only egged him on further, and with time the shock cracked into smiles. We were all laughing, except for Big Jim, who'd turned as red as a beetroot. Ted had no shame, but he certainly had a lot of brass.

By the time he'd started the second verse, half of the plane was singing along. And when he finished with the "hip hip hoorays," complete strangers were out of their seats cheering and pumping their fists in the air. It was a strange glimpse into the power that one highly charismatic individual can hold over others. I was glad he was an aspiring runner and not a cult leader.

We landed in Marrakech somewhat rejuvenated, and when the captain gave his prelanding briefing on the weather and conditions he finished with, "And most of all, I'd like to wish a very warm welcome to Morocco and a very happy birthday to Big Jim."

Yet again, Ted had diffused the tension and put a smile on all of our faces. We were all tired heading into Marrakech, and we needed something to lighten the spirits. He had provided more than sufficient emotional fuel to keep us going, and to keep us bound as a tight-knit group despite the rivalries. It was lucky none of us knew what was about to come.

—ɯ—

We were met in the arrival hall by one of the greats of long-distance running, Mohamad Ahansal. He was a friend of a couple of the runners, and he'd helped set the course for the Marrakech marathon. In running circles Mohamad was definitely in the legends category, and we were equal parts surprised that he would turn up to meet us and starstruck by his presence.

One of the greatest events in the ultradistance stage-racing calendar is the Marathon des Sables. It's pretty much the original, real deal; the race that started it all. Marathon des Sables, or MdS as it's known to most of the grizzled old trail runners, is a six-day, 250-kilometer race. Sure, if you look at it one way that's shorter than the seven days and near-on 300 kilometers that we were doing on our World Marathon Challenge, but it wouldn't be a fair comparison. MdS winds through the hot and barren Sahara Desert in Morocco, and competitors have to carry all of their own supplies and equipment in their backpacks. It is a very different race, a brutal race.

Mohamad, and his brother, Lahcen, have dominated the MdS for nearly fifteen years, and at the ripe age of forty, Mohamad is still regularly competing in and winning the event. He is a celebrity in his home country, and has been awarded by the king of Morocco for his efforts and accolades running marathons and ultramarathons around the world.

Mohamad was in a good mood, enjoying the limelight and happy to be soaking up the attention, but at the same time he came across as quite humble and gentle. He spoke little English, and I spoke very little Arabic, but it never ceases to surprise me how far one can get with a few smiles, handshakes, and gestures. He had bought a few friends to help with organization and transport, and he switched between a flurry of conversation with them in Arabic, and a more enunciated English dialogue with our logistics people.

We were told to take things as they came this trip, and I realized early on that the best policy was to focus on the marathons and let the organizational staff figure everything else out. The other runners and I sat and nervously chatted as we waited for the transport vehicles to arrive. We made small talk and had the occasional laugh, but we all knew there was a job to be done, and the sooner we started, the sooner we finished.

As time passed Mohamad seemed to become more animated and agitated. I suspected he was getting a little tired of waiting as well. It was after midnight and I'm sure he had somewhere he'd rather be, most likely his bed. After a series of phone calls a pair of vans arrived and we were ready to go. We dashed from the airport terminal through the rain to the waiting vehicles. It was important to try to avoid getting our casual clothes drenched; we only had one or two pairs at most, and there was really no way to dry them. Even more important was to protect the luggage. The rain was heavy and if a suitcase became soaked it would mean the clothes for the next three races were wet. This wasn't solely a matter of comfort—wet clothes meant blisters, pain, and problems, and staying comfortable and injury-free at this stage was vital.

As soon as we stepped out of the airport terminal I realized how little I knew about Morocco. I had pictured the Sahara Desert: camel trains, sweeping sand dunes, and remote oases springing from the desert. I had imagined some ridiculous Lawrence of Arabia scene with the twelve of us running through the sand with the sun beating down on us, watched from afar by Bedouins in traditional flowing robes and keffiehs on their heads. In reality, Marrakech felt freezing cold and wet. It was a surprise, and nobody likes a surprise on a race day. If nothing else, it was going to require a complete rethink on strategy and run clothing.

Fitting all of our luggage in two vans was like a giant puzzle, but after some movement and manipulation everything was in, as were we. The logistics plan for this race was similar to Punta Arenas. We were to travel to a local hotel near the race start, drop our bags and get ready, do the race, and then come back to the hotel for a shower, quick sleep if time allowed, and meal, and then on to the next flight. Of course the period of rest depended on the time taken for the marathon, and some of us got much more of a break than others.

—◊◊◊—

We arrived at the hotel at around one o'clock in the morning, but in reality local time had become a little meaningless by this stage, except for the effect that it had on light levels and hence visibility for running. Our brains and our bodies had become so confused. I'd traveled from Hong Kong on one side of the world to South America on the other, where the time is nearly the exact opposite. Then I'd traveled to Antarctica, where there was no night at all, and we started our first marathon at 11 p.m., in the bright sunlight. Following a brief sojourn in Punta Arenas for the second run, I'd then gone to Miami, where we ran in the morning in the Eastern Daylight time zone. I'd totally lost track of where I was and which way was up. I figured not worrying about the time of day was the easiest and most sensible strategy. Trying to keep an anchor on a time zone or continually remind myself of what time it was at home would only make me feel more disjointed and tired. Again, the same race plan took hold—go with the flow, soak it up, take it as it comes, don't worry about it. But that didn't mean it didn't take a toll.

When I arrived at the hotel, I felt exhausted. I guess it all just hit me like a freight train. The temporary mental lift that Ted's plane antics had given me started to fizzle, and the reality that another marathon was soon to be upon me started to dawn. It wasn't one thing—it was everything. It was physical, mental, and emotional.

I was tired. It was the fifth race, and the first four hadn't been easy. The cumulative fatigue had started to set in. I was in the lead up to this point, and I'd held on to my forty-five minutes, but it hadn't been easy. I had done damage. Two of my toes were black at the tips and I was worried they were frostbitten, and my knees and Achilles tendons were starting to get sore, but more than anything my muscles were feeling really tired and flat, just lacking any drive or power.

Three continents within twenty-four hours. On paper it seems like an impossible idea. There was no time to recover, no time to heal. Having the marathons this close together exponentially increased the damage. I guess I hadn't really thought about the scheduling and logistics, but in my head and in my training I'd been planning for one marathon evenly spaced every twenty-four hours. There are extreme runners who have done hundred-kilometer ultramarathons or more in a twenty-four-hour period, but to break that up with a couple of plane flights and all of the associated check-in, check-out, baggage collection, logistics, and so on—well, that was just nuts. Never mind adding in the other four marathons spread throughout the week. I had never prepared for it; in fact, I'm not sure you could prepare for it.

Mentally I was losing the drive. Although we tried to get on as best as we could, it was a pressure cooker, and we all felt it. Smiles, handshakes, and pacts were fine and all, but this was a race, and we all wanted to win. The alliance had been sorely tested in Madrid, and even though we'd come to a truce I had developed a small seed of doubt over Doug's willingness to keep to our bargain. I'm sure he felt exactly the same way about me. We were all thrown in this together and we tried to support and encourage each other, but we all knew that we weren't close friends. We'd all come here to achieve a result—especially those at the front of the pack.

I felt like a target. I was in the lead, and I was the guy everybody was watching. It was that pack dynamic coming into play again. I could sense it forming in Punta Arenas. The tension had been slowly building in Miami and Madrid, and by Morocco the dynamic was stretching to breaking point.

The alpha, the betas, and the omegas. Members of the pack will support each other up to a point, and the leader of the pack, the alpha, has a surprising degree of influence over the others. He's seen as somebody to watch, somebody to learn from, and somebody to listen to. When the leader says, either verbally or through his actions, to take this race a bit slower, generally the pack will slow down and welcome the rest for the day. It's an enjoyable position of influence, and one that can greatly improve the leader's odds, allowing him to play the event to his strengths and counter his weaknesses.

But when the leader weakens, when the pack betas smell blood, there will be no quarter given, no mercy, and no second chances. The hierarchy simply shatters.

Two things happen when that pack comes sailing past the leader on a race. First, and most important, the pack realizes that the leader is no longer unassailable. He's now just another runner. The baton of race leader and alpha is passed to another, along with all of the inherent benefits, including the ability to shape the race to one's advantage. Second, there's the massive damage to the ego of the former leader. He's not in front any more. He's suddenly a follower to a new, stronger, tougher, fitter leader. The legs become more tired, the aches become worse, and the will is broken. I knew this to be true. I'd already seen it happen twice to Doug, once when he started out fast in Antarctica and was the leader for a short time, and once when he tried to get the jump on me in Punta Arenas. Once he got passed, he was soon nowhere to be seen.

It's not just a running phenomenon. It happens in all stage-racing sports, but probably none more so than professional cycling. The setup is the same—the leader in the yellow jersey for the Tour de France, the Maglia Rosa at the Giro d'Italia, or the Maillot Rojo in the Vuelta a España, with the peloton working around him. There is his team, and there are the competing teams, but the mentality courses strongly through all riders in the pack. The informal name for the leader is the pack boss, with good reason. The pack boss controls the race. The pack boss sets the pace. The pack boss determines the attacks. And when the pack boss is attacked and challenged, the only option is to fight back ruthlessly, because once that halo is lost, it's very difficult to recover.

Mentally, I was feeling that pressure—the pressure of being the leader and the fear of losing it. It was weighing on me heavily, constantly reinforced by my aching joints and tired muscles. I knew I couldn't show it, though. It's fine for the leader to slow down. It's fine for the leader to control the pack, to reduce momentum on days when he is tired and then to wind it up faster on days that suit him, helping put a little extra lead or strain on those rising through the ranks and looking to challenge for the top spot. But the leader can never look tired, he can never look weak, and he can never look beaten.

It sounds like an exaggeration, but it's not. It's an odd implementation of natural selection, of survival of the fittest. When that weakness becomes obvious and the pack realize it, the leader is "blown"—out of steam, too exhausted, and too tired to fight on. The next step is to be dropped, left behind by an unsympathetic pack who possibly secretly harbor a little smile that there is one less person in front of them on the way to the podium, one less person who needs to be outsmarted and defeated. Once you're blown and you're dropped, you've lost the support of the pack, and your chances of coming back shrink to virtually nil. It's a cruel reality of stage racing. It's not vindictive and it's not malicious, at least not usually, but it's just how the game is played.

I knew all of this as I stood in the hotel lobby, waiting to get checked in by a concierge who understandably wasn't really in the mood to do the paperwork for twelve runners and an accompaniment of logistics staff in the early hours of the morning. We made a smattering of small talk, but we were all tired, and it was showing on all of our faces. At least I wasn't alone in feeling worn out. With a few passport photocopies, some paperwork, and a couple of signatures, I was handed an electronic room keycard and I was away. I wanted to spend as little time in the lobby as possible, especially when feeling as tired and as weak as I was.

I inserted the room keycard into the magnetic reader on the door and there was a satisfying click. Thank goodness. Even the thought of going back and having more hassles would have been too much. The room was fine. It was simple but there was a clean bed and a modest bathroom. I didn't need creature comforts at this stage; I just needed some privacy and a little time to collect my thoughts.

I wheeled my suitcase into the corner of the room, opened it, and retrieved the ziplock bag marked "Morocco." The contents were a testament to my poor predictions for the conditions of this race. I was expecting warm and hot, and I'd packed a light running vest and shorts. Instead it was cold and wet. Time for a reshuffle. I managed to salvage some basin-washed warm running clothes from Punta Arenas, and my windbreaker from the Antarctic. They'd have to do. I held myself together as I got changed. I had things to do and a race to get to. I wanted to get the race preparation sorted and finished as quickly as possible so I could sneak a few valuable minutes lying on the bed, resting rather than sleeping. I laid out my energy gels, and prepared a bottle of electrolyte drink. I put my shoes at the end of the bed. And when everything was done and I was ready, I laid down.

While lying there, I realized that being in a hotel I might have Wi-Fi and Internet access through my smartphone, and I could see if there were any important e-mails. I pulled my smartphone out of the pocket of the jacket I'd been wearing on the flight and switched it on, still lying on the bed. I waited and watched the phone flicker to life and start searching for that ethereal uplink to the rest of the world. It was like watching a kettle boil. The phone, and the e-mail and text messages it brought, were my only connection with anybody outside the race. In desperation for contact with home I'd even started using Facebook, something I'd stubbornly held out against for years. My daydreaming was suddenly interrupted by a chiming of bells and whistles as the phone signaled new text messages and e-mails.

I quickly scanned through the list. There wasn't a whole lot of time and I had to prioritize the important messages, while still leaving some time for rest. There was one e-mail that caught my attention. It was from my wife, Trilby, and the e-mail title header simply read "Madeleine," the name of my youngest daughter. With a smile I clicked on the e-mail, and when it opened I was greeted by a picture of my five-year-old girl proudly standing in her new school uniform, with the caption "Madeleine's first day of school."

That was the point at which the dam burst. My cup of emotions was full to the brim, and this last drop caused it to runneth over. It was over. My race was over. I was going home.

—⟁—

I lay on the bed, weighed by a combination of paralysis and defeat. Spiraling thoughts of self-loathing raced through my mind.

Why am I here?

Why did I leave my family behind to cope without me while I gallivant around the world at great expense, doing a race that I am hating?

Why am I not a better father? All I am doing is seeking self-recognition and reward.

I am a failure. A failure in the things that really mattered—taking care of my family, doing my job, providing for and helping those around me. This race means nothing compared to that.

When that black dog of despair and self-doubt hits, it's almost impossible to think your way through. We've all been there, and I knew somewhere deep inside that it was a normal part of my stage-racing experience. I always hit a wall, and I generally hit that wall about midway through a race. Midway through you were tired, you were emotional, the excitement and novelty of the start were long forgotten, yet the finish line wasn't even a distant light at the end of the tunnel. I'd been visited by the black dog of despair on every stage race I'd ever done, but this time was unlike any other. This was rock bottom.

On reflection, as strange as it sounds, this part of stage racing was not only inevitable; it was part of the experience. It was part of why I raced—to see how far I could go, how much I could be pushed, how deep I could dig, and still dig my way back out. But this time was too far. I was spent.

With that my mind was made up. It was over. I lay on the bed for a while, and after I'd collected myself I got up, resigned myself to being the guy who pulled out of the race, and started packing my suitcase. I couldn't be bothered getting changed back out of my running gear. I just wanted to get to the airport and catch the first flight out. I didn't care if I had to pay full fare. I didn't care if I was going to lose all of the money I'd paid for the rest of the World Marathon Challenge. I just wanted to get home.

All of the other runners and logistics staff were in their rooms preparing or resting, and in the early hours of the morning the hotel was empty, devoid of regular guests and tourists. I wheeled my suitcase through the corridor, and as I came to the lobby I saw Big Jim sitting in one of the large plush Moroccan leather sofas. He was deep in thought, looking at a nondescript point on the wall opposite. The rattling of my suitcase wheels against the grooves of the tiled floor seemed to shake him back to reality. He looked tired.

I'd gotten to know Big Jim more as time went on. I had come to like him, as well as respect him. He was a quiet achiever. He was the person who truly had come here to run his own race. We all said we were just here for the experience, but for Big Jim this really seemed to be true. No hidden agendas, no games or plans; he'd just come for the personal challenge and the experience.

Compared to the rest of us, Big Jim seemed a giant of a man, as the moniker we'd given him suggested. He would have been more suited to playing seven pro-basketball games on seven continents than running marathons, but he was following his dream and passion just like the rest of us. For a big guy, Jim had a unique knack of blending into the crowd and not drawing attention to himself. He came across as able and experienced, but also humble, and he didn't feel the need to parade his virtues like the rest of us.

I had made an effort to spend some time talking to Big Jim on the trip so far. He was the kind of person you had to seek out and gently question, rather than having him voluntarily open up and display his ego in front of you. He threw small morsels of information out one at a time, leaving you interested and wanting more, but feeling like you never really got a full story. I don't think this was intentional; I just think it was a combination of his self-effacing nature and the fact that he really didn't enjoy small talk. I think possibly that was what drew him to running—those long miles of peace and tranquility without the need or expectation to interact. When I realized that, I could see exactly why he'd chosen the marathons and not the basketball court.

He was a Londoner, a solicitor for a living. He worked in property and apparently had some big clients, but he also had ironclad discretion. He liked the band Dire Straits. He had a girlfriend but no children. He was forty years old today. And that was about all I'd been able to pry out of him.

"Hey," Big Jim said.

"Hey, Big Jim," I replied.

"How are you doing?" he asked.

I figured there was no point hiding it at this stage. I was leaving. There was no need to maintain the facade of the leader firmly in control of his emotions and his race. Plus, I'd have to explain to everyone that I was going and say my goodbyes. I was spent, but I wasn't going to slink off into the night like a complete failure without at least letting the others know, face to face.

"I'm done Jim. It's over."

As is quite often the way with people who aren't big talkers, Jim was a good listener. Intuitive and understanding. His tired eyes met mine, and I could feel him looking intently, probing and analyzing. I didn't need to say any more. He knew.

"You, too, huh?" he replied in a quiet, deep rumble. "You're not the only one. I was sitting out here trying to figure out if I continue. I'm tired. This race is probably more than I've got in me, and it's definitely more than I was prepared for."

This was about the most Big Jim had ever opened up on the entire trip. I was surprised—his wall was also cracking. It was the first time he ever said more than a few words in a conversation, and definitely the first time he did more of the talking than me. It was better for me not to speak, to let him get it off his chest. This was his flood of emotions, akin to mine in the hotel room twenty minutes earlier.

"But I've been thinking," he continued. "We get to that starting line across the road and we start. I can't change what happens after that. If I pull out, I pull out. I tried my best and I couldn't do it. But I can change whether I start or not."

Big Jim turned me around that day. I know for a fact that if he wasn't in the lobby of that nondescript hotel on the outskirts of Marrakech in the early hours of January 21st, 2015, I wouldn't have finished the World Marathon Challenge, and I would be still regretting my decision to leave to this day.

In a few simple sentences he taught me one of the most important lessons I learned on this expedition: you have to focus on what you can change, and you have to let everything else follow. If you never give up, you just may succeed.

I had nothing to say in reply; he was completely right. I left my suitcase in the lobby for pickup in the morning. I extended my hand and helped pull him up out of his chair. We slowly walked together over the road to the start of the race. And after everyone finally arrived, we started.

—m—

Mohamad Ahansal joined us on the starting line, flanked by an entourage of Moroccan supporters. I was already glad that Jim had convinced me to fight on, but I was still very tired and very sore. We all were. Mohamad, on the other hand, was excited, to the point of being skittish. He was a racehorse, and he was having difficulty holding back his competitive instincts. He bounced around, hopping from foot to foot, with a huge grin on his face. He spoke very little English, but he made the effort to go to each competitor, shake hands and utter a few words that were either in broken English or Arabic—it was hard for me to tell.

He then took out a Moroccan flag he'd been carrying in a backpack and unfurled it for the press photographer, beaming with pride that a marathon of this race series was being held in his home country, and proud that he'd been asked to determine the course. The other Moroccan support staff and onlookers couldn't get enough of it. He was famous, he was charismatic, and he was in full flight. He didn't exude unpleasant ego, but instead a mixture of self-confidence and showmanship.

As the crowd began to settle, Richard the race director stood in front of us.

"It's a roughly four-kilometer loop. You've got to run this eleven times. This is the only aid station, but we have food, Coca-Cola, water, and Moroccan coffee. Stay on the pavement if you can. The road can be dangerous, even at this time of the day, and be careful; the surface is uneven."

Matter-of-fact, as always. It's good to know where you stand.

The starting gun fired and Mohamad took off. I'm not sure whether he expected more from us, or it was still his racing instincts at play.

Doug and I hobbled together off the starting line. We'd agreed to stick close on this one. If there was ever a time we were going to need to support each other and work together this was it. Then came James, Big Jim, and Pierre. Behind them a little the rest of the pack had amalgamated, brought up at the rear by Ted. This was the first time Ted hadn't bothered with his usual prank of sprinting off the start line to lead out the race for a few hundred meters, a testament to how tired he was. If I was superstitious, maybe I would have thought this a bad omen.

It took a kilometer or so for Mohamad Ahansal to realize he'd misjudged the pace. I saw a surprised look when he turned around and it dawned on him that this team of hardened marathon runners had been eroded into weary travelers. The grin still remained on his face as he dropped from a canter to a jog and waited for Doug and me to catch back on, with the other runners in tow.

The pace still felt forced, but at least we were back together as a team. Each of the eleven loops was just under four kilometers long. Mohamad was only scheduled to run with us for the first loop. It was going to be a push, but I could hold on for that. I'm not sure if it was a consolation or an added burden, but Doug looked even worse off than I did. I could see the hollow look in his eyes. He was running on empty, too. He'd lost the motivation and I could almost see the self-doubt welling up.

A quarter of an hour later we saw the starting line coming back around, with its table of supplies and small medical tent. The first loop was coming to a close. It wasn't getting easier, but it was starting to maybe seem possible. Everybody else appeared just as tired as I was, except for Mohamad, of course, who seemed disappointed he wasn't continuing on for another loop. I decided the best strategy was to take it one loop at a time. Make it to the end of this loop, then worry about the next. I wasn't going to run a marathon. I was going to run this roughly four kilometer loop eleven times. No, I only had to run it ten times now, as the first was already over. Four kilometers is the distance from my house to my local supermarket. It was the shortest of my regular training runs. It was the run I did when I was feeling lazy and couldn't be bothered doing a proper run. It was my easy run. This was just going to be ten more easy runs.

I told myself all of these things again and again. I thought the words were going through my head, but Doug suddenly asked what I'd just said, and I realized I was mumbling them out loud. My lips were moving as I was thinking.

"Don't stop."

"Four-kilometer loop."

"Just shuffle it."

"It's so short you don't even consider this a proper run."

"It's your normal cooldown after a bike session."

"I don't quit. I never quit before."

"I've been worse before and kept going."

And finally, if am I to be completely honest, the thought that often plagues me the most: "What would everyone back home think?"

I was convincing myself. I was also starting to look like I'd gone a little stir-crazy. The race was affecting all of us, and no one would have been surprised if there was a mental breakdown in the pack. It was getting to that stage of the race. But I wasn't going crazy—I was starting to feel alive again. I persisted with my mumbling as Doug retreated to one side and let me get on with it. I can vividly remember the point where I realized that I could do it, and I would do it. Slowly, not comfortably, but I would do it. Feeling like I had been climbing and climbing up an emotional and motivational mountain, battling against the elements both within and around me, and finally I had reached the summit. If I could crest the summit and conquer my pessimism and melancholy, then the hard work would be behind me, and I could steam down the other side of the mountain with newfound strength and commitment.

Which left me with one other problem—Doug. Doug didn't look great either, and I don't think he'd had as much experience in long-course and ultradistance racing. It was a distinct advantage I had over him. I was older—nearly ten years older—but age isn't such a burden in long course. Much of the research shows that people actually improve at ultraendurance with age, up to a point. Ironman triathlon is a testament to this—guys like Craig Alexander and Chris McCormack won the Ironman World Championship when they were forty years old. This would be unheard of in shorter distance Olympic racing, where the field is dominated by athletes in their twenties, but the longer the race, the more experience and cumulative training over the years counts. Sure, as we get older we do lose a little muscle mass, but regular physical training greatly helps counter these effects. The minor loss in muscle mass is greatly outweighed by the benefits of age in endurance racing. The training over the years teaches your body how to deal with the by-products of exercise such as lactic acid, improving metabolic efficiency. Even more importantly, the training and racing over the years also teaches you how to mentally approach a race, how to pace yourself, how to recognize your ups and downs, and how to deal with them. These days I know that I'll have at least one major down in each race. I also know I have the potential to get through it, and history reminds me that I've never let a down patch stop a race before.

Doug didn't have this. He'd trained well for this, and he'd raced on a number of times before, but when I spoke to him I got the feeling he didn't have those years of long-course knowledge under his belt. Doug had also taken some time off racing, and given that he was making a comeback, his performance up to this point was pretty impressive.

Doug and I had made an accord back in Miami. It was sorely tested in Madrid but it held. Now was my time to make good on my commitment.

—ᚁ—

Doug seemed fairly removed from the situation. He was running on autopilot and he had a blank, hollow look in his eyes. We were all tired but he was more than tired; he had lost his motivation. I knew exactly how he felt. I'd been there less than two hours ago. However, the big difference was Doug didn't know that. And I wasn't planning on letting him know any time soon. There was sympathy and support, but I needed to remain the pack leader. I needed him to continue to think I was in control, even though I was starting to have my own doubts.

"How are you feeling Doug?"

Doug murmured a vague sign of recognition.

"Well I'm feeling it too . . . pretty tired . . . but we'll be ok," I continued.

I wanted to get him talking, and I wanted him to know that he wasn't the only one having a tough day out. Misery loves company, as they say. I wanted him to know I was there to help and to talk. I also wanted to add some credit to my karma account balance, and I wanted to be owed a favor. I had a feeling I was going to need it at some stage in the future.

"Gone" was all he replied.

"Yeah, just count down the laps, that's all you need to focus on. Remember the points you've seen before and mark them off in your head as they pass by. Run from point to point. That's all you need to do. Just get to the next marker," I encouraged, with limited success.

"Gonna listen to tunes," he mumbled, and put his headphones in his ears.

I wasn't sure this was the right choice. Music could definitely keep me going and keep me paced when I was feeling good, but I when I was feeling down I found that I didn't really listen to the music; it just became a drone in the background. With the headphones in ears, the only function the music served was to block the world out. This left one alone with one's thoughts, and the end result was sliding even further into that hole of self-doubt and emotional morass.

I'd gone through the same feelings Doug was now experiencing more than once on a race course before, and the only thing I'd ever found that got me through was trying to strike up a conversation. Talk to someone. Talk to another competitor, even if he's a complete stranger. Chances are the person is in a pretty similar mood and will relish the chance to take his mind off the situation. It doesn't matter the conversation or the topic. Talk about home. Talk about family. Talk about daisies. Talk about anything—just don't talk about the race. Talking takes the mind away and gives it a break, allows it to recalibrate and reconsider, to look afresh. Thinking about the painful situation you're currently in can fell even the strongest will.

I still remember those uniquely random conversations I've had out on the race course. I remember speaking to a dentist, who was also called David, in the latter stages of that Norseman Xtreme Triathlon, back in August 2013. The race had been stunning, but unwaveringly difficult. I had completed the four-kilometer swim through the icy fjord; I had cycled 180 kilometers in freezing, windy conditions; and I'd completed around three quarters of the mountainous marathon. I was exhausted. I'd crossed the checkpoint in good time, and the race organizer told me I was high enough up in the rankings to continue for the special final stage, the climb of the massive Mount Gaustablikk.

Gaustablikk was barren and rocky and looked like something out of Tolkien's Middle-earth. The closer I got, the larger it became, looming on the horizon. Ominous. David the dentist, who I'd never met until this point, was about a hundred meters up the road from me but he was shuffling pretty slowly. He was blown. I was hanging on by a thread myself. I decided to try to move my shuffle up to a very slow jog, and after what felt like half an hour I made up one hundred meters, and we were shuffling together. I asked him if he wanted to walk for a bit and we could recharge our energy. There was a visible look of relief on his face. Because I'd suggested it, in his mind the walking was my idea and it was my fault we'd stopped running. It's strange the mental targets we all set for ourselves.

I remember talking about where we came from, what we did, what our jobs were like, the little details. For those short moments, a complete stranger became a close friend. The race had torn away any barriers and any social pretenses we had. We were just two guys doing some crazy race in Norway. And by the time we looked up again we were at the base of the mountain. We'd burnt half an hour of pain and suffering by talking and forgetting about the world around. It was a tonic. We both hit that mountain fresh. And we both got the legendary black T-shirt reserved only for those who finish at the top of Mount Gaustablikk.

I never spoke to David the dentist again. I can't even remember his surname. But if he knocked on my door today, I'd greet him like a long-lost friend.

—⟨⟨⟨—

Doug was a big boy. I couldn't tell him what to do. It didn't really matter whether I thought he should talk or he should listen to music. It was his choice. Maybe he knew better than me anyway. Push on and give him some time. The headphones would come off at some stage, and I could make another attempt at engagement.

I certainly wasn't feeling tip-top either, and not having to carry someone and encourage him at that moment was somewhat of a burden lifted. I did need to stay very close to Doug, though. Even if he wasn't talking, he needed encouragement. Someone needed to keep him moving, to pace him. We jogged together for another two loops, but he was slowing. I tried to get him to stop and eat something at the food table near the starting line marker checkpoint, but he had something else on his mind. Or someone else. James.

On the overall standings I was currently in first by about forty-five minutes, Doug was in second place, and James was in third, less than ten minutes behind. On the run today, Doug and I were in the front, but James wasn't far behind. To add to the pressure, a big group of James's friends, including all of his running buddies, had turned up to surprise him and encourage him. Marrakech isn't a long flight from his home in England, and they'd decided to take a weekend holiday. It was a really nice gesture, and James was tickled pink. It had given him a real boost both emotionally and physically. His friends were taking turns running with him and pacing him, while the others back at the starting line checkpoint had started quite a wild party, under the auspices of supporting the runners. And support they did—they were out there to help anybody and everybody, and to generally lift the mood of the day. They were a welcome sight each lap and a good source of amusement, getting progressively more loud and lively as they played drinking games based on our lap counts and running.

Doug didn't see it that way though. I think he had it in his head that James had an unfair advantage and was using that advantage with a specific target in place: second place, both today and overall. Doug was angry and stressed in equal measure, and he didn't deal with pressure well. I had my suspicions in Antarctica and Punta Arenas, but it was in Miami that I'd really seen the stress of the situation get to him, and had watched it tear him apart.

Some people use stress and pressure to their advantage. They wrap it up into a ball and use it to make them angry, to make them fierce, and to make them fight. Other people don't seem to acknowledge the stress and pressure, and let it wash over them without a second thought, just happy to run their own race despite their surroundings. But there's a third group who let it get to them. They focus on it and allow it to find a small crack in their armor. They allow it to get into that crack and wedge it open until it's a gaping wound. And from what I could see, Doug was one of these people.

He kept looking over his shoulder, looking for James, just like he had with me in Miami. He let it play on his mind. He didn't focus on his own problems and performance; he focused on an imaginary monster coming up behind him. The only person that served was James, who, when we did get a glimpse of him behind us, had a smile on his face and was laughing with his friends. This only served to worsen Doug's anxiety.

"He's coming. I know he's gaining. It's not fair he's being paced," Doug exclaimed.

"Yep, he's being paced. You can't change it. Don't let it bother you," I replied.

"Yeah, but it's not fair. All his friends are helping him," Doug replied.

"Nothing you can do; just run," I responded.

I wanted to help, but I was dog tired, too. I could keep him going like I promised, but that was about all I could do at that stage. At least the headphones were off. I could try the Norseman trick: talk to him, think about something else, forget about the current problems, get further down the track and then all of a sudden realize we're five kilometers closer to home and feeling OK.

Doug was tired both physically and mentally, as we all were, but he also seemed very vulnerable. A second thought crossed my mind, a much worse thought:. *Break him. Turn up the dial now. Right now. He's tired. He's weak. All I've got to do is pull away from him. That won't take much. I just need to get out of his eyesight. On a dark, winding, miserable wet road. To heck with our accord*, I reasoned guiltily. *If I leave him on his own without any pacing, he'll slow down. He'll start looking over his shoulder more and more. And every time he looks, he'll see James coming, an unstoppable freight train, with all of that peer support and friendship behind him. Doug will slow more and more as his emotions start weighing more heavily. After not such a long time, James will put that final kick of speed in, coming steadily and confidently striding past Doug, entourage in tow.* James wouldn't be rude; he'd turn as he passed, smile and nod. And that would be all it took. Doug would implode under the weight of his own anxiety and self-doubt. I knew because I'd seen it happen twice before to Doug. But this time I had the feeling it would knock him totally out of contention. With no support and no motivation, he'd throw time away by the fistful, and there was a good chance I'd be able to put over an hour onto him in this one race alone. I'd be far ahead in the overall lead, with James a distant second, and Doug even further back in third. There'd be no fight left. Anything from that point on would only be jostling between Doug and James. Barring injury, I'd be unreachable.

I'd like to say the only thing stopping me was our agreement—the Miami accord. Sure, that was a part of it, but it wasn't the only reason. I have always prided myself on racing fairly. I've never broken the rules and I've never broken an agreement, and I wasn't going to start today—although I was sorely tempted. To rule him out of contention would have made my job in the next few days much easier and more certain. However, deep inside I knew there was something else stopping me. I knew that there was the chance I might have the same day as Doug was having, yet to come. I needed him and his support if that was going to happen. I needed him to stick to his side of the agreement. I needed him to owe me. I needed to play this delicate game extremely carefully.

—⚏—

It was time to take control of the situation. Doug was starting to fade and I wasn't feeling the best either, but we had to keep going.

"Doug, let's talk for a bit," I tried to convince him.

"OK."

I wracked my brain for something to talk about, something that would engage him, something that would make him forget about his current problems. I'd always been told that the thing people most like to talk about is themselves. I knew Doug was a very spiritual person. I wouldn't be doing it justice to say I could accurately summarize his beliefs, but I knew he believed in Eastern philosophy, karma, Gaia theory, and universal harmony. He was the kind of guy who took a picture of the sunrise every morning and posted it online, along with a quote from a Buddhist or Hindu teacher. Not quite my area of expertise, but it was worth a shot.

I knew his beliefs extended beyond what I would consider average spirituality and moved further into uncharted territories of mysticism and Shamanism. I got the impression that these beliefs had helped him through some very hard times, and I respected him greatly for this. Many people would have given up and thrown in the towel during those hard times, but not Doug. Looking at the person I saw on the race track, I wondered how he'd gotten through some of his trials and tribulations in earlier life, and I figured that the spirituality was the key.

"So tell me what you believe in Doug. What makes the universe tick?"

No point in padding this one and leading in gently I figured, better to just go in all guns blazing.

"You wouldn't believe me," he replied.

I wasn't going to be dissuaded, and at least I'd gotten him talking.

"C'mon," I cajoled. "We're out in the middle of nowhere at three in the morning running a marathon in the dark. What have you got to lose?"

"It's kinda different. Not many people get it," he replied.

"Yeah . . . and . . . ," I coaxed.

"The universe. We're all connected . . . we're all one. We're not even one at all. We're just thoughts."

He continued on, with an occasional nod, grunt or OK from my side to keep the ball rolling. I'm not even sure I was listening that carefully, but it had worked. He was talking. His running became more fluid and relaxed. He put his problems aside, stopped looking over his shoulder, and put his mind elsewhere. The next thing we knew we were about six kilometers closer to the finish, and he seemed happier. James had melted into the distance, obviously feeling the strain a bit himself. I think his friends, who were all feeling great and running on fresh legs, might have pushed him a little hard, and he was starting to suffer. The tide was turning, and the balance seemed to have been restored.

Then it happened. We were about thirty kilometers into the race and we were feeling fatigued. It was dark. I was in a trance, hypnotized by the white striped markings on the brick paving tiles of the path as they flashed past under my feet. I wasn't paying attention. The sidewalk that we were running on was patchy and poorly maintained. There were regular potholes and hazards. They needed to be avoided or side-skirted, and I had done neither. I landed with my right foot square in a hole, and it twisted with a sickening crunch. I fell to the ground, sharp pain shot up my leg from my ankle.

"You OK, man?" Doug asked with a look of surprise and concern on his face. I think he'd been daydreaming too, and my tumble had shaken us both back into the real world.

"Yeah, fine, just a spill," I tiredly replied.

"OK, good, let's take it easy for a bit."

It was hard to tell what was wrong. My ankle really hurt, but I wasn't yet sure if it was just one of those short, sharp pains that tend to resolve and be forgotten about over the space of a few minutes, or if it was something more serious. There wasn't really a lot to do apart from take it a little easy and give it some time. Right now it was hurting, and hurting badly.

I could run, or at least lope. Loping was good enough to keep up with Doug, who obviously wasn't feeling particularly shiny either. The ankle was supporting weight, it wasn't obviously crackling, and I could feel and move all of my toes. Every time I landed on it I could feel that fire deep inside the bones, but I could run. It took another day of swelling and throbbing pain before I realized I might have broken it—maybe a hairline break, a nondisplaced stress fracture.

The pain of the ankle was tough, but it did have one benefit. It made me forget about the pain in my hips, quadriceps, knees, feet, and toes. The thought made me laugh. Glass half full. If you look at the glass as half full, you'll get through. If you see the glass as half empty, you'll give up. Keep positive, keep a smile on your face.

—⚉—

We kept running, and the pain of the ankle slowly transitioned from acute stabbing to more of a dull but deep burning and throbbing, which I interpreted as a good sign. The other aches and pains weren't faring quite so well. Both of us were slowing down, the muscles and the bones were so very tired. We were coming toward the thirty-five kilometer mark, and we'd done ten laps. One lap to go by my count.

Somewhere deep inside I had an uneasy feeling—something was wrong with the distances. The course distance I had in my head seemed to be out and the closer we got to the finish line the more obvious the discrepancy became. I put it down to being dazed and confused, and not thinking straight. I thought maybe I'd gotten my math wrong, maybe my GPS watch hadn't picked up the signals, maybe it had accidentally stopped or paused and hadn't counted all of the running. Maybe I'd gotten it wrong and didn't realize. Whatever the case I didn't really care. I just wanted this to be over.

We got to the end of lap and Richard the race organizer pulled us to the side for a talk. *Oh damn,* I thought. *We've been penalized for something.* Thoughts raced through my mind. *Did we accidentally cut the course? Was there something we didn't see? Did one of the laps not register? Was somebody else out on the course injured or missing?*

It was none of these, which in a way was good news. But in a way it was much worse. We'd miscalculated the distances. Maybe there had been a lost-in-translation moment between Mohamad Ahanasal's Arabic and our English. Mohamad had set the course and measured the distances. I think the mistake arose from the fact that Mohamad counted the first loop as zero, whereas in English I'd count the first loop as one. I still don't entirely understand to this day. But the long and the short of it was that we had to do a total of twelve loops, not eleven, and we had two more to go rather than the one we had expected.

There are very few things in the world that you could have told me at that moment that would have deflated my sails and my emotions further. Two more loops felt like twenty. It was an agonizing blow. My ankle was throbbing with pain. Doug was completely out of gas. We were both asleep on our feet.

The show must go on, and if one thing was for certain, I wasn't running 90 percent of the hardest marathon of my life and giving up. We both knew it; it was time to accept it and deal with it. We had about eight more kilometers to go, but we were both completely smoked. There was nothing left. We needed to figure out a way to conserve. So we made a plan. We settled on a run walk. It was the first time I've walked in a marathon in my entire life, but there was no other choice. We decided to measure out the distances on our Garmin running watches. Run nine hundred meters, walk one hundred meters. Do this eight times, and we would cross the finish line. It was possible. The cycles of run and walk would allow us to build back our strength and energy, then spend it, and then build again. It was the most efficient and fastest option we had.

So we started. We made the unanimous decision that we should both start off with the walking component; that wasn't a hard choice. It had the side benefit of being less taxing, so we had time to talk some more. Just small talk, but enough to take our minds off the situation at hand. It was a shame that there was only one hundred meters of walking each cycle—it seemed to be over so quickly. Before we knew it we were on to the fourth cycle, and passing through the loop checkpoint for truly the last time. I even found enough energy to make a wisecrack to the organizer about maybe adding in another loop just to really test myself, because we were enjoying ourselves so much out here.

As we passed the checkpoint and started running again, Doug glanced over his shoulder and his face fell to a look of horror. James. He wasn't far behind at all. Our run-walk strategy had helped keep us going, but it had obviously really affected our average pace, and James had steadily clawed time back from us. James had played his hand very cleverly today. Sure, he'd had support and friends, but he hadn't let them overpace him and overexert him. He'd realized he had to slow down, and he'd obviously told his friends to jog at his pace and not tried to run at theirs. It was a strategy that had served him very well indeed; he'd obviously planned this better than we had.

James also knew this was his chance, and he had to make it count. He was going to give every last scrap he had in him to win today, and a large part of me thought maybe we should let him win in front of his friends. It wouldn't have been a gift. Doug and I had worked together, and to some degree this was more beneficial than James working with his friends. Doug and I were in the same mental place. We understood each other. We could pace each other. We weren't going to overstretch each other like running with fresh runners could do. James had run a very good race and he deserved it as much as anybody.

Doug didn't see it the same way. I mentioned the idea to him, and there was absolutely no chance he was going to allow James to have any time. I reminded myself that James was a threat to Doug, and he was quite close in overall time, much closer than Doug was to me. It was easy for me to be magnanimous when the outcome of today really wouldn't affect me much, as long as we all roughly finished together. To Doug it meant much more. It meant the possibility of losing second place overall, and I could see why he was going to fight tooth and nail to the finish. Understood, and our agreement was in force. If Doug needed it, I'd do everything I could to work with him.

"We go now," I stated.

Doug just looked at me.

"He's catching. No more mucking around. We go now or we lose this. You decide," I continued.

I started running, and Doug started running with me. We only had about three and a half kilometers to go. I just kept telling myself three and a half kilometers to go. I told Doug. And I kept telling Doug.

"Three."

"Two and a half."

"Don't look back. Keep looking forward."

"Two."

"I said don't look back."

"One and a half."

"One."

"Eight hundred."

We got to the final corner and James had drifted back. I suspect he was surprised by our last flash of effort and speed and realized it wasn't his day. Once James lost the will with this realization, his race was lost. He was in the distance. Doug and I kept to our agreement that I let him take this one, as he had let me take Madrid. For me, that was the most vital part of our accord. It kept us even. And it helped preserve my time gap. I was going to play fair, but I was playing to win.

Doug crossed the finish line exhausted, and I pulled in around twenty seconds later. We shook hands and had a brief man hug and congratulated each other, and then congratulated James as he crossed the line a few minutes later.

—⁂—

The press photographer took a photo of me when I crossed the finish line in Marrakech. I look ruined. My face looks twenty years older. My eyes are shrunken back into their sockets with dehydration and fatigue, my cheeks and chin are hanging limp and baggy, seemingly devoid of any collagen or muscular energy. I look like the life has been drained out of me, exhausted and withered.

Normally I'd delete such an unflattering picture without a second thought. Yet I keep this photo because in a strange way I'm proud of it. In fact, it has become one of my favorite photos from the whole race. It reminds me of how far down I went on that day, of how deep I could burrow within my own physical and emotional reserves, of how bad things can get.

And still dig my way back out. On top.

Sometimes, your worst days can become your best days.

MARATHON 6: ASIA

Dubai, United Arab Emirates: When to Win Alone Would Have Been a Loss

As far as I can see, it no longer needs to be a race for you. You can afford to start enjoying the scenery and the wonderful places you are visiting.

—Lindsay Gething, my long-suffering mother

I was quite emotional after Marrakech. So much had happened in that twenty-four-hour stretch. We had been on three continents—North America (Miami), Europe (Madrid), and Africa (Marrakech)—all within that short period. It hardly seemed possible. More than just touching the ground and continuing, we'd run a marathon in each. And each marathon, each continent, had been an incredibly intense experience. In a strange way there was so little similarity between any of those races. Sure, on paper they were all forty-two-kilometer runs. On the ground, however, each one was so very different, so very challenging in a unique way. Each had been a struggle against demons internally and externally, physically and mentally.

A large part of me was exhausted. But for the first time I could also see the light at the end of the tunnel. Dubai was the second-to-last marathon. At last it was seeming like this event might actually be something I could finish, and somewhere buried deep inside there was also that glimmer of hope that it was something I could win. I had always tried to keep that idea locked up and suppressed. Trying to focus on the overall goal was too all-encompassing, too big. When the thought occasionally bubbled up into my conscious mind it served more to build a fear of failure and anxiety rather than to spur me on. I knew, even though I had a forty-five-minute lead, that things could change very quickly. To become cocky or overconfident would serve only to lessen my chances, as would becoming complacent. No, it was better to take it in bite-sized chunks. One marathon at a time, and on the tough days, one lap at a time. Unfortunately, they were all tough days.

I'd had a hard time in Morocco. It was one of the toughest days of my life. But it also left me with the confidence that if I could get through that, I could get through anything. It seemed like nothing could be worse. I knew that however bad things now became, I had already surmounted greater obstacles. It had reinforced that old sardonic rule of stage racing: you'll have the greatest times, you'll have good times, you'll have bad times, you'll have the worst times.

The tide ebbs and flows. It builds and rises to finally reach a peak, a nirvana where everything seems easy. But it won't remain easy for ever. Small cracks will form and that bubbling and boiling energy hisses out of the fractures and seams, slowly draining the will and sapping the strength, eventually cooling down into the valleys of a low moment. This was completely acceptable, and this was normal. Whenever I hit a low moment, I knew the best way was to understand it and embrace it, and to realize that with some time I'd come back out the other side, ready for the cycle to start again. I don't think it's possible to prevent or even control this cycle, but the hard-fought lessons I'd learned in the past twenty-four hours taught me that it is possible to shape it. In Dubai and in Sydney, this lesson was to become very important indeed.

—⟋⟍⟍—

The injuries were mounting. The ankle I now believed I had broken in Morocco was stable and hadn't displaced, but it was certainly painful to walk on and even more painful during the toe-off period of the running stride. It was manageable as long as it held together and any possible crack didn't progress into a full break. My toes still looked very unpleasant after getting so cold in Antarctica—black, desiccated, and numb—but on the bright side they weren't painful; in fact, I couldn't feel the tips at all. I figured there wasn't much I could do there. It didn't seem like treatment would have much benefit anyway.

Of more concern was the generalized wear and tear that seemed to be developing. There was no one focus of pain or damage, but a blanket of fatigue and degeneration of leg muscles, ligament, and joints. My Achilles tendons had started an odd creaking and rubbing feeling when I flexed my ankles. I could feel the tendon moving and catching against the surrounding sheath, with a slightly troublesome clicking sound. It was something I'd never experienced before, the result of truly prolonged overuse. Being a completely unfamiliar injury, it was also an unknown variable. I had no experience with the progression or treatment. I figured there wasn't really much I could do except accept the problem was there and monitor. I did have anti-inflammatory ibuprofen that I was taking as needed. I also had good friends back home who run a large physiotherapy practice. I was tempted to send them an e-mail to ask but I knew what their advice would be: stop putting strain on the tendon, stop running long distances, rest, and stretch; it'll heal. Very true, but not particularly useful right now.

My knees were also becoming sore. I could feel my old bugbear patellofemoral syndrome on both sides but especially on my right. Patellofemoral syndrome is also sometimes called runner's knee. I'd had it before, but it had been a long time ago. It occurs when the kneecap (patella) rubs excessively against the groove in the leg bone (femur), causing inflammation and irritation. This slow, rasping erosion of the groove by the kneecap resulted in an intense throbbing pain on the inner aspect of my knee whenever I ran. Some people are just prone to patellofemoral syndrome, and I was one of those unlucky ones. It's generally a combination of genetics and lifestyle. In my case I had fairly flat feet, which caused the kneecap to shift over to the inside of each leg. In addition, I did quite a lot of cycling, resulting in the upper leg quadriceps muscles developing an imbalance, further pulling that kneecap off-center. The stage was definitely set for knee problems.

In reality, as with all of these types of injuries, a large part of it was overuse. Experts say that you should increase your running distance by a maximum of 10 percent per week. What I'd done in the last week had paid absolutely no respect to that old adage; in fact, it had thrown it out the window. On a race like this overuse was a given—it was how you helped offset and manage the inevitable injuries that was going to count.

I knew patellofemoral syndrome well. It had dogged me in the earlier days of my running, when I was full of enthusiasm but lacked that deep reserve of strength and development of the connective tissue, the ligaments and tendons, bones and muscles. That only came after years of training. Back then it had taken about six months to get completely better. Through a combination of working with a physiotherapist and a large dose of Internet research and couch science, I'd developed a regime of stretching, leg strengthening exercises, muscle rebalancing exercises, and glucosamine dietary supplements, as well as time to rest and heal. The only problem was that I didn't have six months. What I did have was the memory of another race, an ultramarathon done too soon after that initial bout many years ago, where the patellofemoral pain became so bad that I had to hop to the finish line on the one good leg. If that happened this time I could certainly kiss good-bye any chance of a win.

I needed a plan, a therapeutic program to get myself through this. I didn't want to go off and find a doctor—there was too little time between each race when I included the flight, recovery, eating, packing, and everything else that needed to be done. I figured, with a little foolish hubris, that I'd treated enough musculoskeletal injuries in animals over my career as a veterinarian, and I'd be able to sort myself out just as well a "human" doctor.

It probably wasn't very smart, but I also didn't want anyone else to know. I didn't want Richard or any of the logistics and support staff to know as they might, very sensibly, tell me I needed to pull out of the race. I wasn't willing to get this close and then not finish. And I didn't want the other runners to know, partly because we were all sore and stiff by this stage and I didn't want to be that person who complains and moans, but mostly because I didn't want to show any weakness. That old pack dynamic was playing over in my head: when the alpha shows weakness the betas will move in to finish him off. Unfortunately, however, some injuries were becoming hard to hide.

I mumbled that running injury acronym to myself. RICE: rest, ice, compression, elevation. I didn't have any ice, so I figured I'd substitute ibuprofen. I reasoned that the acronym still worked perfectly. I also had a faint memory of reading a medical research paper that threw doubt on the benefits of ice anyway—apparently it delayed healing by slowing blood flow, preventing new healing elements being brought to the injury side, and removing damaged tissue components. I told myself maybe no ice was actually a lucky break.

Rest. I was certainly doing as much as I could. Like my old coach Max used to say, don't run when you can walk, don't walk when you can stand, don't stand when you can sit, and don't sit when you can lie down. There was that small exception that I was still running a marathon every day, but that was unavoidable.

Ibuprofen. I never really liked to take medication while I was running. On the other hand, ibuprofen's pain-relieving effect is due to reducing inflammation, not just masking the discomfort, and I decided that reducing the inflammation should reduce further damage and help prevent any longer term injury. I could mitigate the medication-related risks of dehydration and stomach upset by taking the ibuprofen with food and drinking lots of water. And when it all came down to it, I figured I didn't have much choice. I needed to run, and it was already starting to get difficult to even walk.

Compression. I immediately put compression tights on after each race, and I usually kept them on for at least a few hours to reduce the swelling in my legs and help push out any toxins. There are many opinions on how effective this compression clothing is for recovery, but it certainly didn't hurt, and I was willing to jump on the bandwagon even if it was only a glimmer of hope.

Elevation. I tried to elevate my legs on a pillow or two when sleeping, but in reality it was difficult to get much leg elevation. Especially in an airline seat. Some of the lounges had recliner couches, but even these were generally sloping downward. I tried lying on them backward, with my head where my feet should have been, but succeeded only in making myself look foolish, as well as red faced and dizzy.

It wasn't perfect, but it was a system. If I followed the RICE system, I had a shot at staying injury-free enough for two more marathons. I'd done five. I only had two to go. It must be possible. At least the flight from Morocco to Dubai was a long one.

—⟋⟋⟍—

The only way forward was backward, at least initially. We had to fly on Ryanair back to Madrid, then collect our baggage and check in to a new flight on Emirates. There was going to be a couple of hours between flights, but a little breathing room was never a bad thing. It would allow us all to have some downtime, get a bite to eat, and maybe even socialize together. Then again, if my memories of Madrid airport served me correctly, it was probably going to take a few hours just to walk from one side of the terminal to the other.

The Ryanair flight back to Madrid was quick and painless, but it was much more somber than the trip over. We had all been emotionally and physically stripped bare by our experiences in Morocco. After we boarded and took our seats, I looked from face to face and saw eyes that seemed shrunken back into their sockets, surrounded by gray, baggy skin. Most of all Ted. He'd taken the longest out there on the road in Morocco, finishing in the daylight a few hours after I'd come in. There had been no time for him to rest or recover after the race, and he looked exhausted. It was one of the only times since I'd met him that he wasn't angling to be the center of attention or looking for some new mischief. In many ways he'd done the toughest race of the lot of us over the last five days. He was on his feet for the longest, he had the least time for recovery, and by his own admission he'd trained the least.

Big Jim, not forty for one day, now looked fifty. Creases seemed to have developed overnight, stretching across his forehead and from the corners of his eyelids. Young Pierre was sore. He wasn't making a fuss, but watching him get in and out of his seat painted a very clear picture of where he was physically. We were all exhausted. Sometimes at least there's solace in the fact that you're not alone.

There were only a couple of sentences muttered between the lot of us on that whole flight, and not an hour later we were in Madrid. Not long after that, administrative tasks accomplished, we found our way to the Emirates departure lounge, tucked in the far corner of a disused section of the terminal reached only via a maze of stairs and corridors. At least Madrid airport was consistent in its design. We stuck together, fearing wandering off down the wrong corridor only to emerge months later unshaven and gaunt, having finally navigated the labyrinth.

The lounge was oddly divided, with a quiet room for reading and resting in the center of the common lounge area. Most of the other runners settled in the main lounge, quickly grabbing some food and then settling down to answer e-mails, read, or rest. Doug disappeared into the quiet area, but not before giving me a curt nod and gesture toward the room. First things first—I went to the food area and took a container of pasta salad, a roll, and some Spanish omelet. Nothing spicy, nothing risky, but I needed to eat and keep my nutrition up.

I wandered across to the quiet area and pushed the door open. It was spacious, but oddly empty. The wall dividers didn't extend to the high ceiling, somewhat negating the concept of a quiet space. Doug was sitting on a sofa eating what looked like a vegetarian paella, Marianna was sitting on a chair on the other side of the room, tapping away e-mails on her iPhone. They had bonded as friends during the trip, and I wasn't surprised to see them together. Marianna was supportive and kindhearted, and I think Doug found her much easier to be around than some of the more jokey blokey runners.

Doug invited me to sit, and almost immediately started talking about strategy for Dubai. His tone was excited but also anxious, and his conversation was focused on our fellow runners. Given our lack of true privacy, I quickly raised an index finger to my lip to try to get him to quieten down, and I can't believe that the others didn't hear at least some fragments of his opening conversation. It wasn't a good idea to have the others thinking we were planning, forming a cabal, even if to some extent it was true. By that stage I'm sure all of the runners had paired up to a greater or lesser degree, but some things are better left unspoken.

Doug was fixated on James. James had clearly rattled him in Morocco, coming so close to beating him. Part of it was anger—I think Doug believed it wasn't fair of James's friends to cheer him on in Morocco. More than that, James was holding together very well. Relatively speaking, James seemed to be getting stronger as the week went on, and that was playing on Doug's mind. Doug wasn't worried so much about winning any longer; I think he figured that was unlikely. He was worried about protecting second. It's an odd testimony to the human psyche that we are hardwired to worry far more about losing what we already have than considering what we might gain. In economics they call it loss aversion, and it is an integral component of the cutting-edge areas of decision and game theories.

Loss aversion isn't a rational behavior, but it is part of the human condition and it is fascinating. The classic example is that a person feels more dissatisfaction when they lose twenty dollars than they feel happiness when they gain twenty dollars. Doug's case was a specific form of loss aversion called "the endowment effect." People place a much higher value on what they already own than they do on something they do not own. We are much more upset at losing one of our items than we are if we're not given a new item, even if it's identical or in some cases better. It's been proven time and time again in psychology experiments. And specifically, for Doug, the thought of losing that second place that he already had was much more of a pressing concern than the possibility of gaining first place.

Rationally speaking, this didn't make sense. Gaining the first place would have been a much bigger prize, but in Doug's mind it was time to hold the fort, batten down the hatches, and formulate a plan to keep things as they were. I could understand how he felt. I was roughly forty-five minutes ahead at this stage, and it would be difficult for him to make that up in two races unless something went badly wrong. James wasn't that far behind, and in Doug's view losing second place was a possibility. It suited me just fine. I certainly had a strong loss aversion; being in the lead, the only place for me to go was down.

I had seen loss aversion before. I'd seen it in myself many times. I'd definitely felt it toward the end of races. It's that paranoia about holding your position and being worried about people coming up from behind, all the time failing to realize that the person ahead is slowing down and with a little effort you could catch them. It's the rationalization that it's OK to slow down as long as you don't lose your place. I'd seen it with investments, continuing to back a clearly losing stock or investment strategy because I'd already put so much in and figuring I'd just see how it goes now, rather than accepting the loss, selling the investment, and salvaging any remaining value. And I'd seen it before with employment, being willing to stick with a job that I didn't really like because it was a sure bet, rather than cutting my losses and trying to find something better.

The funny thing about loss aversion is everybody feels it. Doug was worried about losing a spot to James more than he was about trying to catch me, whereas James was more concerned about losing his spot in third to Marcelo than he was about beating Doug. Marcelo was most concerned about Pierre, and so on. It wasn't something we talked about, but it was clear: we all knew where we stood, and we all worried about losing what we'd spent the last five days building.

So I sat with Doug and discussed. Whether he realized it or not, his conversation kept coming back to James. Personally, I liked James. Sure, he played a few games on this trip, and he wasn't above setting the pieces up to fall as he pleased, but didn't we all, in some way or another? James was honest, he was always keen for a chat, and above all, he loved his running. I got the impression, though, that Doug was starting to see James as the enemy, as someone who was after Doug's spot and needed to be watched carefully.

We talked gently as Marianna continued to text, occasionally cocking her head or throwing in a nod or "uh-huh." If I'm to be honest it was very useful for me to strengthen my alliance with Doug. I needed him to stay close, not to gain time on me in the overall standings. The closer I could get to that finish line in Sydney with the two of us running together, the less chance I had of him running away from me and taking my place.

It was classic loss aversion yet again. Maybe I could have struck out on my own in Dubai and tried to increase my commanding lead to a point that couldn't be beaten. If I was completely Machiavellian, I could have tried to work with James and pace him up to seriously threaten Doug's second place. That would have given Doug much more to worry about, and he might have cracked again. But first, that wasn't fair; it was going too far. Second, I'd made an agreement with Doug to work together, and although it had frayed initially, it seemed now to be holding. And lastly, I was simply too averse to losing that first place to try new tricks. I would like to think the first two choices of ethics and fair play were my prime influences.

Doug and I talked and discussed, and we settled on a plan. There had been a lot of talk between the other runners and the logistics staff about Doug and me and the dynamic between us. Was there only competition or was there also camaraderie? Being in first and second place had made us the most watched runners, both from within the group and online by friends, families, and the wider world. I gave up reading Facebook soon into the race. Most comments were way off target, and many served to make one of us angry rather than helping to build a cohesive team. Some online said he was toying with me. Others said I was letting him win a couple, and he wasn't pulling his weight. In reality neither of these statements were even close to the truth. We decided there was one way to settle it. We would run Dubai together. We'd finish it together. He had a flag that was a composite of the flags of all the countries in the world. We'd hold a corner each as we crossed the line together. It was a symbol that we didn't want to fight. At least not today. We wanted to work together, to win together, and maybe people would finally get it and figure out what was going on. Maybe we were just tired, but at the time it seemed meaningful.

Of course it also served a deeper purpose that scratched both of our itches. Doug would be kept ahead of James if the two of us won, and I knew I wouldn't lose any cumulative overall time. Whether we realized it or not, our loss aversion genes were doing all of the talking.

—∿∿—

Flying from Madrid to Dubai made me realize I had spent too much time in airplanes recently. I decided, after sitting in a business class seat on the Emirates flight, that there was far too much polished rosewood. Everything was framed in rosewood: the seat-back tray, the head rest, even the audio-video control unit. For some reason it irritated me. And then, in a complete emotional backflip, a laugh erupted from deep within. Marianna, sitting next to me, gave me a quizzical look. The realization hit me that I was annoyed by the luxury wood in my business class seat. It was time for a reality check. Either I was flying far too much or I was losing my sanity or, most likely, a combination of both.

I chatted with Marianna while our in-flight meal was being served. I hadn't really had a chance to get to know her before now, but through the random chance of seating assignments, we were now thrown together for nearly eight hours. Marianna was somewhat of a mystery to me. I'd painted entirely the wrong picture of her in my head before we met. From the prerace information and discussion, I only knew three things: she was from Finland, she'd been a star on the Finnish version of the *Big Brother* reality show, and she was pretty. I'd put these pieces together and had assumed she'd be a Paris Hilton type, needing constant affirmation and pampering, and only coming on the trip to try to rekindle some public stardom in her home country. I couldn't have been more wrong.

I'd come to realize during the week that she was a quiet person, supportive and caring rather than self-centered and loud. She didn't seem to want to be the center of attention, and she seemed as concerned about those around her and the cohesiveness of the group as she was about her own well-being. I knew already that the tête-à-tête Doug and I had in Madrid had upset her; she sought harmony and peace within the group. What I hadn't realized, until talking to her now, was that she was ten years younger than me, yet had behaved at many times with more wisdom and grace. Make no mistake, Marianna was competitive. She was here for a reason, but that reason seemed to be solely to challenge herself.

Despite the fact that we were both tired, the conversation flowed easily, only interrupted while the flight attendant served the meal and when Pierre hobbled over to ask if I had any suggestions to help reduce the pain and inflammation in his knees. Pierre was getting quite banged up. We all were, but I think he was a little less prepared. I think he'd decided that because I was a veterinarian I'd have the best idea of how to treat injuries, and maybe a couple of secret tips. I gave him a tube of anti-inflammatory gel to apply and an ibuprofen tablet and told him to rest—it was really all that could be done.

As nice as the conversation was, we both had a more pressing need: rest. I put a pillow under my head, pulled the in-flight blanket over me, and rolled on my side, smiling at my previous foolishness as I carefully avoided bumping my head on the rosewood-paneled armrests. It couldn't have been more than five minutes before I was out cold. The next thing I knew I was being gently rustled back out of my dream world by the flight attendant as she put my seat upright for landing.

—∿—

Dubai. It had been more than a decade since I'd last visited. It was a different country. I'm sure that's true for many places; a decade brings much change. In Dubai's case, it was a complete metamorphosis. Gleaming towers of glass and steel vied for space with a tangle of cranes and machinery, an urban skeleton rising out of the desert. It was the true embodiment of build it and they will come. The tales of Dubai's accomplishments—and in some cases excesses—are well-known. Resort islands built out of land reclaimed from the sea, indoor ski fields in the desert, the world's tallest building, the world's most luxurious hotel, and the massive desalination plants to feed it all. In some respects, it was an ostentatious showcase of mankind's efforts to dominate nature, and at least at the moment, it appeared that mankind was succeeding.

We had arrived in the midmorning, and Dubai was truly stunning. It was a cloudless blue sky, shimmering heat haze rising from the tarmac and surrounding desert sands. And bone dry. The brightness was quite a stark contrast to that midnight run in Morocco or the dull gray winter of Madrid. It lifted the spirits and made me feel awake and alive again. I was still sore and rickety, but it felt like a brand-new day and a new beginning. Doug and I had agreed on a plan for this race; it was just a matter of getting through the day, and then we'd be onto the final marathon. The race series was slowly winding toward a finish. I didn't know what was going to happen tomorrow, but at least I knew where we were headed today.

A minibus waited for us outside the terminal, engine idling in a valiant effort to power the air-conditioners and keep the cabin cool. With bags loaded and passengers buckled in, we were away, fighting through the Dubai morning traffic, surrounded by a melee of taxis beeping and black Mercedes S-Classes with tinted windows. Apparently we were heading to a running track along the beach with a view over the Persian Gulf. The track was just over two kilometers in length, and the marathon would consist of ten out and back efforts. I figured at least this run would be scenic.

As we pulled into a dusty unpaved car park near the beach, there was a lone figure waiting for us: a short, petite dark-skinned man. I didn't really take much notice—I was more engrossed in trying to determine how hot it was going to be, the risk of sunburn, and how to stay hydrated in the desert. It was certainly hot, but it was a dry heat. Sweat would rapidly evaporate and keep the body cool. As long as there was enough to drink, overheating was unlikely. I figured sun was more of a problem than heat and opted for a hat, a shirt, and a thick layer of sunscreen.

I suddenly realized I was the only one left on the bus. I'd been preoccupied, and as I looked out the window I saw the others on the running track, encircling the little man. My curiosity was piqued, and in any case, I didn't want to be left behind if they suddenly started the race. As I approached I realized that everyone was having photos taken, and as I got closer again my jaw dropped. It was Haile Gebrselassie, one of the most, if not *the* most, famous distance runners of all time. Haile had won multiple Olympic gold medals and had victories and world records at distances ranging all the way from 1,500 meters to the marathon. His victory in the Sydney Olympics against Paul Tergat was nail-biting, one of the moments that sealed the Games as one of the greatest Olympics ever. For a marathon runner, meeting Haile was like meeting a living god. Apparently he was in Dubai for the upcoming Dubai Marathon, a race that he had won three times previously, and had decided to come down to meet us and wish us luck. It was an incredibly kind gesture and spoke to the person that he was, grounded and genuine despite his stellar career.

The fact that he had taken time out of his training and preparation to meet us meant a great deal. He truly loved running, and I think his curiosity was also piqued—who were these twelve crazy fools who had decided to run around the world? Haile was very generous with his time, allowing each of us to get a photo and shake hands, although conversation was limited. Haile's English wasn't the greatest, and our Ethiopian Amharic was completely nonexistent. Still, as is often the case, a smile and a gesture carries more goodwill than a paragraph of words.

Unfortunately, though, both we and Haile had our races to run, and we couldn't stand around taking photos all day. We lined up on the starting line, and in what I'm sure was a strange juxtaposition for him, Haile stood at the side holding the starter's air horn. He raised one hand in the air, allowed the tension to build for a few fleeting seconds, then gave a long loud blast. Once again, we were off.

— ⁓ —

It didn't take long to realize there was something unusual about the track. It felt easy to run on. I looked down and realized the green tarmac surfacing of the track was actually slightly rubberized, absorbing the energy from each footfall to return it back with a slight spring into the up step. You had to hand it to Dubai. This wasn't designed as a professional running track—this was a winding jogging path along the beach—but they'd still constructed it to absolutely this highest quality standards using the latest technology and materials. Cost was obviously not an object—the only desire was to have the best.

With the gleaming bright sunlight, the meeting with Haile Gebrselassie, the bouncy running surface, the plan to run together, and the incredible Dubai backdrop, life was good. Today was going to be a good day.

Doug and I set off together. There was no need for jostling this time. We had a plan; we just needed to stick to it. I think both of us also wanted to make clear that today was a truce. We were both tired, but more than anything else, we were tired of fighting each race. The peace of a truce was comforting, relaxing. Today could be a run between friends, rather than a fight for supremacy. Of course it wasn't quite as simple as that. We still had to hold on to our positions, we had to run a strong race, we still had to defend against those behind us, but with a bit of luck it wasn't going to involve the same draining mental battles and brinkmanship that had dominated some of the previous days.

What neither of us wanted to admit, was that the real reason we were both taking it a little easier today was that this was the calm before the storm. We both knew that Sydney was going to be the real contest, the decider. We both wanted to save our strength, because at the end of the day we were only fair-weather friends, and when it came down to the wire, we both knew that we were fierce competitors.

My goal from the start was to control the pace. If nothing else I was still the leader, and the other runners would fall into line to some degree. They'd spent the last week forming a hierarchy. We all knew where we stood, and subconsciously we ran in that same hierarchal order, determining our speeds relative to each other. If I started off a little slower, my hope was that the others would fall into line, each keeping their appropriate positions.

As Doug and I ran side by side, I gave him a gentle, almost imperceptible downward wave of the hand. It was a signal. Slow down, control your effort. Doug was still a little twitchy, concerned about James, who was not too far behind. I had to convince him not to worry and to let the race play out. Even if he could run at this pace I certainly couldn't, at least not for a full marathon. My knee joints were sore, my potentially broken right ankle was throbbing, and my quadriceps and calf muscles felt drained and weak. As much as it was bright and sunny and beautiful, I knew I had to be very careful. A hard effort today would leave me in tatters, and when it all came down to the wire in Sydney I needed to have some gas left in the tank.

We chatted between breaths for a kilometer or so, but after a while Doug became silent and seemed self-reflective. He was a quiet one, and I'd seen him struggle in group situations a number of times during the week. He preferred his own company; relating to others didn't come easily to him.

"Let's listen to music," he suggested.

That sounded just perfect to me. Making small talk took an effort, and I couldn't really find the enthusiasm either. Mostly, I just wanted this run to be behind me; it was a matter of getting through and keeping the status quo, and the best way to do that was to zone out, look at the scenery, and let my mind wander.

Old habits die hard. I let my mind drift and started taking mental notes on waypoints. This course was certainly one of the more interesting. If Dubai wasn't a mostly alcohol-free country, I might have thought whoever designed the running track had been inebriated. The path weaved and bobbed up and down the beach, snaking up the shore and then back down much closer to the water. This meant some changes in gradient, which is never much fun on a long run, but it also made it much easier to make checkpoints to count off the distance on each lap.

The track initially looped down toward the sea, and then wound back up in a wide arc along the top of the beach. There was a brown-stained wood and stone gazebo at the top of the arc. It was my first checkpoint. As we continued on, the gradient became progressively more forgiving, and after a few hundred meters, it started to slowly wind down the beach again. We passed a small working party dressed in overalls, setting up some decorative ornaments and sprays of flowers on the beach. Interesting, definitely a second checkpoint.

Doug and I continued to run side by side, maintaining a very measured and conservative pace. I noticed he was looking over his shoulder. His tell. He was getting concerned. I figured James was playing on his mind. James wasn't far back, but we were only a short way into the marathon. This had been Doug's self-imposed weakness on more than one occasion during the week. He'd sprinted off the starting line in Antarctica, he'd put on a ferocious pace in Punta Arenas when I ducked off to the bathroom, he'd tried bursts of speed at the turnarounds in Miami, and in Madrid he'd lead out for nearly a whole lap at a tempo that would have been reserved for a fast ten kilometer race. It was his biggest hurdle as a distance runner, the understanding of conservancy and timing. Each marathon was a long day, and time and time again he'd burnt himself out with self-destructive efforts. On previous days I'd used it to my advantage, waiting him out until he tired, but today I needed to put a lid on it. The idea percolating in his head was going to ruin the plan.

"Don't worry about James," I said quietly between puffs.

"He's catching us," Doug replied, quickly looking over his shoulder again.

"No, he's not. It's a long day coming. Take it easy, control your pace. I'll watch James."

Doug looked relieved, or at least mollified. James had now become my problem, and Doug could put him out of his mind.

The running track continued along the top of the beach, passing in front of another dirt and gravel car parking area. There was the normal mixture of cars, normal for Dubai at least: a shiny new BMW, a fairly worn Toyota, and a Hummer. Then at the end I saw my third checkpoint. There was a beat-up Bedford van that had been converted into an RV-styled campervan. It was straight out of the seventies, and completely out of place in Dubai. Tasseled curtains hung from the windows, and the owners had spray-painted the sides and tailgate with a variety of stick figures and icons. The number plates were from Iran. Up to that point I'd had no idea it was even possible to drive from Iran to Dubai. I was certain that I'd be able to find an interesting feature on that one each time I passed.

Finally, after another kilometer or so, we reached the turnaround. Thankfully there was a local runner with a shade tent covering a supply of water and Coca-Cola. Coke was something I'd never drink in normal life—I found it sweet and sickly—but toward the end of a long race it was like nectar. At those times, the combination of sugar and caffeine was rejuvenating and strangely delicious. Seeing it there gave me a little boost, knowing that I had a pick-me-up in reserve if I started to tire.

We both stopped for a quick drink at the turnaround. I insisted. Doug was worried about James, but in the desert I figured dehydration was a far bigger problem. With the air so parched, the sweat evaporated almost instantly, and even though neither of us was damp, I knew we must have been losing large amounts of water. Salt marks were already forming on my arms. Water was going to be essential, as were electrolytes. Failure to keep up both would lead to cramps, or worse. I tilted my head back to get a drink down as quickly as possible, and as I looked up I saw it—we were a stone's throw from the Burj al

Khalifa, the world's tallest building. Built from a bundle of cylindrical towers bound together, each of a different length, topped with a spire reaching up into the sky, a finger seemingly scraping the upper atmosphere. It was colossal, and I had no idea how I hadn't seen it before now. It was a lesson in the dangers of looking at your feet the whole run, how much of the scenery and beauty could be missed by only looking at the track five meters ahead.

I turned about-face to head back the way we came, and then I noticed in the distance was the Burj al Arab, the massive sail-like and magnificently opulent hotel that jutted out into the Persian Gulf. The Burj al Arab was legendary. There are no rooms, only suites. The service is described as seven star, a jewel in the desert, a modern-day palace. It is a hotel that has drawn as much criticism for its excesses as it has praise for its state-of-the-art construction and design. The Burj al Arab and the Burj al Khalifa are collectively seen as the embodiment of Dubai, the conquest of practicality by wealth. It was only now that I realized these two monoliths were bookends to our run. I certainly had my last two waypoints.

—⟋⟍—

As we headed back from the turnaround we saw James approaching. I gave him a smile and a nod. He gave a grin back. Doug, however, was much frostier.

"He's not that far behind us."

"He's far enough back. Don't worry," I replied flatly. "We need to keep our cool."

"OK, OK," Doug finished, and put his headphones back in.

He was still anxious, but at least he was trying to block it out.

We doubled back down the track the way we'd come. I mentally ticked off the checkpoints, playing my game of finding something new in each of them, and gave a wave or a nod to the runners coming the other way. I looked at the Iranian camper and noticed it was rusting around the wheel arches. Strange, I wouldn't have thought metal would rust in such a dry climate; must have been the sea air. I waved to Marcelo and gave Pierre a smile. The working party on the beach had put some carpeting down and were arranging the flowers and wooden ornaments into a large arch. I nodded to Big Jim; said hi to Tim and Jon, who seemed to be running together; and stifled a laugh at Ted as he did a little dance for our benefit—maybe the last, but definitely the most amusing. I passed the wood and stone structure and realized it was a public washroom. The thought came across my mind that I'd paid good money to stay in less fancy-looking hotel suites than that public washroom. Again, only in Dubai. Finally, we came across Marianna. She was sitting on the side of the running track. Tears were streaming down her face. Something had gone badly wrong.

Doug shot me a concerned glance. By this stage we had a team mentality, a group spirit born from the experiences of the last week. Sure, we all wanted to do well and there was competition, but we also all wanted everybody to finish. It would have felt like a blow to all of us if any one of us had to pull out, especially this far through. For Doug, Marianna's situation was even more of a concern. I got the impression Doug felt he owed Marianna. Marianna had been his support on a number of occasions. He'd spent much more time with her than he had with any of the rest of us, and I think her caring and supportive nature gave him the confidence he sorely needed.

Doug slowed down to a jog as we approached, and then dropped into a walk. "What's wrong?" he asked.

Marianna shook her head. She must have put on mascara before the race. It was running down her face, streaked across her cheeks carried by the tears.

"My leg. I can't. Go on."

"No we'll help," Doug replied.

"No, I want to be alone," Marianna finished, and looked out across the ocean, making it clear the conversation was over.

There wasn't much that could be done. She needed time alone. We continued on, but agreed to stop and make sure she was OK each time we passed. We'd try to encourage her and see if there was anything we could do to help.

By the time we reached the starting point turnaround Haile Gebrselassie was long gone, replaced by an interested local Arabian bystander dressed in a flowing gray robe with an equally flowing white beard, and a small circular cap atop his head. Richard, the race director, was standing nearby, preparing some drinks for the runners on a table set up near the path.

I grabbed a drink and nodded to Richard.

"Marianna's in some kind of trouble. She's down the track, only about a kilometer away."

"Yeah I know," he replied. "She's got a bad Achilles. She can't run."

"I've got ibuprofen in my bag. She can have it," I said.

"Don't worry, so do I. You guys run. I'll take care of it."

There was no denying the inevitable, and however much I tried to placate Doug he was right—James wasn't that far behind. It was time to go.

As we came around the first long bend, we saw Marianna again. She was further up the road, propelling herself down the track with a hobbling, shuffling gait. She looked sore, but somehow she'd pulled herself together and found the inner strength to continue. We both smiled. She may have been gentle and caring, but she was also tough as nails. It was impressive. I knew then and there that she'd finish, even if she had to drag herself across the line. It was a worry lifted off both of our shoulders, but Doug especially looked relieved. I don't know whether he would have pulled out of the race to help her, but I think he would have at least considered it.

Doug gave Marianna a pat on the back as he ran past, and I uttered one word: "Respect."

——

We continued on, passing the landmarks one by one, alternating between staccato breathless conversation and listening to music. The laps passed by, the effort required felt like it was increasing with each lap. I'm not sure if the day was heating up or I was running out of energy, but either way it was becoming difficult—difficult for both of us, but for the first time I was acutely aware that it was feeling more difficult for me than for Doug. In a role reversal, I realized Doug was pacing me. I was slowing too much, I needed him to control the run speed, to balance us on that fine line where we were not overexerted, but fast enough to cross that line in first. And he did it perfectly.

Doug carried me for much of that second half of the run, and any favors I did him in Morocco were paid back in full. I sat a half-stride back from his left shoulder, using a combination of my landmarks, music, and trying to think about happier times to take my mind off things. I suddenly realized the problem—I was blowing up. Once you're blown, it's very hard to come back. Maybe I'd be able to recover by Sydney, but the next hour or two were going to be really tough.

There is a stack of euphemisms for it: hitting the wall, bonking, the hunger knock, blowing up. It is a point when metabolic supply can no longer keep up with demand and the body loses the ability to adequately fuel itself. It is a derailment of that complex physiological interplay of muscle glycogen, fat stores, blood glucose, insulin, and glucagon. Glycogen is the easiest reserve for the body to convert back into blood sugar, the body's fuel. However, the body only has the capacity to store enough glycogen for around forty-five minutes' exercise. After that, it's a matter of either switching to burning fat, which is much slower and less efficient, or relying on energy drinks and sugary gels consumed to provide the glucose. In reality there is always a mixture of fat-burning, glucagon usage, and oral carbohydrate nutrition, but the proportions of each change as time goes on.

Blowing up was a feeling that every distance athlete has experienced at times. A weakness in the legs, numbness in the feet, dizziness, and even trembling of the hands. Once that metabolic train derails it is notoriously hard to get it back on the tracks. Twenty-four hours and a big bowl of pasta would fix it, but I didn't have twenty-four hours. I needed to keep running now. Running and racing. As kind as Doug was to take the lead and pace me, I didn't expect him to stop and walk with me while I regained strength.

I figured I'd blown up through a combination of not eating enough during the race to supplement my glucose stores, and a cumulative drain of fat and carbohydrate stores over the week. My joints and tendons had already rebelled. Now it was my metabolism's turn. At least I could recognize my signs, acknowledge the problem, and start trying to sort out a solution. The deeper the bonk became, the more impossible it became to reverse. I had to act now.

I had a couple of gels stuffed in the back pocket of my running shorts. I'd put them in there to remind me to eat as I ran, but I realized now I'd been woefully neglectful. I'd taken on plenty of fluids and a fair amount of electrolyte drink, but my sugar supply had clearly been inadequate. I took both gels out and squeezed them down my throat in quick succession. It was like eating treacle with a dry mouth. My tongue stuck to the roof of my mouth as I tried to swallow, cemented by a sugary gum. I'd read somewhere that the body releases its final reserves of sugar into the system as soon as the tongue registers sweetness, signaling the arrival of new energy. I wasn't sure if it was true, but it was something for me to hold on to. I knew it was going to take at least fifteen minutes for those gels to make their way down from my mouth, move into my stomach, pass into my bloodstream, and then finally arrive at my muscles. I was going to have to just tough it out, and I knew having a pacer in the form of Doug was a huge advantage to beating the bonk.

At the back of my head there was only one goal right now: get to that Coca-Cola. There is nothing finer, at least not in my knowledge, to get the metabolism back on track. It was a combination of that sugar substrate for the metabolism, the caffeine to kick-start the internal chemistry, and the water to wash it all down and flush it into the system. I knew if I could just get there I'd be able to pull through the marathon.

On the other hand, part of the problem with being blown is that those low blood sugar levels affect the brain as much as the muscles. Thinking became clouded, decisions became difficult, plans were not clear. I knew I had to remain focused on that Coke. That was now my only checkpoint. And once again, like so many times before over that last week, it became about putting one foot in front of the other.

There was no conversation. I didn't have the energy. Doug could certainly sense what was going on, and he stood by me. He gave the occasional word of encouragement, but for the most part he was one more for action than words, and didn't seem entirely comfortable being the person who was now required to be the crutch for others to lean on. Nevertheless, he got me to that turnaround. I broke my own rule and upped my pace as I saw the turnaround drinks tent, cantering at speed toward my promised land. I grabbed three cups of Coke. The race marshal had been kind enough to put ice cubes in each to keep them cool in the baking desert air. Maybe it was physiological or maybe it was psychosomatic, but that Coke hitting the back of my mouth made me feel like my batteries had suddenly been replaced. I guzzled cup after cup, until Doug finally said enough. I think he was worried I was going to bring it all back up, and he was probably right.

We jogged off together, my stomach sloshing back and forth, belches loudly emanating from deep within. I wasn't perfect, but I was fixed enough to finish. I slapped Doug on the back with a "Thanks, man."

He looked at me and nodded. We both knew that we were square.

—⁓—

We jogged down the track, passing James coming the other way. He was still a distance behind, not a threat. I suspect Doug was quite relieved that his charity toward me didn't appear to be costing him the race. We passed my mental checkpoints, checking off a new feature on each. I rounded the corner and saw a man standing on the beach in a full tuxedo. I must have been losing it. That Coke obviously hadn't worked. I was hallucinating. Then the penny dropped. He was standing at my third checkpoint, standing between the flowers. And walking toward him, down our running track, was a lady in a flowing white dress—a wedding dress. We both smiled as we passed, and she smiled back. They were both European. There was only one answer—they were expatriates working in the Emirates, today was their special day, and they were getting married on the beach. They seemed to be quite alone apart from a few curious onlookers and the setup staff; I could only imagine they'd be heading back to repeat the ceremony in their home country.

Seeing the happy couple was certainly a boost to our spirits. We continued on with smiles on our faces, and as we came around that wide arc Marianna was running toward us. We all slowed down.

"Looking good," Doug said to her.

"Richard motivated me. I'm sore but I'll make it," she replied, with a hint of a smile starting to creep across her face.

The day I had expected to be so easy and relaxed hadn't been so easy at all, but the problems were being dealt with, one by one. There was only one issue remaining—we had one more loop to go, and to his credit James was putting in a big effort, seeming to be making up some ground.

"You OK to speed up for the last one?" Doug asked.

"Yep, don't worry about me; I'll hold on. But keep it controlled," I replied.

We reached the starting point turnaround, had one more sip of drink each, then headed off for our final loop. For once, nothing went wrong. We paced each other evenly, both knowing the course's ups and downs a little more intimately by now. We both zoned out for most it, running on autopilot, only stopping again at the far turnaround to grab one last Coke, one for the road. I thanked the race marshal for all of his help today, told him he'd been a lifesaver, and then continued on that final length of track knowing it was soon to be over, with a spring in my step additional to that provided by the track.

Doug and I were running quite fast, making sure to hold James off, but we knew we were on the home stretch, and at least for today, there was no need to keep anything in reserve. I think James must have realized, because he appeared to drop right back, sensibly saving his energy for the next race. I said farewell to my checkpoints one by one, a collection of oddities that as a group were special to nobody but myself. The wedding had finished and the workmen were packing back up as we passed.

Finally, we made the last turn on the beachfront and ran up the finishing straight. The bearded bystander in the flowing robes had been co-opted in to the event, and was now holding one side of the finisher's ribbon across the track, standing opposite a race marshal on the other side of the track. Exactly according to plan, Doug pulled his flag out from under his shirt. He must have grabbed it at the last turnaround while I was drinking. He unfurled it and gave me the top left corner, while he held the right. A couple of meters from the finish line we both slowed to a walk, stretching the flag up high between us, looked up at the finishing camera and smiled as we both cut the ribbon at exactly the same moment. Equal first. We'd won, and we'd won together. It was a feeling unlike any win I'd ever had.

We gave each other a nod and a knowing smile, then waited at the finish line for James, who wasn't far behind. He'd run a tough race today, and he'd done it solo. If the truth were told, I don't think I could have managed that. He had a big grin from ear to ear. He was delighted to have finished. We all stood for some photos, then gingerly limped down into the Persian Gulf for a cool, relaxing soak and flap about.

Nearly three hours later, Marianna crossed the finish line. She'd battled pain, exhaustion, and self-doubt. She'd emerged victorious. She was the last person to finish on that day, but without a doubt she was the bravest. That was the day that I truly learned never to judge a book by its cover.

MARATHON 7: OCEANIA

Sydney, Australia: The Final Showdown

Now just don't stuff it up. No pressure though.

—Mark Peters, old friend

An hour or so after emerging from the Persian Gulf I found myself in the Dubai Oberoi. The minibus waiting at the race finish had taken the three earlier finishers—Doug, James, and me—to the hotel to get showered and changed before the next flight.

The modern luxury of the Oberoi, and Dubai in general, seemed completely at odds with our other destinations on the trip. Polished fittings glittered and shimmered in the midafternoon sun, another pristine structure mushrooming up out of the sand. Expensive artwork hung from the walls, massive crystal chandeliers were suspended from the roof, and marbled floors shone back up at us as our dirty running shoes squeaked across, leaving a trail of sandy footprints.

There was, however, one similarity. Hotel staff the world around aren't impressed when a bunch of bedraggled runners turn up in their lobby. More so than ever we were such a contrast to the suit-wearing staff and finely dressed patrons that we all felt quite self-conscious and silly. At least I wasn't madly dashing in to use the bathroom this time. I wondered whether the race logistics staff had a friend at the hotel or had been sponsored for the rooms; such opulent lodgings seemed like an odd choice otherwise. Odd, but certainly impressive.

James and Doug both seemed a little out of their element. Five-star hotels weren't common in the farming country James came from, and I got the impression Doug preferred the simple life to the high life. If nothing else, living in Hong Kong for fifteen years had taught me that sometimes the best policy is to not blink. I walked straight up to a smartly dressed lady at the reservations desk, stood tall, shoulders back, looked her in the eye, and gave a friendly smile. I made a conscious effort to try to speak the Queen's English with clarity.

"Hello, I'm here with the party of runners. I believe our rooms have been reserved by our staff."

She didn't miss a beat. A true professional. I'm sure in her place I would have started laughing.

"Yes sir, of course. Your rooms are ready."

She slid three room cards across the counter but the corner of her mouth curled up into a genuine but mischievous smile, betraying her efforts at remaining completely nonchalant. I smiled back.

I gave Doug and James a card each, and we proceeded off toward the elevators and our respective rooms. The room didn't disappoint, with floor-to-ceiling windows that revealed sweeping vistas over the Dubai metropolis. I looked out over the horizon. Seeing the Burj al Khalifa at the far end I spared a thought for those of us still out there on that running track; I was certainly glad to be finished. The room was divided into a living quarters and an expansive adjoining bathroom, with a full porcelain bathtub resting near the window. The moment I saw it I knew I couldn't resist. A long nice hot bath would revitalize me, slowly leaching away the sweat, dirt, and lactic acid accumulated in the previous hours and days. I figured there wasn't much else to do; we had to wait for the other runners anyway. I set the taps to run and slowly immersed myself into a long, dreamy soak overlooking the hustle and bustle of Dubai, the comings and goings of an army of ants attending to their twenty-first century mounds.

Sometime later in the afternoon Tim, my fellow runner, Antarctic tent-mate, and now apparently Dubai changing-room-mate entered. I was dried, changed, and asleep on the bed by the time he arrived. He looked like I felt about three hours ago, drained and exhausted, but happy to be finished. I, on the other hand, felt better than I had in days. Tired, sure, but finally properly clean and somewhat rested. I made the decision to allow Tim some privacy, and went off in search of some late-afternoon lunch.

A few hours and one Dubai-style Arabic mezze platter of food later, I found myself sitting in the lobby with my fellow runners. Less than an hour after that we were at the boarding gates, embarking on the final and longest flight of our trip: Dubai to Sydney, via Kuala Lumpur in Malaysia. It was a Malaysia Airlines flight, and the carrier's relatively recent air-safety troubles weren't lost on some of the runners. The way I saw it, what were the chances that lightning would strike three times? And if it did, at least I would have gone out peacefully—I was passed out in my seat for the entire flight, minus the short stopover, of course.

—⁓—

By the time we got to Sydney, we all knew the routine. Get the bags. Get into the van. Get to a hotel. Get changed. Get to the race start. Run. There was only one thing different this time: this was the final race, and everything was on the line. I did have a forty-five-minute lead on Doug, with James not too far behind. Forty-five minutes seemed like a lot, but it would only take one major problem to completely upset the balance.

I'd seen how much time an injury had cost Marianna in Dubai, and my ankle felt like it was one good thump away from breaking properly. I also knew this time there would be no mercy from any of the runners, and none would have been expected. Sure, we were all friends to some degree, but it was a competition, and when it comes down to the wire, people's true instincts and desires bubble to the fore. More than that, being the front-runner I had everything to lose. It's that old rule about the leader never showing weakness. The moment you do, the lieutenants start circling, looking for the kill. You are the target. And at that moment, I felt the burden more heavily than ever. Doug had put on a strong showing in Dubai; he was certainly stronger than me on that day. If he could continue that streak, and I continued to weaken, the results were going to be very, very close indeed, too close to call.

By the time we arrived at the airport, I'd started to realize I was in trouble. Sydney was Doug's hometown. Despite the fact that we'd arrived very late on a Sunday evening, there was an armada of friends, relatives, and supporters at the airport to greet him. As soon as he emerged from customs into the arrivals hall, that tired look on his face vanished, to be replaced by an ecstatic grin. Doug was a good runner. There was no doubting that. Doug was fit. Doug was, from what I could gather, relatively uninjured. There were only two things that Doug lacked: the ability to pace himself effectively, and the self-confidence to go through with his pacing plan. When I saw his entourage a few steps out of the airside terminal, I realized that had all changed.

"My friends are going to run with me for this last one," Doug said, smiling.

With that one sentence, the solid emotional ground I was standing on began cracking, making my mind stumble and sway, conspiring to open right up and swallow me whole.

I didn't take it as an intentional threat. I think he was truly happy that he was finally around people he felt comfortable with. Even if it wasn't meant as a threat, it certainly was one. With Doug being paced by multiple runners, I'd just lost any strategic advantage. I knew I still had those forty-five minutes, but I was injured, and the injuries seemed to be worsening. I was going to have to be careful—really careful. It was a fine balance between restricting further damage, not losing too much of that cumulative lead, and getting to the finish line in one piece. Winning today was not important, and in truth a win today was probably not possible anyway given the circumstances. What mattered was winning this week. I realized then and there that I was about to live one of the toughest days of my life.

In fairness, I should also say that Doug acted completely openly and honestly. There are different views on the subject of external pacers in races, and different conventions between the sports. In triathlon it's considered unsportsmanlike and unfair, whereas it's commonplace in cycling, and for distance running races, especially marathons, it's pretty much the norm. Pacers in competitive marathons even wear different colored clothes, usually brightly contrasting stripes with a PACER sign to distinguish them from the professional runners. Most of the world records in running have been set with pacers. The idea pretty much started back in 1954 when Roger Bannister broke the four-minute mile using pacers. In fact, in marathon running they're so ubiquitous they have a nickname—"rabbits." The last thing I needed was Doug surrounded by a bunch of rabbits, stopping him going off too hard yet keeping him up to speed in the final few kilometers, and buoying up his confidence the whole way through.

No, not helpful to my cause. But completely fair. And if we landed for that last race in Hong Kong, my home town, I'm sure all of my friends would have turned up with exactly the same idea. Anyway, I figured there was nothing to stop me running with his pace group, if I could keep up.

Not two minutes after arriving in the exit area of the terminal, my phone rang. It was one of those few moments in my life when I've believed that karma may exist. I thought I recognized the number. A smile crept across my face. The first smile for some time.

"Hello?" I asked, somewhat surprised.

"Chap. How are you?"

My smile widened. It was my good friend and training buddy from back home, Richard Hall. He was one of the people who got me started down this path over seven years ago. He was one of the guys who met me huffing and puffing on my bike up that hill and invited me to join his ride. He and I had trained together solidly for more of my life than I care to remember. At times I think his wife and my wife became worried that their husbands were cheating on them. With each other. Now he was finishing the story with me too. He and another close friend, Jan Skovgaard, were running seven marathons in seven Hong Kong districts in seven days, parallel to my races. It was a touching gesture, something only true friends would be willing to do. They ran those marathons in solidarity, not for recognition, and only told our closest friends and family. Of course it wasn't all altruistic. Richard was as driven as I was, probably more so. He planned to do an eighth marathon on the eighth day, just to prove which of the two of us was truly the real man.

"Pretty rough. I'm banged up," I replied.

"Me too. Forget about that though. We're all back here cheering for you. Rachel's made a spreadsheet. All of the guys and girls here can't take their eyes off the screen. You've got this."

At that moment I felt so vulnerable. Fighting this battle by myself seemed manageable. Up to now we'd been strangers in faraway lands, completely isolated and separated from the rest of the world. Suddenly I felt violently thrust back into our civilizations with all eyes watching, watching to see the only really important thing: who wins. It's a sad truth, but nobody really cares about who comes second. This conversation made me suddenly realize I wasn't carrying my own hopes; I was carrying the hopes of all of my friends back home, and if I failed today I'd be letting them all down, returning home with my tail between my legs.

I think the silence on my end of the line told Richard he'd better say something fast. He was supportive, but we'd always operated on a "harden-up toughen-up" policy when dealing with problems out on race course. Richard didn't do mollycoddling.

"Listen. You've got forty-something-minutes lead. He's got to run a three twenty marathon or faster. Which he's never done. You've got to run a four hour or slower. Which you've never done. Stop talking to me and get out there and win it."

"Thanks, man. I'll let you know," I replied.

With that, he hung up. Maybe he was running late for his own marathon. Maybe he was feeling the strain himself, and nobody was there boosting him up. I'll never know. But I do know that his words not only hit the nail on the head; they drove it right through the timber. I'd never been one for self-doubt, and now was not the time to start. There was only one thing that needed to be done, and that needed to be done in less than four hours.

—⚏—

The Menzies hotel in Sydney's central business district was the destination for dropping off the bags, getting changed, and getting ready. It felt a little dated, but given that our last experience was the polished sparkle of the Oberoi Dubai,

I think anything might have felt old. I dragged my luggage up to the room; opened up the small roll-on that I'd previously packed with today's race clothes, shoes, and energy gel sachets; and got changed. Taking my jeans off was agony. My legs would hardly bend. I looked at myself in the wardrobe mirror. My legs had really swollen up. I'm not sure if it was the flying at altitude, the lack of solid nutrition, the marathons, or all of the above, but something was clearly wrong. I'd lost any muscle definition, my limbs were comically engorged and creased with cellulite-like marks. I knew what it was: edema, leakage of body fluid into the tissues. My veterinary training told me there were three main causes of edema: heart failure, toxicity, and severe tissue damage. There wasn't a good option there, but I hoped it was only tissue damage.

From my reading after the race, I know now that I had developed chronic exertional compartment syndrome. When the muscles are used excessively, day after day in a high-stress exercise like running, they swell. The pressure within the muscle increases. This reduces blood flow to the muscles, preventing new, fresh, oxygenated blood from supplying the tissue and preventing old, used blood from carrying away toxins and metabolites produced during exertion. The resultant muscle damage increases the swelling, worsening the problem. It makes the muscles rigid and inflexible, hampering the normal contraction and extension and preventing the legs from properly bending and flexing. More than anything else, compartment syndrome and the related tissue damage results in a throbbing pain, an intense fire in the muscles emanating from deep within the leg. Walking was difficult. Running was going to be agony. This was going to be a problem. Another problem.

I figured I didn't have a lot of options. I figured I had about forty-five minutes in that hotel room and I needed to make the most of it. That old mantra of RICE came back to me. First, two ibuprofen tablets should help with the swelling. The next step was to elevate those legs—get them higher than my torso to encourage the fluid to flow back into my circulatory system. I laid down on bed with my feet perched up over the headrest. Lastly, I figured I needed something to push the fluid out. Compression tights weren't going to help me this time. The tights were a slim fit when my legs were a normal size, but in their current swollen state, it would have been like pushing a watermelon into a deflated balloon. Necessity is always the mother of invention, and at that moment I decided that despite no formal training or experience, I was going to try my hand at sports massage. I rested a pillow under my chest to help raise my arms a little, and placed my hands on my right quadriceps. I pressed one thumb on top of the other to help build pressure, and to my surprise, my lower thumb sank deep into my leg. Pulling both hands away, there was a puffy thumb-shaped crater remaining in my thigh. Pitting edema. That couldn't be good.

Richard Hall's words about hardening up came back to me, not for the last time that evening, and I placed both hands back on my upper leg. I began to massage, gently at first and then with more force, pushing the internal fluid back toward the circulation in my chest. I can't say whether it was the ibuprofen taking effect or the massage, but my legs started to feel slightly better. I had another thirty minutes or so before we had to meet in the lobby of the Menzies for our final race departure, and I was going to spend all of that time as productively as I could, getting myself ready to race. I put my headphones on to listen to some music while I tried to knead and work my legs.

Five minutes later I opened my eyes and had the fright of my life. My wife, Trilby, and my father, Tim, were standing at the end of the bed. I knew they were both going to try to make it for the final showdown, but only having limited e-mail and phone contact, I wasn't exactly sure whether they'd been able to arrange flights and accommodation.

So there I was. Eyes closed and in a trance, puffy legs thrust up the wall, thumbs furiously rubbing my muscles. I'm sure it didn't look good. I could only hope they'd been there long enough to realize nothing untoward was happening. I flopped my legs down to my left, the resultant momentum acting to catapult my torso upright. I smiled weakly.

Trilby slowly looked me up and down. I must have appeared haggard. Face gaunt and lined. Eyes glazed over with a hollow stare. Chin covered in a motley five o'clock shadow. Legs swollen and puffy. Possible frostbite in two toes. A right ankle swollen up to the size of grapefruit, and knees that wouldn't bend.

She paused for a minute to collect her thoughts, raised her head, and looked me straight in the eye with a smile on her face. Four simple words came out of her mouth.

"Honey, you look great."

She made me smile. It was probably the only time in our twenty years together that she'd lied to me, but right now it was the one sentence that made everything seem OK. I was clearly feeling the emotional and physical scars from the preceding week, and I knew things were going to get even worse in the next few hours during that last marathon. I felt like all eyes were on me, and there was risk I was going to let everyone down. I was struggling to hold myself together. I opened my mouth to talk and nothing came out. I didn't know what to say. I was so tired and drained at that point, and part of me knew that if I thought about the whole situation any more I was going to crack. If I was there with just my wife, I may have cried. But big boys don't cry, not in front of their fathers at least.

We all sat and talked for a while. Talked about anything except the race. Talked about the girls, Amelia and Madeleine; talked about home; talked about plans for tomorrow after this ridiculous race had finished. But before everything was done we also talked about one more thing. Winning didn't matter, they assured me. Getting to this point has been an incredible success and an amazing journey. Nobody would be upset with me if I didn't win.

As much as I wanted to believe it, I knew it wasn't true. At this stage for me, winning overall was the only thing that mattered. I didn't care how much my body hated me afterward, how long it took to recover, and what it took mentally to get through today. I had to win. And to win I had to plan—plan to sacrifice today and lose this one marathon, but with the intention of preserving enough strength and finishing fast enough to win overall. It was a strange gambit. I'd never played to lose before. I wasn't even sure I knew how to plan and execute that properly.

—⁂—

As the three of us headed down into the lobby Trilby let me know one more secret. She knew it was Doug's town. She knew his friends were runners. She was smart enough to put the pieces together days ago—far smarter than me. She knew they were going to pace him. She knew she had to do something to flatten the advantage. She couldn't pace me—she was fit but she wasn't a marathon runner. But she could do it on a bicycle. Apparently she'd arrived in Sydney a day early and arranged a hire bike, complete with a cycle computer to measure time and distance, and a small basket on the front to carry snacks and water.

If there were no other reason in the world, I knew at the moment why I loved her.

She was going to work in combination with my dad, Tim, who had a car. He would wait at the significant checkpoints to make sure we both had enough water, fuel, and supplies.

A smile crept across my face once more. I was back in with a shot. Having support out there lifted a massive weight off my shoulders. If nothing else, she was my emotional shield against Doug's pacers. Seeing her would keep me strong and keep me paced and on track to that ultimate victory. I returned to that lobby a different man. Gone was the crestfallen warrior, replaced by a tired but spirited distance runner, with an ace up his sleeve.

I made some quick introductions between my new running friends from the race and my family, but everybody was too preoccupied for anything more than superficial niceties. We all had our own reasons to fear that last marathon. My dad and Trilby quietly wandered off to allow us some time to get ready. Some calm before the storm. It wasn't long before an aging Holden station wagon pulled up in front of the Menzies. I smiled. It was good to be back in Australia. It wasn't my hometown anymore, not like Doug, but half a lifetime ago I'd spent my childhood years in the Sydney suburbs. The memories were mixed, but nostalgia has a way of tinting all glasses in a rose color.

The local race organizer, Dave, opened the driver's side door and strode into the hotel. As far as runners go, he was clearly the real deal. Lean and sinewy, his arms and legs wrinkled and tanned from hours in the sun, parched skin stretched over taut muscle and bone.

"G'day. Let's get going," he announced to the group.

I appreciated the directness.

By the time we'd gathered ourselves, two other cars had arrived outside the hotel, driven by other members of the Sydney marathon team to help ferry us out to the starting point. I jumped into the front passenger seat of the Holden, next to Dave. Although the car was hygienic, nobody would have suggested Dave had specially cleaned or organized it for guests. I discretely corralled some pamphlets, advertisements, and newspaper cuttings that lay on the seat into a small pile and transferred them to the car door pocket. Dave didn't seem to mind. A copy of Gregory's Road Atlas and Street Directory rested in the foot well, along with a copy of the *Daily Telegraph*. I decided to not upset the applecart too much, and carefully rested my legs on the other side.

Once we were all in and buckled up, he fired up the engine and we were away, the other cars following in convoy. We turned right into a side street almost immediately, and then left onto a road that seemed to roughly follow the shoreline of the harbor. We were driving out from the city and into the suburbs, to a bay on the Parramatta River called Iron Cove. The plan was to run an eight-kilometer loop around Iron Cove four times, then peel off for a mad dash back through inner-city Sydney in the early hours of the morning and onward to the finish line under the Sydney Harbour Bridge.

Dave the organizer turned around and looked at Marianna, Pierre, and Ted, who had squeezed themselves into the back seat.

"We're driving back along the run course you'll be taking," he remarked, a friendly smile on his face.

All of us perked up and looked intently, trying to remember any important points on the road, potholes or disturbances, hills or dips, intersections or signs—anything that might become significant later in the day.

Dave was quiet for the rest of the trip, despite a couple of awkward attempts by his passengers to get conversation rekindled. He was a thoughtful man, but one who didn't waste words. Our only alternative was to watch the distance markers roll by on our way out to Iron Cove, all the time knowing each kilometer was to be paid back in full by foot on the return run. The expressions on all of our faces gradually became more drawn. It seemed like he was driving a very long way indeed. It was going to be a long night.

I have always loathed that period immediately before a race. To me it feels like standing at the end of a long dark tunnel with a train rapidly approaching. At first there is just a distant spot of light on the horizon and I tell myself everything is all right, there's still time to get ready, it's not on yet. But deep inside I know that time is inevitably slipping away, that spot of light is slowly getting larger and larger, the train is steaming ahead coming nearer and nearer. An uneasy feeling starts to build at the base of my stomach. Yet I stand there, rooted to the ground, mesmerized by the glow of that light approaching. I can't stop the train, I can't alter its path, I can't even slow it down. It's coming straight for me, and I can't move. The light gets brighter and brighter until it's almost blinding, the mechanical screech of the train becomes louder and louder until it's a roar. All of a sudden everything becomes deafeningly silent. I'm standing on the starting line with that bright light staring deep into my eyes.

And the gun goes off.

—❧—

Ironman World Championship, Hawaii, October 14, 1989. The scene of arguably the greatest battle ever in endurance sports. It became known as "Iron War." Mark Allen and Dave Scott were two of the best long-distance triathletes in the history of the sport. They'd faced off against each other a number of times previously, and they'd never seen eye to eye.

In 1989, triathlon was still in its infancy. The sport was rapidly developing, and for the first time it was truly starting to attract an audience outside the hardened enthusiast or sportsperson. The general public were captivated, and no race was more famous or more watched than the Hawaii Ironman. It starts with a 3.8-kilometer swim off the Kailua-Kona shore, followed by a 180-kilometer bike ride through the blisteringly hot lava fields of the big island of Hawaii, and then culminates in a brutal 42-kilometer run in the tropical heat. The race had taken its toll on a number of competitors in previous years, with heatstroke, collapse, and exhaustion being commonplace. Truth be told, this toll was a large part of what made the event such a media frenzy—the chance to see elite sportsmen and women throw themselves into the blender and see who was still standing at the end of the day.

Most did the Hawaii Ironman simply to finish, to be able to say they'd battled the odds and the elements and come out victorious. But right at the top end of the field, there were a few that didn't consider it a test of survival. To them it was a race—the greatest race.

There were a handful of legends already carving a name for themselves, but none as polarizing or as fiercely competitive as Dave Scott and Mark Allen. Their whole ethos and philosophies were diametrically opposed. Dave Scott was the all-American athlete. He'd grown up the high school and college sports star, playing basketball, football, and swimming, and then turned his attention to triathlon. He competed in his first Hawaii Ironman in 1980, which he won, finishing almost two hours ahead of the previous year's winning time. The race was broadcast on the ABC Network, and his incredible skill, tenacity, and speed captivated viewers. This race and his performance in it are widely credited as the spark that lit the fire of modern triathlon. Dave Scott was the textbook athlete, with a rigorous scientific approach to training, racing, and nutrition.

Mark Allen was everything that Dave Scott was not—neither better nor worse, just different. Mark Allen always considered himself a regular person. He had no formal run training, and his cycling experience prior to Ironman mainly came from riding his bike as a practical means of getting to college and back. He entered his first Hawaii Ironman in 1982 with only six months of coaching, and it took six more years before he truly cracked the secret of Ironman. Mark Allen approached Ironman with an entirely different focus. He saw it as a mental and spiritual journey more than a physical ordeal, and despite his immense fitness he spent as much time training his mind as he did his body.

Triathlon was a very small world back in those days. Mark Allen and Dave Scott had lined up against each other a number of times before that Iron War in 1989. Scott won the Ironman World Championships against Allen five times prior to that epic race, and along the way they had built up one of the most intense and hard-fought rivalries ever seen in the sport. They both came into that '89 race on the back of their best seasons ever in the sport. Given his history, Dave Scott was tipped to win by a nose. But when Allen lined up next to Scott on that morning, he believed he had solved the Ironman equation, and he now knew how to reverse Dave Scott's winning streak.

The race got off to a shaky start. State governor John Waihee, who was tasked with officially starting the race, accidentally fired the blast from the canon early. There was a mad dash as unprepared athletes who were still warming up scrambled for the starting line. Mark Allen and Dave Scott were both caught off guard, but were excellent swimmers, and accelerated off the line like they were racing a sprint, not a 260-kilometer Ironman. They swam side by side, reaching the bike transition together, just a minute or two behind the fastest swimmers in the pack.

They mounted their bikes and began a two-man war of attrition. It was the first time in the Ironman's history that it had truly become a race, and suddenly the world sat up and paid attention. Scott's strategy was simple: race, and race hard. Go out full blast, and make sure the others can't hold on. Allen, on the other hand, played a mental game. In his opinion, the race only started at the six-hour mark, nearly three quarters of the way through. Until then he needed to stay calm and stay focused. Scott rode strongly, and immediately put a lead on Allen. In a postrace interview Scott said his plan was to dominate the bike field, and that he'd left Allen in his dust. Mark Allen saw things very differently. He was playing the long game. He saw no value in trying to outride Scott on the bike. It was a waste of energy. It was better to keep Scott close but not force the pace and to save his energy for the run. His plan was to lull Scott into a false sense of security, only to strike when the time became critical. It was a dangerous strategy—letting Scott put some distance between the two of them meant that he had a cushion when Allen finally attacked. But saving himself until that final strike was Allen's only chance.

They arrived at the bike-to-run transition, Dave Scott leading. His plan, and his hope, was that he could maintain that cushion of time and distance between himself and Mark Allen and prevent a head-to-head battle on the run. Allen wasn't going to let that happen. When he got off his bike, he was still feeling fresh. Allen had trained for this moment, both mentally and physically. He'd set the trap, and now he was preparing to let it spring.

The two athletes ran shoulder to shoulder, cresting the hill out of transition together. Both Allen and Scott had blank, distant stares on their faces. They were both summoning their inner reserves. It was now going to be a battle of wills as much as physical strength. They ran the next forty kilometers side by side, each testing the other's resolve with attack after attack, pushing the pace to the limit of possibility. They both knew it was going to come down to the last couple of kilometers, a race of many hours where mere minutes and seconds were going to decide the victor.

Dave Scott pushed, and pushed again. This had always been his strategy. Turn up the heat until nobody else can stay in the kitchen. Every kilometer his pace increased, rapidly approaching a breaking point. Mark Allen held on, running off Dave Scott's shoulder, patiently waiting. Allen knew that Scott was a strong flat surface runner, but he wasn't as strong uphill. Allen also knew that there was one more uphill, only a kilometer or two from the finishing line. He knew he was leaving his final attack until very late in the game. There would be no room for error and no chance for another try if the plan didn't work. They came around that last corner, trailed by an entourage of official race motorcycles, stewards, and camera crews. And when Dave Scott least expected it, Mark Allen sprung his trap.

Allen summoned up the last of his remaining strength from deep within for one final push, and attacked that hill with everything he had. Scott could see a gap opening up. First it was one meter, then two, then ten. Scott knew it was over. He had no riposte. His energy was drained and his body was spent.

Mark Allen didn't look back. He grabbed a small American flag from a spectator and held it high as he ran down the finishing straight, surrounded by a raucous crowd. His face was a mixture of exhaustion and elation, his lips curled into a small, awkward smile. He never was one for crowds, and yet he'd just sealed his place in the triathlon history books.

Allen looked up at the clock and realized he'd shattered the Ironman world record, previously held by Dave Scott. Possibly more importantly, he'd shattered any lingering self-doubt he'd had about his credentials as a world-class athlete. It had taken him seven tough years to crack, but now that he knew the secret, he would go on to win the Ironman World Championship five more times.

In keeping with his humility, Mark Allen gave a postrace tribute to Dave Scott that day. He lauded Scott as the greatest of all Ironmen, and anyone who beat Dave was only borrowing the title from him.

Yet again, the sport of triathlon was changed forever.

—⚒—

I'm sure the length of that journey in the Holden station wagon to the start of our seventh and final marathon was magnified by the nerves and the unpleasant realization that the longer Dave drove, the longer we were going to have to run. I looked at my watch and realized it was getting very late. I was starting to wonder whether Dave was trying to wind us up by taking the extra-long scenic route, or whether he was as disoriented as we were. I was about to discreetly sneak a look at the Gregory's Street Atlas at my feet, when Dave suddenly announced flatly that we'd arrived, and turned into a car-parking area adjacent to the UTS Haberfield Rowing Club. The club was a small but modern two-story building, sitting on prime riverfront real estate. The upper floor was entirely devoted to recreation and dining, dark and quiet now, the last of the revelers having left hours ago. The lower floor was all action, with large bay doors opened and floodlights casting a glare over stored rowing boats and sculls of all shapes and sizes.

I thanked Dave for the ride and lumbered over toward the bright lights, looking around for Trilby and my dad, but it seemed they hadn't arrived yet.

As it happened, they never did arrive before the race. They actually got lost on the way to the starting point. Not sure what else to do, I picked up a small disposable plastic cup of sports drink and wandered around looking a little overwhelmed.

The media had clearly been alerted to our presence, and reporters from different outlets jostled and rejigged their equipment, trying to capture an angle that would simultaneously cut through the darkness of the lake while not getting blinded by the floodlights. Throw together a combination of international reporters, the local logistics staff, curious bystanders, and onlookers, and it made for quite the carnival atmosphere. Partygoers talked excitedly, punctuated with the occasional loud laugh or back slap. New friends and old. The only people who weren't in the mood for a party were the runners. We were all filled with the ironic combination of not wanting to start and yet wishing it was over.

Doug was surrounded by his entourage of friends and family, and was excitedly chirping away about the week he'd had as the television cameras watched. It was his moment, and he'd earned it. These kind of moments are best left unshared. I wandered off into the night, hoping for a few minutes' peace and quiet to steel my nerves against the upcoming onslaught.

I sat on a rock wall next to the water's edge and tried to collect my thoughts. I had walked down a path next to the wall with an icon of a jogger and a cyclist stenciled in white paint. Well, I guess I'd stumbled on to the run course.

I sat and thought about nothing and about everything. I tried to avoid thinking about the upcoming race. That would only serve to build anxiety. Anyway, since I had no idea where the course would go or what would happen, there didn't seem much point in making foolhardy guesses and suppositions. The most effective choice right now was to work on what I could control. Try to stretch out those tight tendons and massage some blood back into the limp muscles. Eat a sports bar. I had an all-natural nut and date bar in my pocket; that would provide slow-release energy and keep me going, without being too heavy. Sit and let the brain idle in neutral for a while. Soon enough there would be plenty to occupy my thoughts.

Out of the corner of my eye I noticed a tall, thin man shyly walking toward me. I really didn't feel like talking to a random stranger, and I wasn't quite in the right frame of mind for an interview.

"Dave? Is that you?" the stranger gently called.

That voice. That sounded vaguely familiar.

"Uh. Hi?" I replied.

The stranger picked up his pace slightly, coming close enough for me to finally make out his face. Toby Store. One of my oldest friends. In fact, he was my oldest friend. I'd known Toby since we were eight years old, classmates in junior school. We used to get up to mischief together, but truth be told Toby was as harmless as I was—none of the trouble really amounted to much more than smoking a purloined cigarette behind the school sheds or cutting a class. We'd once skipped a whole day of school together. I remember we were so concerned about getting spotted and caught by a teacher that we spent the day in a public car park beneath the Hornsby shopping center. By the end of the day hanging around in a basement we both realized we probably would have had more fun if we'd just gone to school like we should have.

"Toby. Bloody hell. Is that you?"

There was a brief moment when I thought I must have finally cracked and was now seeing things. I hadn't seen Toby in years, and we only spoke on the rarest of occasions. However, the ties that bind old friends bind strongly. I'd always be there for Toby, as he was now for me. I had to smile. It was a truly pleasant surprise that, at least for a moment, absorbed me in a spell of reminiscence, allowing me to forget about my current anxieties.

Toby wandered up and sat on the wall.

"How are you doing, man?" he asked calmly.

Toby was a mellow soul, a quiet and easy-going character who didn't seem to let the trials and tribulations of day-to-day life affect him. Happy, contented, and relaxed, he was the exact person I needed to see right at this moment, a complete antithesis to my current mental state, and a wonderful counterbalance that would help drag me back into a frame of mind to get through this final ordeal of a marathon.

"Not bad, man," I replied.

A slight flicker of a smile came across his face. He knew me well enough to know that statement was a complete lie.

"So, it seems that you got into running and exercise."

Now it was my turn to smile. "Uh, yeah, I guess so."

We talked for a while as only old friends can. For some reason spending time with Toby didn't leave me with that same feeling of pressure as I would have had with any other friend or training partner. Anyone else would have discussed the race, what I'd seen, my ranking position, how I was going to run today, my plan of attack, how I was going to win. Toby didn't even mention the race. For all of his affable facade he was also a deft judge of character, and he knew which buttons didn't need to be pressed. And frankly speaking, I suspect he really didn't care about whether I won. He wanted me to succeed and achieve, but Toby never really saw the world in terms of winners and losers; just being there and experiencing it was enough. I honestly couldn't say whether we sat for five minutes or thirty, but I came away feeling emotionally refreshed.

I was jolted out of my recollections of the past by a bright shining light focused on the two of us. A television crew were standing a little way down the path back toward the rowing club. They'd done well to hold off for so long, and they'd definitely done their best to give Toby and me some time to chat, but it appeared they'd finished all of their other interviews and discussions. Their report wouldn't be complete without speaking to the guy who was currently in the lead.

I turned to Toby.

"I better go take care of this. Thanks for coming. I'm in Sydney for a few days. Let's catch up over the weekend if I can still walk."

"Go well, man," he replied with a nod and another gentle smile.

I walked over to the reporter, who greeted me with a friendly smile and a handshake while his cameraman fiddled with the intensely bright LED spotlight panel mounted to the top of the camera. I couldn't help but smile as the reporter and I discussed all of the race subjects that Toby had cleverly avoided, the two conversations contrasting yet complementing, yin and yang.

A secret signal must have been sent at around half past eleven in the evening. Organizational staff and logistics crews stopped their buzzing and arranging, onlookers fell quiet, and my fellow runners and I had gravitated toward the large bay doors of the UTS Haberfield Rowing Club. As a group we all seemed to have come to an unspoken consensus that it was time to get going.

Dave the local logistics organizer stood on a small grassy mound near the carpark.

"Alright. Everyone here? Good. I'll make this short." He spoke with quiet calm authority.

"You're going to run four loops around Iron Cove, and then you're going to run into the city.

"Each runner has a guide on a bike. They're from the local cycling club, so thanks to them all for coming out tonight to help. They know who their runner is. They'll come and find you now."

With that, the race briefing was over. We all stood there awkwardly, like the new kids standing at the front of the gym class waiting to be picked for the team, each needing to feel wanted, but trying not to show any emotion or apprehension. The runners and riders paired off to shake hands and spend a few minutes getting to know one another. And in a strange parody of my school days, yet again I was the last kid standing on that line, waiting for acceptance. As I started to feel really uncomfortable, Dave the organizer sauntered up.

"Dave? I'm Dave. You're with me."

I smiled. Dave was the kind of guy you couldn't help but like. He didn't waste words, he didn't tolerate fools, but I got the distinct impression that he was a person I could rely on to lead me around the course. This would be perfect. I wasn't looking to have a chitchat and to be honest, I wasn't looking to make a friend; neither was Dave. He was here to help get me over the line, I was here to get the race done. We were a team. And what's more, being the organizer I figured he would be the best informed about the route and anything to watch out for.

Dave walked over to an old rusty cruiser bike leaning up against the side of the path: nine-speed rear cassette, double-ring crank on the front, rim brakes, and a basket on the handlebars. It was superb, a time-warp from the eighties. I don't think they've even made nine speeds for the last two decades. The only thing it was missing was a playing card wedged into the back wheel arch to rub against the spokes and make that clattering "engine" sound we all thought was so cool when we were nine years old. Still, I figured at the speed I was running he wasn't going to need a racing bike.

Dave grabbed a couple of bottles of water and a bottle of Coke and put them into his basket.

"Off we go then," he said flatly.

—w—

Twelve runners stood at the starting line, facing westwards away from the club. We each held up our country's flag, provided to us by the race organizer. There's a superb photo of the starting line that was taken by a photographer from Reuters. I am standing bang in the middle, and although I felt physically wrecked, I had a big smile on my face. Nearly all of us did. We'd made it this far. We were nearly there, nearly finished now. Uma and Krishna from India stood directly on my right; James, Ted, and Jon were together all sharing a British flag on my immediate left. The others all fanned out on either side, happy to be at that final starting line.

There was only one person in the photo who wasn't smiling. Doug was standing on the far right, looking directly at me with an intense stare. Not anger, not frustration, not fear. He was sizing me up, steeling himself, planning. Planning how to leave every fiber of his being on that race track, sacrifice every element of himself, and claw back those forty-five minutes to win in front of a home crowd. This starting line wasn't a celebration for Doug, at least not yet. Celebrations would only be determined by how the events of the next few hours played out. We were all acting like the race was nearly over. Only Doug was smart enough to realize that the real race hadn't yet begun.

Richard Donovan, the race series organizer, raised his right arm, lifting the starting air horn high. He waited a few seconds to build excitement. Television cameras recorded silently under the bright self-contained spotlights mounted above their lenses and banks of dials and switches. Organizers, supporters, and the occasional curious bystander lined the path for the first fifty meters. For a few moments, everything was silent. Time seemed to hang. Finally and abruptly, the silence was punctuated by the blast from that air horn. Time suddenly realized it had been unpaused. The next minute or two was played out at double speed in an urgent need to catch back up. Spectators shouted and cheered. The crowd parted down the center. The guides mounted their bikes. And for one last time, we ran.

Doug set the early lead with a blistering pace right off the blocks. I figured he had to—he was in front of a home audience, and he needed to be the local boy made good. To give him his credit though, he did look good. His stride and gait were clean and natural, far removed from the lumpy, loping style my injuries were forcing on me. Injuries be damned, I knew that I had to keep up. I was surprised to realize I wasn't the only one. James was running next to me, sharing a look of strain on his face.

It was at that moment that it finally struck me. Everything was in play, and everything was left to play for. I'd occupied myself with thoughts of winning and holding off Doug. All that time, James hadn't given up on second. Heck, maybe he hadn't given up on a win. James was smart; he was probably the best race strategist of the lot of us. He knew I was injured, and he knew Doug had a tendency to go out hard and then blow up. A smart man, a calculating man, well, he might just surprise everyone.

The course started with a short dog's leg run up the shoreline and then across a road levee over a narrow section of the bay. There was a hairpin turn at the end of the levee and the course doubled back on itself, passing the rowing club for a second time and continuing onto a much larger loop of the other side of the bay. As we passed the rowing club that second time, we picked up our bike escorts. Unexpectedly, we also picked up a large contingent of support runners, most of whom were Doug's friends.

The three of us continued to drag out the early lead, pulling away from the second pack of Big Jim, Pierre, and Marcelo, followed fairly closely by the remaining runners. The path was fairly narrow, weaving and bobbing close to the shoreline. There was little talk; the race took all of our focus. It was a difficult course to race. The further we drifted from the roads and traffic the darker the path became, with only an occasional light acting as a beacon to guide us from point to point. A half-moon hung high in the evening sky, but was too dim to provide much more than a silvery glint from the water in the bay.

The three of us ran in a line, with Doug leading out and James bringing up the rear. I was sandwiched in the middle at a forced pace. I would have rather set the pace, but I contented myself that sometimes it's easier to sit in and not think too much. Dave, the local organizer and my race guide, led out in front, a blinking red tail light acting as a hypnotic beacon for us runners. Following behind James was a cavalcade of supporters, both official and unofficial. I hoped most of them would lose interest after a few more minutes.

The tapering path made it difficult to pass one another, and running side by side would have risked an accidental excursion into the bay as we jostled around a corner. But the serpentine path wasn't the only reason for our silence. This race had a very different feeling from the camaraderie of the past few days. It was the glaringly obvious but unspoken truth: today we were nothing more than competitors.

A little over a kilometer and a half down the road from the Haberfield Rowing Club, Dave waved his left hand, signaling a turn. He continued up onto a suspension footbridge that had clearly been designed by an architect, large planks of treated timber suspended from raw steel cables and trellises. For a structure that appeared so ornate it was remarkably solid, with little give or sway yielding from our footfalls, but the incline to the middle was taxing on already tired legs.

Dave turned sharply left as he reached the opposite side of the footbridge, continuing along the shoreline running track on the opposite side of the bay. The downward slope of the second half of the bridge allowed no relief, only serving to allow Doug to increase his pace further. James was struggling to hold on, and I wasn't feeling much better.

It took another kilometer or so of winding riverside path to convince James that this wasn't his day. I looked over my shoulder and he was a couple of meters back, looking strained. When I checked a minute later he was fifty meters back. The next time I looked I couldn't see him. Well, I guess that just left two. The race wasn't over, though, not by a long shot, and for all I knew James could have been playing the smart game, the long game, conserving his energy and waiting for the two of us to bury each other in a deep hole of fatigue. By my reckoning, the look on his face said otherwise. He was spent. He'd made a play for it, but he'd come to the conclusion that it was better to hold on to third, and a podium, than overstretch his abilities and have now fourth-place Marcelo give him an unpleasant surprise.

As we continued around the bay, the running track parted ways with the river and slowly climbed up the embankment, joining with a footpath on the side of the road. Two hundred meters further we split from the road again, descending down what appeared to be a private driveway and back onto the river front. The climb made my hamstrings burn, and the descent inflicted equal discomfort on my quadriceps. We were still running at a mad pace. Something needed to be done. I needed to try to try to talk some common sense into Doug.

"Doug, we need to pace it. We're going way too hard on these hills. We've got a marathon to run."

Doug didn't reply, but he did give a slight nod. He was feeling good, but he wasn't feeling invincible. We were about five kilometers into the race, less than one eighth of the way through, and we were both running at our physical limits. Our efforts were starting to catch up with both of us. We'd outrun nearly all of the friends and family supporters; our only company now was our bike escorts. I mentally breathed a quiet sigh of relief as Doug slowed down a little.

Once more Dave the local race director peeled his bike off to the right, joining a side-track that climbed sharply, circling up the side of the embankment and onto the road, doubling back on itself as we ascended to meet a bridge crossing the bay. As we ran across the bridge Dave broke his self-imposed silence.

"Last lap you blokes will go the other way up that hill and on to the city and finish line," he commented matter-of-factly.

Half of me didn't want to think about the last lap right now. It was too far away and there was too much that needed to be accomplished before then. The other half wanted to hang that mental image as a carrot right in front of my nose to keep me going. I kept telling myself I only had to see this point three more times ever in my life—just keep going. Three more times did strike me as quite a lot though.

We turned at the end of the bridge and ran back across the river. Doug started speeding up again, his pace building as he came down the embankment and back on to the shoreline. It was a test. I knew then and there that he was trying to quietly assess how much I had left in my tank, how far I could go. A test that needed a response. Doug was running very well. I'm not sure where he found the strength after such an intense week, but he was well on the way to running the fastest marathon of the whole week. It was uncanny. I couldn't fall off the back, at least not yet. I knew a win today was going to be unlikely, but a win today wasn't my primary concern. The only thing that mattered to me was a win overall. It was going to be a fine balance between running fast enough to not lose more than that forty-five-minute difference, while at the same time not overdoing it and blowing up in the process.

I figured the best way to answer Doug's subtle challenge was to up the ante. I was injured, but he didn't know how badly. For better or worse I was still the race leader and the pack boss. It was time to act like it.

"Let's run this flat bit harder, then take it easy on that hilly section up and down from the road," I suggested.

My plan was to slow the race down when we got to the hills. That was going to be the most taxing on the legs, and by the look of things Doug had a lot more left in his muscles than I did in mine. Again Doug remained silent, but nodded in acceptance or agreement.

It wasn't long before we came across James running the other way, followed by a procession of the other runners, all fairly evenly spaced, each accompanied by their cyclist. Last was Marianna, painful and hobbling, but resolutely smiling. I remember thinking right then that she was the only one of us who I guaranteed was going to finish. With what she'd been through already there was no stopping her now.

—⟋⟍⟍—

Doug put on a sudden burst of speed when we got close to the architectural suspension bridge, and it didn't take me long to realize why. A cluster of friends and well-wishers were waiting there, letting out a raucous cheer as he passed them in the lead. Six or seven of his friends started running with us again, joining for the return leg to the UTS Haberfield Rowing Club.

As I approached the club I heard a familiar cheer. "Go Davy." There was only one person in the world who called me Davy. He had done so since before I could walk, never mind run. It was my dad. I guessed he'd finally found the race start. I mustered the effort for a wan smile. It was great to see him. I'd been feeling a little outgunned and outnumbered on this marathon.

"Trilby is out on her bike. She'll meet you," he yelled.

"Thanks," I mumbled.

I stopped quickly to grab a drink from the table set up by the organizers. It may have been the middle of the night but the weather was still unpleasantly warm and muggy. I was dripping sweat and cramping was going to be a risk if I wasn't careful. I looked around and couldn't see Toby, but I knew he had to work and it was getting close to one o'clock in the morning. We'd planned to catch up the day after, and I'd told him not to wait around.

It wasn't until I started running again that I realized Doug hadn't stopped. I looked up ahead and caught a glimpse of him around a hundred meters up the road as he passed under a streetlight. His friends had thought this through, and they'd been quite clever. One of them was now running next to him with a drink bottle, passing it every so often for a drink. That meant he didn't have to waste time on drinks stops. Smart.

It also dawned upon me that only four of his six running friends were with him. Two of them were now running with me. Maybe they'd also stopped for a drink, I guessed. A young female runner fell into line with me, running stride for stride on my left as we continued up to the levee.

"Hi, you must be David," she offered.

I replied with a weak smile. I didn't want to be brusque but I was somewhere between physically exhausted and mentally drained, and being sociable wasn't high on my list of priorities.

She talked for a while about how she was a friend of Doug's, she'd watched the race and how interesting it had been, trying to drum up some conversation. I'd be the first to admit that conversation on a run can be fantastic. It can engage the mind, allowing thoughts to drift and time to pass. Today, I didn't have the stamina to chat. I needed to just focus on the race. My replies were limited to an assortment of smiles, nods and the occasional "Uh-huh."

"You know, Doug's looking really strong today," she continued.

"Uh-huh," I replied.

"I dunno, he's not that far behind in time is he?" She let it hang before proceeding. "It's about thirty minutes or something right? The way he's running, it's going to be close."

It can be difficult to make accurate assessments when you're deeply emotionally attached to the subject, and I've thought about her conversation and the overall situation many times. I've tried to convince myself that I took it the wrong way. That it was an innocent comment by somebody who wanted the best for her friend, somebody who completely lacked tact.

But at the time, I saw red. Bright red.

As I let her words sink in, I started building a mental picture, an assessment of facts as I knew them. In my mind I put the pieces together the way I saw they fit. I might have been right; I might have been wrong. The way I saw it, these people had come this evening to run. They were dressed in running gear so they'd clearly planned to be out on the race course. They had waited at that architectural suspension bridge and then they'd run back to the rowing club with us. They had drink bottles with them, so they'd planned to continue through the support station without stopping, even though it was only a kilometer or so from where they'd started. They had split up when Doug and I had split up, most of them continuing on to pace him and give him supplies, but a few of them hanging back with what I now imagined were less noble intentions. The way I figured it, they'd hung back with two objectives: to sow the seeds of self-doubt in my mind and to pace me down so I wasn't running as fast. It was a calculated move.

I'll never know whether any of my assertions were true. I'll never know whether I was emotionally brittle after one of the toughest weeks of my life, and my judgment was sorely affected. I'll never know.

At the time I was furious. This was not fair, I told myself. It was way beyond not fair. Pacing in a marathon may be acceptable, but purposely splitting the pack and intentionally advantaging one runner while disadvantaging the other was very far removed from fair pacing. If my conclusions were correct, their actions were not OK by a long stretch.

"Don't want to talk anymore," were my first and final words to her.

I'm not sure if she replied. I'd put in my headphones to try to block out any outside interference. My blood was boiling. I knew I needed to keep my mouth shut. Any more I said wouldn't have been helpful to my cause, and in any case I needed to save every drop of energy I had left. I knew I needed to focus. I knew I needed to play it carefully. If I ran off at speed to prove a point, I was just as likely to overcook myself as I was to catch him. But I knew that now I had a mission. I desperately wanted to use her words against her, bury them deep in the pit of my stomach and allow them to smolder away, fueling a furnace of angry energy that was going to pull me through when this race became tough. I never liked to race angry; it made for rash choices. Yet I told myself today was different. I told myself today I was going to give them a demonstration of the law of unintended consequences.

—ɯ—

Doug rounded the hairpin turn at the end of the levee a short distance ahead, and by the time we were back at the rowing club, we were pretty much neck and neck again. I've never harbored any ill will toward Doug for the episode with his support runner friends, not on that day nor ever since. I truly believe he had no idea. It wasn't like him to plan something like that, and even if he wanted to I don't think he could have planned that far ahead, especially not knowing the course or the race variables. In reflection maybe his friends didn't specifically plan it either. I think a set of circumstances presented themselves, and they wanted to help their friend. Sometimes a situation just plays out the way it plays out. Sometimes people make the wrong choices with the right intentions. But when I got to the drinks station at the rowing club, I wasn't going to make the same mistake twice. I grabbed a drink as I was running through and didn't even slow my stride.

His running buddies pulled to the side again at the suspension bridge, leaving us with just the blinking red tail light of Dave the local organizer's bike, and

Doug's bike escort bringing up the rear. The pace hadn't let off much, and my swollen and crunchy right ankle was really starting to throb despite the ibuprofen. On a more positive note, it wasn't too long before I got some welcome relief in the form of Trilby, sitting on her bike at the side of the embankment near the road waiting for us.

"Good work guys," she yelled as we ran past.

I smiled and nodded, somewhat amused by the contrast of how enthusiastic and happy she looked, and how unenthusiastic and woeful I was feeling.

We continued along the shore and up and over the far bridge, running shoulder to shoulder. It wasn't until we were nearly back at the architectural suspension bridge that we saw third-place James, a testament to how fast the two of us must have been running.

Doug's runners rejoined us at the suspension bridge again and ran the dog's leg loop up past the rowing club, across the levee, and back again, but this time were much more sedate and well behaved. I figured maybe they'd started to realize that Doug was running out of time to make up that deficit. Maybe they had decided the last time we'd run together wasn't handled in the best way. Maybe they were tired themselves. It was close to two in the morning after all.

This time we both stopped for a drink at the rowing club aid station. It was a brief truce in a war of brinkmanship. We gave each other a nod and continued on. Winding path. Architectural suspension bridge. Path up the embankment to the road. Wave at Trilby. Path back down to the foreshore. Steep curved path up to the road. Cross the bridge. Turn around and head all the way back again. I hadn't even realized it but I was subconsciously counting off the landmarks. When the chips are down I guess you rely on what works.

Doug was still surging at times. He seemed to relish the hills, putting on a little turn of speed each time we hit an incline. The testing continued. We were over a third of the way through, and we were still neck and neck. I knew I just had to hold on as long as I could. Leave as little of the race as possible for him to cut into my overall time. The longer I could hold out, the more difficult it was going to be for him to make up those forty-five minutes. But there was still a long way to go, and I knew things were bound to happen. I knew I needed to stick to my original plan of focusing on winning the week, let come what may today.

Doug was no fool, though, and he knew as well as I did that his time was limited. He knew what he wanted, and piece by piece he was assembling a plan to get it. Each time he pushed up those short climbs I fell a few meters behind, and Doug was starting to realize that the once strong runner was now looking rather vulnerable. The title of pack boss was being challenged, repeatedly prodded and tested to look for weakness. Each time he attacked, I was weakened a little further. We all knew that if the crown fell it was going to fall hard, and I'd no longer have any control over race pace, drink stops, or strategy. It would snowball away from me and then I'd be the one fighting for position.

I should have seen it. I should have anticipated it in advance. But I didn't. There was only ever one place where he'd make a move, where he'd have the confidence and the support to break away and hold his lead. In retrospect, it was so bleedingly obvious.

We reached the architectural suspension bridge, and it was like a gun went off in Doug's head. He suddenly and unexpectedly changed gears, slipping into a ferocious pace, then used the slight uphill incline of the bridge to put a sizable gap into me before I even knew what'd hit me. He continued down the other side of the footbridge, using momentum and the gravity of the downhill to stretch his legs out into wide lunging strides, further increasing his lead. His friends cheered. This is what they'd come to see. They'd hoped for it on the first lap, but they'd had to wait until the third. We were seventeen kilometers in. Maybe there was enough time, they thought.

Doug's bike escort battled to squeeze past Dave and I, then to navigate through the throng of supporters. He was as taken by surprise as I was. Doug's friends then all fell into line with him, running with him and offering him support. This time it was all for one—they all wanted to be part of the breakaway, and nobody remained behind to run with me, for better or worse.

And when the crown finally fell, it shattered. Being left behind in such a spectacular fashion was gutting. The remaining emotional and physical energy hemorrhaged out, leaving my body feeling broken and confused. Only Dave the organizer was left, and suddenly everything felt very silent.

The restrained cheers from my dad fell on deaf ears when I ran past the rowing club. I was on autopilot. I knew I needed to keep going, but I could feel my pace dropping. As I came up to the start of the levee, Doug and his entourage passed the other way. There was no recognition on his face, just a thousand-yard stare. His race had now just begun.

You never realize how important a positive mental attitude is until it's gone. Part of me knew this moment was coming. Even before I started the race today I had a very strong feeling I wasn't going to win. Some might say I'd talked myself out of winning today before the starting horn sounded. I'm not sure I'd agree. I knew I was carrying injuries. I knew I was tired. I knew I wasn't looking as good as Doug, or quite a few of the other runners. And I knew I only cared about one thing: winning the overall race. Today's marathon was only a piece of the puzzle. I knew I had to play it smart to try to hold off Doug for as long as I could, and then minimize the damage when he did take off.

I knew all of this, and yet when it happened it felt so very different from what I'd expected. It wasn't just a plan anymore; it wasn't a strategic retreat. I was getting thoroughly trounced, and it hurt. The night seemed to become darker. My feet became heavier. The track became steeper. My injuries ached and throbbed with a newfound intensity. I was slowing down, and I couldn't pick my pace up despite my best efforts.

The fourth loop was hard. It was the toughest time I'd had all week. Madrid had been hard. Morocco has been awful in parts. Heck, every race had its moments. But I'd always had someone to share the good times and the bad. Now I was alone, following the blinking red light of one of the nicest but least talkative people I'd met. Time was slipping through my fingers. I looked down at my watch. I was running at over four-hour marathon pace. And then my friend Richard Hall's words during our phone call earlier in the day came back to me: "He's got to run a three twenty marathon or faster. Which he's never done. You've got to run a four hour or slower. Which you've never done."

Well, never until now old friend.

Everything I'd fought for this week was steadily running away from me, at a three-fifteen marathon pace.

—m—

Dave finally broke the silence.

"You don't have to catch him. You just need to keep running mate. You'll be alright."

He was a man of few words, but when he opened his mouth he knew exactly what to say. He was right, I figured. This was part of the plan. Just keep going. His words helped, but they weren't a solution. I was going slower and slower, settling into not much more than a shuffling jog. The kilometers were ticking over painfully slowly, both literally and figuratively. Maybe my mind was playing tricks with me, but my right ankle felt like it was burning, making me imagine a crack in the ankle bone rubbing back and forth, back and forth with every step. The only good news was it was so painful that I'd forgotten about the wails of suffering from my knees, tendons, and muscles.

By the time I was heading down that foreshore for the last time I was at a pace that wasn't much more than a fast walk. My candle was nearly extinguished, and there was still over fourteen kilometers to go. Trilby had packed her bike in the back of my father's car by the time I came back up the embankment. She hopped back across the road to wave as I passed. My face clearly told the story. She gave me no false assurances or claims about my appearance this time. She knew I was in trouble. It was time for damage control. She knew the train was derailing, and she needed to get it back on the tracks. She was all business.

"I'm smoked," I said to her wearily as I approached.

She started to jog beside me, with Dave leading us out a few meters ahead.

She looked at her watch, then looked back up at me.

"Look, he's eight minutes up the road," she stated analytically. "You've got about fourteen kilometers to go. You currently have a thirty-seven-minute lead. He has to make over two minutes per kilometer on you. You know you can hold that off. I'm driving to the finish line, then I'll ride back out and meet you, bring you home. You need to decide what you're going to do next. Oh, and I love you."

With that she turned around and jogged back to her car.

I was somewhere between awestruck and dumbfounded. I think I was just given a talk about toughening up from my wife. She always knew exactly what to say, and yet again she didn't disappoint. It was probably the only thing that could have kept me going. A hard, unemotional analysis of the facts and an ultimatum. Make a choice; it's yours to win or lose.

I continued my shuffling jog behind the blinking red light of Dave's bike, my face blank. I might have appeared still dazed, but on the inside my mind was racing, digesting the new information and weighing up the choices I had just been presented.

The facts were these. I was feeling almost totally exhausted, and my pace was dropping. The right ankle was becoming excruciatingly painful, and the other injuries weren't much better. Doug was eight minutes ahead. I started doing the calculations in my head. He'd left me at seventeen kilometers. We had a little over fourteen kilometers left in the forty-two kilometer race. That means that Doug and I had been separate for the last ten kilometers, which meant he was making about a minute and a quarter on me per kilometer. I figured that wasn't too bad. However, I knew I was slowing down, and I knew that my injuries were worsening. That time gap could easily increase to two and a half minutes per kilometer, which would mean that he'd be able to gain enough time to take the overall win.

I only had two options. First, I could be sensible. Slow down my pace to a fast walk and jog shuffle. Protect and preserve that ankle. Hold myself together. Get to the finish line. I wouldn't be in first place, but I'd be in second, or at worst in third. That means I'd be on the podium. And that's a pretty amazing result. Me, the guy who only a few years back considered exercise to mean flexing my bicep to lift a pint of beer to my lips, would now be on the podium of a most amazing race around the world. I'd had unforgettable experiences; I'd seen and experienced situations that I never thought possible. Not only had I traveled the world in a week, I'd run seven marathons in the process. I could hold my head high and be proud of having done something that very few people in the world will ever be able to say they've accomplished. No one would be upset with me, I told myself, they'd understand. They'd be amazed that I was even able to finish.

Or.

Or I could be foolish. I could be rash. I could throw all caution to the wind. I could go for it. If I did, there was a chance I could win. But there was a better than even chance that I could break. That ankle felt like it was one bad footfall away from a complete crack and split. If that happened, I could forget about running; I couldn't even walk on a fully broken ankle. The race would be over in one cruel moment. I would have to withdraw, quit. And I would forevermore be known as the only guy who couldn't do it. The guy who didn't finish the last marathon. The guy who wasn't strong enough or smart enough to run seven marathons on seven continents in seven days. I'd return home a failure, and although all of my friends would be kind enough to remain positive, I'd spend my foreseeable future explaining to people what went wrong and why I wasn't good enough. However, I knew that wasn't truly the bitter pill that would burn me deep inside. It was the fact that I'd have to spend the foreseeable future explaining to myself what went wrong and why I wasn't good enough.

Sometimes a decision is easy. It isn't really even a decision. I knew the answer even before I'd finished weighing up the options in my mind. I've always been a fool.

I was going to go for it.

—⟋⟍⟍—

I started thinking about everything that had happened during the week. Every moment I had suffered, and every time I'd been filled with pride and satisfaction. I thought about what it would mean if I turned my back on all of that now. I also thought about how much a win would mean to me, and to those people who'd come out to help me. One by one I thought about everybody who had thrown their hat into the ring to help me, train me, encourage me, support me. My cycling friends who took me into their circle when most others probably would have had a chuckle at my expense and continue riding—Richard Hall, Tim Kremer, Jan Skovgaard, Matt Baile, and later Steve Purcell. My coach, Nigel Gray, and coach Max Shute before him. My true friends like Toby Store and Mark Peters. My parents Tim and Lindsay Gething, who spent forty-odd years up to this point never giving up on me, despite the regular frustrations I imparted to them. My two daughters, Madeleine and Amelia, who gleefully supported their daddy's crazy adventures and rather unsocial training schedule, despite the fact it didn't seem to be what other more normal daddies did in their spare time.

But, of course, there was one person who was central to my thoughts: Trilby White, my wife. It was her unexpected but well-deserved reprimand of my behavior a little over seven years ago that started the chain reaction of events that led me to this point. Even more importantly, it was her love, support, acceptance, and unwavering belief in me that actually got me here. She had been beside me every step of the way, and she had also made many sacrifices. I wasn't going to let her down now.

I could feel my resolve building. For the first time that night I was feeling positive. This had to be done. I only needed one more thing. I needed a spark to light the fire. A lick of flame dropped into that dry tinder-box to ignite the inferno. I'll never understand how our minds work, or why they work the way they do, but at that moment I thought about that female support runner who ran next to me a couple of hours ago, seemingly trying to sow the seeds of self-doubt in my mind while slowly reducing my pace. That made me angry. It made me determined. Those negative emotions crossed wires against the positive feelings about all of the people who had supported me, who I now needed to do right by. And as those wires came close enough to touch the energy jumped across in a blinding arc. The spark had been lit, an intense fire started to burn. Enough talk, it was time to go.

—⁓—

I've read stories about runners, especially the great ultrarunners. They talk about achieving a runner's high. Being in the zone. Some kind of feeling that was part spiritual, part out-of-body experience, part euphoria. Personally, I had always thought it was nonsense. Sure, I'd felt great after a good run, and I certainly felt special after a personal best or a win, but I'd never had some wacky mythical high before. I figured people were probably just experiencing a combination of dehydration, physical exhaustion, mental fatigue, and maybe some endorphins and adrenaline, the body's neurochemical coping mechanism.

I couldn't say whether I finally got my taste of the runner's high that night, partly because I can't remember most of what happened after I made that decision to go for it. I can only remember flashes. Mental postcards.

I remember climbing up that hill from the foreshore for the last time, and finally turning right toward the city instead of left.

I remember running down a street with late-night bars and pubs open, revelers in various states of inebriation spilled out on the streets, rubbing their eyes to make sure they weren't hallucinating when an exhausted hollowed-out runner raced past them as fast as his legs would carry him.

I remember running across Pyrmont Bridge in Darling Harbour, meeting Trilby halfway as she was cycling back up from the finish line car park to find me. In my delirious state I still recalled that it was here standing on this bridge with a bottle of Piper Heidsieck Champagne that I proposed to her over fifteen years ago, just before we moved to Hong Kong. How life rolls around in random but uncanny circles. She said she had no idea it was the same place, that was so long ago now. But she did remember the champagne.

I remember her riding beside me for the last few kilometers when I was becoming increasingly unhinged and confused, telling me I was on track and it was going to be OK.

I remember crossing the finish line, under the Sydney Harbour Bridge, my dad standing to one side cheering, Trilby with a tear in her eye, news cameras rolling, flash photographers shooting.

I remember the race organizer telling me I'd won the World Marathon Challenge and giving me the large glass trophy plate and a medal. The moment was a combination of supreme satisfaction and plain relief it was all over.

And I remember urgently handing that glass trophy to my father as I fainted and fell to the ground just to the left of the finishing line.

The next thing I remember is waking up in my hotel room.

EPILOGUE

Hi Anneliese, tell Jeff that I've just traveled 88,000 kilometres, traveled to seven continents in seven days and run seven marathons . . . and in the process possibly set two world records. But I can understand if he's a little too tired to get up.

—My e-mail to an old friend in Sydney, the day after the race, who wanted to postpone a planned breakfast together because he was a little tired from a late night out. Apparently his party days weren't yet behind him. Happily, we ended up having our breakfast reunion as planned.

The press photo shows me out cold, lying on the grassy bank covered in sweat, with my arms wrapped around my head, a very concerned wife on my left side and a very excited cameraman on my right.

Five minutes later, apparently, I came to, although I still don't really remember it. Trilby has told me the story more than once. I'm starting to feel like I now know it well enough to say I can pass on a reasonably accurate version of events. I hauled myself up off the ground into a sitting position and looked around confusedly. The muscles in my legs were involuntarily twitching like they had a life of their own. I tried to get up and stumbled. Somebody grabbed my elbow and held me steady. I did a short postrace interview with Reuters. I don't remember it. Trilby tells me they asked me how I was feeling now that I'd won the World Marathon Challenge, and apparently I simply replied, "I feel f***ed." Unsurprisingly, they didn't use my postrace interview footage, but Trilby tells me it gave everyone a good laugh.

I shook myself off and saw Doug standing about twenty meters back. I walked over to him and gave him a man hug, congratulating him on his outstanding effort today. He'd been a good running companion over the week. We'd had our moments of course, but all said and done we left as friends, both the wiser for having known each other. I thanked Richard Donovan and the other organizers, and we all stood for some photos.

I wanted to wait to see some of the other guys finish, but I didn't have the strength, and Trilby was worried I was going to collapse again. She and my dad decided it was time to get me back to the hotel. My memories of that time are very clouded, but I know my dad and Trilby loaded me into the passenger seat of the car. My dad drove me back and Trilby cycled the bike—there wasn't enough room for her and the bike in the car. I think my dad must have got lost again, because Trilby said she had ridden back to the hotel by the time we got there. I decided it was better not to mention this small fact to my dad on future recollections.

Trilby and I adjourned to our room and my dad to his. My mother was flying into Sydney later in the morning. She was clearly upset to miss the finish and had relied on constant updates from my father, but her travel schedule couldn't be changed. I think she'd secretly hoped we might have got pushed back a day flying out of Antarctica, and she would have made it to the finish, but it was not to be.

I gingerly contorted my aching limbs out of my running clothes and with some satisfaction placed those running clothes into a ziplock bag for the final time on this journey. I had a shower, then lay in bed.

And for the first time in a week, I couldn't sleep.

—⋙—

I slowly recovered my vitality and energy as I rested. After lying for about an hour I realized sleep wasn't going to happen, and my mind started to feel much more clear and alert. I looked at the ceiling for a while, and then, having nothing else to do, I started to write the first page of this story.

Two hours later Trilby's phone rang. It was the *South China Morning Post*. Apparently it was breaking news. They were running pieces on CNN, Reuters, and Al Jazeera, and the media wanted to know the inside story. Trilby patiently sat on the phone at what must have been four in the morning giving interviews and sorting out facts and figure. I was still too dazed to be of any real use. By the time she was off the phone it was almost daybreak. After a short rest, we got changed and ambled across to my father's room to greet my mother when she arrived.

We spent the next day in Sydney, having one last catch-up with my fellow runners and saying our goodbyes, and then spending the rest of the day with family and friends over breakfast, lunch, and dinner dates. As promised, I met up with Toby again that afternoon, and together with his girlfriend, Lynn; Trilby; and my parents, we sat under the Sydney Opera House and drank what tasted like the coolest, most refreshing beers of my life while we watched the sun go down.

It was time to get home, though, and the following morning we arrived at the airport to catch our flight back to Hong Kong. I hobbled through the boarding check-in gate and down the ramp to the plane, Trilby patiently waiting by my side.

I passed the tray of newspapers next to the airplane door. Trilby offhandedly picked up a copy of the *Sunday Post*. She unfolded it to check the headlines.

The front page was running a full centerpiece spread entitled "New World Champion: Hong Kong runner conquers seven marathons on seven continents in seven days," with a big photo of me running the first marathon in Antarctica.

Trilby looked the stewardess in the eye with a broad smile on her face.

"That's my husband."

APPENDIX

The Final Standings

When the dust settled and all were held to account, the race was a resounding success. Despite our personal hurdles, setbacks, and potential problems, we all finished, and we all ran our seven marathons on seven continents in seven days. This is a testament to the physical and mental fortitude of all of the racers, and the meticulous planning and preparation of the organizers and logistics staff.

Overall Rankings for World Marathon Challenge

Rank	Name	Country	Total Time	Average Time
1st	David Gething	HKG	25:36:03	3:39:26
2nd	Douglas Wilson	AUS	26:08:14	3:44:02
3rd	James Love	GBR	28:24:09	4:03:27
4th	Marcelo Alves	BRA	31:11:40	4:27:23
5th	Pierre Wolkonsky	FRA	32:21:56	4:37:25
6th	James Danaher	GBR	33:57:14	4:51:02
7th	Tim Durbin	USA	37:39:18	5:22:45
8th	Jon O'Shea	GBR	37:49:43	5:24:15
9th*	Marianna Zaikova	FIN	40:22:45	5:46:06
10th	Ted Jackson	GBR	45:29:35	6:29:56

Source: www.worldmarathonchallenge.com/html/results/16.html
* First female marathon runner

Detailed Results for Each Marathon

Athlete	Antarctica	South America	North America	Europe	Africa	Asia	Australia
David Gething	03:21:35	03:23:01	03:41:49	03:36:06	04:20:55	03:43:06	03:29:31
Douglas Wilson	03:52:52	03:36:40	03:41:28	03:36:21	04:20:36	03:43:06	03:17:11
James Love	03:56:55	04:06:21	03:46:15	04:07:56	04:36:01	03:54:17	03:56:24
Marcelo Alves	04:10:38	04:20:02	04:04:38	04:37:44	04:43:13	04:42:24	04:33:01
Pierre Wolkonsky	04:08:22	04:03:21	04:21:31	05:00:33	05:32:57	05:21:09	03:54:03
James Danaher	04:53:25	04:54:17	04:19:41	04:31:47	05:57:21	04:27:16	04:53:27
Tim Durbin	04:36:25	05:40:55	05:23:04	05:24:35	05:58:24	05:40:21	04:55:34
Jon O'Shea	05:40:33	04:47:18	04:44:20	04:53:14	06:19:33	05:32:23	05:52:22
Marianna Zaikova*	05:16:55	05:14:34	05:29:31	05:29:31	06:05:50	06:32:45	06:36:08
Ted Jackson	05:59:07	06:22:13	06:36:01	06:16:56	07:45:53	06:17:25	06:12:00

Source: www.worldmarathonchallenge.com/html/results/16.html
* First female athlete in the marathon competition

Rankings for World Half Marathon Challenge

Rank	Name	Country	Total Time	Average Time
1st	Krishna Chigurupati	IND	20:59:38	2:59:57
2nd*	Uma Chigurupati	IND	21:36:43	3:05:15

Source: www.worldmarathonchallenge.com/html/results/16.html
* First female half marathon runner

Detailed Results for Each Half Marathon

Athlete	Antarctica	South America	North America	Europe	Africa	Asia	Australia
Krishna Chigurupati	03:11:36	02:52:29	02:34:40	03:01:12	03:08:46	02:37:01	03:33:54
Uma Chigurupati*	03:15:39	03:05:26	02:41:01	03:05:05	03:08:46	02:46:52	03:33:54

Source: www.worldmarathonchallenge.com/html/results/16.html
* First female athlete in the half marathon competition

NEW WORLD RECORDS SET

David Gething: Fastest cumulative time to complete seven marathons on seven continents in seven days. This record has recently been broken.

David Gething: Fastest marathon ever run on the Antarctic continent. As of publishing, this record still stands.

Marianna Zaikova: Fastest cumulative time to complete seven marathons on seven continents in seven days for a female athlete. This record has recently been broken.

Krishna Chigurupati: Fastest cumulative time to complete seven half marathons on seven continents in seven days. As of publishing, this record still stands.

Krishna and Uma Chigurupati: Fastest husband and wife team to complete seven half marathons on seven continents in seven days. As of publishing, this record still stands.

INDEX

ABOUT THE AUTHOR

The spark that lit the fire—On the approach to middle age, **David Gething** had lived what could optimistically be termed a good life, going out far more than he should, eating, drinking, and certainly living the party life. He was very overweight, unfit, unhealthy, and possibly, inside it all, unhappy. And then came the moment when everything changed. David's wife caught him outside, sneaking a cigarette after he'd promised he'd quit for the umpteenth time. She was not long away from giving birth to their first baby, a daughter. She painted a picture of this child being born with her father, her role model, being unfit and overweight, and asked if that was what he wanted for her, and for himself.

Starting from the bottom—His wall of denial and rationalization came crashing down, and he embarked on his personal race to transform himself into a world-class athlete, starting from scratch to competing in Ironman triathlons up to world championship level, including qualifying for both Ironman 70.3 Las Vegas World Championship and Ironman 140.6 Hawaii World Championship; some of the world's most famous marathons, including the Boston Marathon; and ultramarathons and transcontinental bicycle stage races such as Raid Pyrenees and London-Paris Bike Race. David's transformation culminated with his participation in the 2015 World Marathon challenge, which encompasses seven marathons on seven continents in seven days and which he won, setting two world records in the process.

Making the ordinary extraordinary—David has always prided himself on being an average person. Married with two children, two dogs, a cat, and a regular day job, David has spent years developing a system to juggle and perfect a balance of work life, family life, and sporting life, and trying to make the best out of every situation.

David says, "My story is one that isn't just about racing, but about following and achieving your goals, whatever they might be. It's about planning, collaboration, determination, spirited focus, overcoming obstacles and naysayers, how to build a team and how to build yourself, and how to work with your colleagues and your competitors to give yourself the competitive edge to win."

In his other life—David is a veterinary surgeon and owner of one of the largest private practice groups in Hong Kong. David grew up in Australia, holds dual United Kingdom–Australian passports, and gained full-time residency in Hong Kong. He and his wife, Trilby, who is his equal partner in his work, family, and sporting adventures, have two young daughters.

He raised over HKD$100,000 for Sunbeam Children's Foundation when running the World Marathon Challenge, and aims to found an environmental nongovernmental organization funded in part by revenue and PR raised as a result of his next superhuman feat. David is sought after on the public speaking circuit, and has presented at numerous events including TEDx and the Hong Kong Foreign Correspondent's Club and has featured in many television and print media segments including CNN, Al Jazeera, ESPN, *South China Morning Post*, and *Peak Magazine*. He also serves as a trustee to Outward Bound Hong Kong, is an international member of the Explorers Club, and continues to race across the world in ultradistance endurance events.